Amy Qiu

Metaphors, Trauma and Symptoms

Applications of Cognitive Linguistics

Edited by
Gitte Kristiansen
Francisco J. Ruiz de Mendoza Ibáñez

Volume 56

Amy Qiu

Metaphors, Trauma and Symptoms

A Mixed-Method Analysis

DE GRUYTER
MOUTON

ISBN 978-3-11-149051-9
e-ISBN (PDF) 978-3-11-134650-2
e-ISBN (EPUB) 978-3-11-134654-0
ISSN 1861-4078

Library of Congress Control Number: 2024935484

Bibliographic information published by the Deutsche Nationalbibliothek
The Deutsche Nationalbibliothek lists this publication in the Deutsche Nationalbibliografie;
detailed bibliographic data are available on the internet at http://dnb.dnb.de.

© 2024 Walter de Gruyter GmbH, Berlin/Boston
Typesetting: Integra Software Services Pvt. Ltd.
Printing and binding: CPI books GmbH, Leck

www.degruyter.com

Abstract

Traumatic events such as natural disasters, shooting accidents, war, and social un-rest can bring about intensely and complex subjective experiences, such as emo-tional afflictions, cognitive disturbances, and physiological discomfort (American Psychiatric Association 2013). As it is difficult to address such experiences using purely literal expressions, trauma victims often resort to metaphorical language to bridge the gap between what they have truly experienced and what they are able to express with words. This book presents three case studies of metaphor use by 46 mainland Chinese trauma victims of the 2019-2020 Hong Kong Social unrest. The aim is to explore the contextual characteristics of trauma metaphors and the inter-actions between metaphor use and psychopathological experiences.

Existing trauma metaphor research mostly focused on systematic patterns of metaphors in describing personal traumatic experiences or psychopathological ex-periences. While the studies provided rich and detailed descriptions of semantic fea-tures of trauma metaphors, very few have examined presentational features such as conventionality, emotional valence, and speakers' perspectives-taking in meta-phorization, which capture the speakers' preferred ways of organizing and present-ing metaphorical ideas (Kövecses, 2010). Even fewer studies have examined the systematic interactions among multiple presentational and semantic features in large-scale data, which reveal how specific vehicles and topics are "packaged" in ac-tual metaphor use. If we see different semantic and presentational features as dis-crete points in a three-dimensional space, the relationships among multiple features can be conceived as different facets formed by connecting the points, and the con-textual characteristics of metaphor use can be accessed from different facets that are connected by different sets of features. Contextual characteristics revealed by this approach are conceived by this book as the "multifacetedness" of metaphor use.

Combining categorical data analysis and discourse analysis, Study 1 of this book (presented in Chapter 3) probed into the multifaceted nature of trauma metaphors by examining the interrelationships among EMOTIONAL VALENCE, CONVENTION-ALITY, TARGET CATEGORIES, and PSYCHOLOGICAL PERSPECTIVES. Results show that metaphors about the eight therapeutically interesting topics and those gener-ated from the two psychological perspectives often differ in terms of CONVENTION-ALITY and EMOTIONAL VALENCE. The findings underline the potential for both semantic and presentational features to capture metaphor usage patterns shared by a given speech community. The relationships between CONVENTIONALITY and EMOTIONAL VALENCE varied when the expressions were examined at different lev-els of semantic specificity. This reveals the capacity for semantic and presentational features to capture different contextual dynamics of metaphor use, highlighting the theoretical and practical value of looking into the multifaceted nature of metaphors.

https://doi.org/10.1515/9783111346502-202

Another research gap is the lack of attention to the role of subjective experiences in metaphor variations. Much like metaphor research in general (Littlemore 2019), existing trauma metaphor studies concentrate mainly on the commonalities underlying metaphor use. Much less attention has been paid to metaphor variations, especially the roles of differential experiences that arise from spontaneous yet emotion-laden events. While some studies have shown that nuanced differences in emotional, cognitive, and physiological experiences can be discerned from metaphor variations, these experiences were rarely assessed in structured and quantifiable ways, which constrains the investigation of the systematic relationships between subjective experiences and metaphor use. In contrast, in clinical studies of trauma narratives, psychometric data that capture individual differences in subjective experiences are routinely taken as an important source of linguistic variations. However, metaphorical language is often regarded as ornamental, vague, and idiosyncratic, and is therefore excluded from clinical research.

Study 2 and Study 3 (presented in Chapters 4 and 5) addressed this research gap by incorporating psychometric data and relevant clinical observations into metaphor analysis. Contextualizing metaphor analysis into the scenario of trauma evaluation, Study 2 examined how trauma victims' metaphor usage patterns varied with their overall degrees of trauma and severities of the five ASD symptoms, measured by the Stanford Acute Stress Reaction Questionnaire (SASRQ) (Cardeña et al. 2000). Results of correlation analyses show that severities of the six clinical conditions, each characterized by a distinct set of emotional, cognitive, and physiological features, were significantly correlated with distinct sets of metaphor variables. The significant patterns were then illustrated using authentic linguistic examples and interpreted from a qualitative discourse analytic perspective. Study 3 contextualized metaphor analysis into a more specialized clinical scenario of Acute Stress Disorder (ASD) symptom diagnosis. It examined how trauma victims above the diagnostic criteria of ASD, as measured by the SASRQ, used image schematic metaphors to describe their experience of the five major ASD symptoms. A correspondent analysis that juxtaposed linguistic data and clinical observations was accomplished jointly by the author of this book and a clinical practitioner who is experienced in trauma treatment. Metaphors produced by qualified participants were examined for their relevance to the five ASD symptoms and analyzed in terms of underlying image schemas.

While previous studies established long-term, recurrent human experiences as the primary source of conceptual elements for metaphorical meaning-making, the two clinically situated studies revealed that subjective experiences arising from spontaneous, emotionally charged events may influence how these conceptual resources are accessed and presented with metaphors. Both the severity and variety of psychopathological experiences were identified as key factors in shaping metaphor use.

The three studies constitute a multi-level analysis of trauma metaphors (see Chapter 6 for the framework). Study 1 presents a text-level analysis that examines the interrelationships among linguistic variables without considering clinical input. Study 2 is an individual-level analysis of the relationship between personal metaphor usage profiles and psychometric profiles. Study 3 is a disorder/symptom-level analysis of clinically interesting metaphor usage patterns. The multi-level analysis offers a feasible approach for cross-disciplinary studies of mental health communication. It can be applied beyond the study of metaphors and trauma language to other mental health contexts.

Acknowledgement

My deepest thanks go to my husband, Mr. Yulin Wang, who served as the very important second coder in the interrater reliability tests, the first reader of this monograph, and my personal therapist during moments of self-doubt and stress. His support gave me the strength and resilience to hold on to this journey. I am forever grateful for his unwavering presence in my life.

I am profoundly grateful to Prof. Dennis Tay, who inspired me on this research topic and provided immense intellectual guidance in developing this monograph. As my PhD supervisor, he offered invaluable insights and encouragement like a beacon of light. I am indebted to Mr. Zongmo Wang, who guided me all the way through data collection and analysis as an expert in trauma therapy and my supervisor in psychotherapy. I am also thankful for the academic and life suggestions provided by Prof. Bernadette Watson, Prof. Kathleen Ahrens, Dr. Phonix Lam, Dr. Margo Turnbull, Dr. Jenny Jieyu Chen, Joanna Zhuoan Chen, Zoe Yuan Zhou, and many others at the Hong Kong Polytechnic University.

Special thanks are due to Prof. Jeannette Littlemore and Prof. Wen Xu, who provided constructive feedback on the first draft of this monograph when it was still my Ph.D. thesis. I am thankful for the anonymous reviewers, who provided detailed and critical suggestions for the whole monograph and individual chapters previously submitted as journal articles.

My heartfelt appreciation goes to my mother, Ms. Yuzhen Zhang. Her support and understanding have been a constant source of comfort and encouragement. She never gives up learning and practicing new ways of understanding people and changes in the world. The progress she makes has always inspired me to approach new challenges with courage and optimism.

Any errors or inaccuracies in this book are entirely my own.

https://doi.org/10.1515/9783111346502-203

Contents

List of tables

https://doi.org/10.1515/9783111346502-205

List of figures

https://doi.org/10.1515/9783111346502-206

1 Trauma, language, and metaphor

1.1 Preliminaries

Individuals who have experienced or witnessed a traumatic event may undergo a mixture of overwhelming emotions such as anxiety, anger, depression, and confusion. They may also encounter various cognitive and physical disturbances, including intrusive thoughts, flashbacks, and nightmares about the traumatic event, difficulty in sleeping and concentrating, and physical reactions like headaches and nausea. These symptoms usually disappear within days or weeks after the traumatic event (Cardeña & Carlson 2011). However, it is also possible that these disturbances persist for months and years, leading to trauma-related mental disorders such as adjustment disorder, Acute Stress Disorder (ASD), and Post-traumatic Stress Disorder (PTSD), according to the Diagnostic and Statistical Manual of Mental Disorders (5th edition, DSM-V; the American Psychiatric Association, 2013).

Trauma victims' linguistic accounts of their personal experiences and subjective feelings provide crucial information for clinical assessment and treatment of trauma (Carlson 1997; O'Kearney & Perrott 2006). A particularly interesting linguistic phenomenon is metaphor, which is defined by some linguists as "the phenomenon whereby we talk and, potentially, think about something in terms of something else" (Semino 2008: 1). Traumatic experiences, being intense, complex, and sometimes difficult to describe using literal language, often lead trauma victims to metaphorize their thoughts and feelings in terms of more vivid, concrete, and widely shared experiences. For instance, Wilson and Lindy (2013: 45) noted that trauma victims might describe their perceived sense of deprivation as "I am empty inside" and their difficulties in engaging in meaningful interpersonal communication as "No one can get close to me".

Compared with literal expressions, metaphorical expressions in mental health communication can be more emotion-laden and closely related to the speaker's complex cognitive activities (Gelo & Mergenthaler 2012). Metaphors are also more likely to arouse stronger emotions in the hearers (Tay, Huang & Zeng 2019), potentially exerting a greater impact on the subsequent conversation. The intentional co-construction of metaphors can be beneficial to the therapeutic relationship and bring a positive impact on the therapeutic outcome (Mathieson 2015). Therefore, the use of metaphors in diagnostic and therapeutic contexts has always been an interesting topic for clinical practitioners and researchers.

Systematic patterns of metaphors in long stretches of talk can provide valuable information about the speakers' emotions and thought processes. In the context of trauma diagnosis and therapy, the patterns can offer valuable insights into

https://doi.org/10.1515/9783111346502-001

the speakers' personal and implicit ways of interpreting their own experiences. For example, the two examples above reveal the speakers' tendency to conceptualize the self as an empty container or in a secluded space. For this reason, systematic metaphor usage patterns in trauma narratives, which extend beyond the speaker's immediate control, are often adopted by therapists as a useful tool for exploring the client's[1] psychopathological experiences, promoting adaptive insights, and evaluating therapeutic progress (Kopp 1995; Kopp & Craw 1998; Tay 2013; Mathieson et al. 2018). Numerous studies have demonstrated how therapists can build upon trauma metaphors produced by the client or generate new metaphors for therapeutic purposes (e.g., Grove & Panzer 1989; Haen 2020; Rhodes & Jakes 2004; Stott et al. 2010; Witztum, Dasberg & Bleich 1986).

Apart from playing conceptual and communicative roles, metaphors also serve a scaffolding function in the restructuration of self-identity and re-organization of fragmented narratives. According to Wilson and Lindy (2013), re-organization of personal experiences through metaphors can be an essential step toward trauma recovery and post-traumatic growth. From the perspective of post-traumatic growth (PTG; Joseph & Linley 2006; Tedeschi & Calhoun 1995), re-evaluations of self-identity, emotional states, and the surrounding world represent trauma victims' active attempts to address the discontinuity in self-identity and make meaning of their traumatic experiences. In this process, metaphorical expressions, especially those connecting traumatic experiences with culturally shared myths, rituals, and personally meaningful stories, serve as a particularly useful tool for navigating the post-traumatic world.

Through the use of metaphors, trauma victims' suddenly altered sense of the self and their confusion about the surrounding world can be interpreted by drawing upon concrete world knowledge and familiar life experiences. The metaphorical mapping creates a middle ground between trauma victims' secluded inner experiences and their readily available cognitive resources. The metaphorical interpretation of the self and the world can then be integrated into existing storylines and assimilated into the previously developed life narratives. This process may reduce the amount of new information to be processed during post-traumatic reflection; this may facilitate the integration and re-calibration of the self in light of the traumatic experience.

Apart from interpreting and extending client-generated metaphors, therapists can also apply metaphors as new narrative elements to assist trauma victims in accommodating new changes in their lives (Wilson & Lindy 2013). The collabo-

---

1 Individuals seeking therapeutic treatment are referred to as *clients* or *patients*. The two terms are often used alternatively in clinical mental health research. As the present research context is not therapeutic in nature, the two terms were avoided when referring to the participants. When reviewing previous research, the term used by the researchers was adopted.

rative construction of metaphors between the therapist and the client can facilitate the formulation of adaptive strategies and enhance their working alliance (Mathieson 2015).

Examining trauma victims' metaphor use can provide important insights into the nature of metaphors. As mentioned earlier, the experience of trauma involves a mix of physical and physiological experiences, and emotions and cognitive disturbances that follow. According to previous literature, all aspects are crucial contextual factors in structuring metaphor use (Kövecses 2010, 2015, 2020; Lakoff & Johnson 1980; Lakoff & Johnson 1999; Littlemore 2019; McMullen 2008; Tay 2013). As the experience of a traumatic event introduces unexpected, profound changes in these aspects, these changes are very likely to be reflected in trauma victims' metaphor use. Studying trauma victims' metaphors, therefore, can provide valuable clues about the roles of these contextual factors and their dynamic interactions with each other in real-world metaphor use.

Because trauma-related emotional, cognitive, and physiological experiences examined by metaphor research are also the foremost concern of clinical practitioners, systematic patterns of trauma metaphors may provide useful information for trauma diagnosis and evaluation. The patterns revealed by metaphor-based analyses, especially the interaction between metaphor usage patterns and specific clinical symptoms. can provide useful clues about trauma victims' experiential worlds and their characteristic ways of information processing. The findings may be informative for trauma victims' families as well, especially those with no professional background in psychology and psychotherapy. Reflections on the patterns can open up new lines of communication, which may help to create a more positive atmosphere for trauma victims' self-expression and recovery and provide better social support (Littlemore 2019; Turner et al. 2020).

1.2 Two research gaps

In response to the recent contextual turn in metaphor research (Low et al. 2010; Steen 2011; Zanotto, Cameron & Cavalcanti 2008; McMullen 2008; Tay 2013), numerous studies have provided context-situated analyses of metaphors elicited by specific traumatic events, such as pregnancy loss (Beck 2016, 2017; Littlemore & Turner 2019, 2020; Turner et al. 2020), traumatic combat experiences (Foley 2015; Witztum, Van Der Hart & Friedman 1988; Wilson & Lindy 2013), natural disasters (Tay 2014; Rechsteiner, Tol & Maercker 2019; Rechsteiner et al. 2020), and bereavement during the COVID-19 pandemic[2] (Guité-Verret et al. 2021). A major focus in existing research is how victims of a given traumatic event use metaphors in systematic, convergent ways. The analyses focused mainly on the two semantic aspects of metaphors: *metaphor topic*, which is the abstract issue being interpreted using the metaphor, and the *vehicle term*, which is the concrete, vivid, and physical experience that helps to interpret the topic. Patterns about these two semantic aspects reveal what conceptual resources are used by trauma victims when metaphorizing their emotional, cognitive, and physical/physiological experiences.

In contrast to the attention paid to semantic aspects like vehicles and topics, very few studies have talked about *presentational features* (Kövecses 2015: 187) like the emotional valence and conventionality of metaphors. Instead of revealing what conceptual resources are involved in metaphorical meaning-making, presentational features capture how a metaphorical idea gets organized and delivered. Even fewer studies have examined the systematic interactions among multiple presentational and semantic features in large-scale data, which reveals how specific vehicles and topics are instantiated in actual metaphor use.

If we see different semantic and presentational features as discrete points in a three-dimensional space, the relationships among multiple features can be conceived as different facets formed by connecting the points, and the contextual characteristics of metaphor use can be accessed from different facets that are connected by different sets of features. Contextual characteristics revealed by this approach are conceived by this book as the *"multifacetedness"* of metaphor use. This research gap will be discussed in greater detail in Section 2.3. It will be explored in Chapter 3 based on interview data produced by 46 trauma victims of the 2019–2020 Hong Kong social unrest. More details about the traumatic event and participants will be provided in Section 1.3.

Another notable research gap is the lack of attention to the role of differential experiences in metaphor variations. Much like metaphor research in general (Littlemore 2019), existing trauma metaphor studies concentrate more on the commonalities underlying metaphor use than metaphor variations. The few studies that investigated metaphor variations focused on the impact of recurrent sociocultural experiences and entrenched religious beliefs (e.g., Rechsteiner et al. 2019, 2020; Meili et al. 2020; Wilson & Lindy 2013), or changes brought about long-term recovery or treatment (e.g., Costa & Steen 2014; Foley 2015; Wilson & Lindy 2013).

---

2 Although COVID-19 pandemic has induced widespread stress and uncertainty, the experiences are usually not regarded as traumatic following the DSM-V criteria, as most situations did not involve an immediate threat to life. Nevertheless, exceptional cases like exposure to life-threatening situation, bereavement, death, which particularly affected families of severely ill or deceased patients and medical professionals, may be considered traumatic.

This raises a compelling question: do different subjective experiences arising from spontaneous yet emotion-laden events play a role in metaphor variations? In fact, numerous studies have shown that nuanced differences in emotional, cognitive, and physiological experiences can be distinguished from metaphor variations. However, those studies rarely assessed the subjective experiences in structured and quantifiable ways, which constrains the investigation of systematic relationships between subjective experiences with metaphor use.

In contrast to the trend observed in linguistic studies, clinical studies of trauma narratives take psychometric data that capture individual differences in subjective experiences as an important source of linguistic variations. However, metaphorical language is often regarded as ornamental, vague, and idiosyncratic, and is therefore excluded from clinical research. Whether and how different subjective experiences can be systematically captured in metaphorical language remains an intriguing question to both metaphor researchers and clinical practitioners. This research gap will be further discussed in Section 2.4. It will be addressed in this book by integrating linguistic data with psychometric data generated by the same group of participants. Metaphor variations associated with different severities and varieties of psychopathological experiences will be explored in Chapter 4 and Chapter 5, respectively.

The following section introduces the research background, including the traumatic event, participants, linguistic data, and psychometric data. Section 1.4 introduces the linguistic and clinical aims, and Section 1.5 provides an outline of chapters and an overview of the research design.

1.3 Research background and data

1.3.1 The traumatic event

The traumatic event examined in this book is the social unrest that occurred in the Hong Kong Special Administrative Region (HKSAR) of China from 2019 to 2020. This section provides a brief review of the traumatic nature of this event and its psychological impact on local residents.[3] Special attention will be paid to residents from the Chinese mainland, who are the trauma population under examination in this book.

---

3 The social unrest was highly political in nature (Shek 2020). This book will not elaborate on the underlying causes of the social unrest, as they are not the major focus of the research. Readers who are interested in the political and sociocultural aspects of the event can refer to Shek (2020) and Ni et al. (2020) for more information.

The social unrest began in March 2019 in response to an extradition bill proposed by the HKSAR government, which aims to facilitate the transfer of fugitives to jurisdictions not covered by existing laws, including the Chinese Mainland and Taiwan. Pro-democracy activists accused the government of undermining Hong Kong's autonomy under the "one country, two systems" constitutional principle.[4] Initially, pro-democracy activists organized peaceful demonstrations such as sit-ins at the government headquarters. Starting in mid-2019, a series of more violent protests were launched, urging the government to address the five core demands proposed by the protesters.[5] To allay public concerns, Carrie Lam, the Chief Executive of the HKSAR government, withdrew the extradition bill in September 2019 (China Daily 2019b). However, the pro-democracy camp did not see the response as sufficient and soon launched even more massive and intense protests to push for the realization of all five demands (Kuo & Guardian reporter 2019).

Protests escalated into violence and destruction and grew further into major terrorism events towards the end of 2019 (He & Zhang 2020; Zhang, Zhang & Dai 2019). From June to December 2019, extensive damage was inflicted on the city. A total of 740 sets of traffic lights were vandalized, 52.8km of railings along walkways were damaged, and about 21,800 square meters of paving blocks on footpaths were removed (Yau 2020). Additionally, 85 Mass Transit Railway stations and 68 Light Railway stations were damaged. Protestors used weapons such as metal bars, tear gas, catapults, and petrol bombs, and some resorted to physical and verbal assault as a means to "informally settle interpersonal conflicts" (Shek 2020: 621) with people who held different political opinions. Massive protests were also launched to occupy public places such as the Hong Kong International Airport, railway stations, the Legislative Council Building, and several local universities. In response, riot police employed tear gas, rubber bullets, bean bad grounds, and pistols to disperse radical protestors. This, in turn, triggered even more aggressive attacks from protesters.

Given the intense situation, numerous countries issued travel warnings or raised the alert level for Hong Kong, including but not limited to the US, UK, Aus-

---

4 "One country, two systems" describes the governance of Hong Kong and Macau, which became Special Administrative Regions of the People's Republic of China in 1997 and 1999, respectively. It indicates that while the Mainland of China adopts the socialist system with Chinese characteristics, the two special administrative regions, under the principle of "one China", could retain their own governmental systems and legal, economic, and financial affairs, independent from those of the mainland.
5 The five demands include the withdrawal of the extradition bill, universal suffrage, inquiry into alleged police brutality, amnesty for arrested protestors, and retraction of the classification of protesters as rioters.

tralia, and South Korea, (China Daily 2019a). At the most violent stage of the social unrest, classes at schools and onsite work had been suspended for safety concerns, and the public was urged by the government to avoid outdoor activities (The Government of the Hong Kong Special Administrative Region Press Releases 2019). The social unrest caused enormous economic losses and disruptions in the social order, leading to a sharp decline in public confidence in the Hong Kong government (Keating & Reinhart 2020).

The social unrest gradually died down towards the end of 2019. The society was eventually restored to peace and stability after the National Security Law was implemented on June 30, 2020 (The Government of the Hong Kong Special Administrative Region Press Releases 2021). However, its impact on Hong Kong citizens' mental health well-being and interpersonal relationships persisted. Exposure to violence and physical assault caused widespread fear, frustration, and lack of certainty, leaving a significant impact on residents' psychological well-being. Excessive emphasis on political viewpoints further added to social polarization and disintegration among family and friends (Ng 2020). According to a longitudinal study on Hong Kong residents' mental health well-being (Ni et al. 2020), exposure to traumatic events during social unrest was a crucial factor leading to probable depression and suspected PTSD. The weighted prevalence of depressive symptoms among adults was 37.4%, and the probable depression rate of 11.2%, surpassing levels observed in the past decade. The weighted prevalence of post-traumatic symptoms rose from 16.6% to 31.6%, and the rate of suspected PTSD was 12.8%, with approximately 810,000 people being affected. The psychological impact of the social unrest was largely comparable to what was previously found for the experience of large-scale natural disasters, armed conflicts, or terrorist attacks (Ni et al. 2020).

A wide range of individuals reported stress symptoms, including residents of the affected areas, individuals who were exposed to trauma-related media reports, and those working in protest-related occupations such as doctors, nurses, police, media workers, and street cleaners (Mogul 2019). Those who participated in the protests also reported sleep difficulties, intrusive thoughts, and dissociative experiences (Mogul 2019). Individuals with a history of other mental health issues reported heightened flashbacks, hypervigilance, and dissociation due to media exposure to street violence (Ng 2020). Violent protester-police confrontations during the social unrest were largely comparable to military conflicts in frontline war zones. Clinical researchers warned of delayed or long-term psychological effects, as the psychological impact of such conflicts can sometimes manifest weeks or months after the events (Ng 2020; Ni et al. 2020).

This book focuses specifically on a large-scale protest activity during which a local university was illegally occupied and vandalized by pro-democracy activists.

The occupation lasted 13 days, from 17 to 29 November 2019 (Yiu 2021), marking one of the most violent phases of the social unrest. During the illegal occupation and the subsequent confrontations with riot police, rioters used dangerous chemicals, petrol bombs, and several other weapons (Mok 2019). Buildings, teaching facilities, and laboratories on campus were severely damaged, leading to immeasurable loss in research projects; the neighborhood of the campus also experienced extensive vandalism (Cheung 2019). The adversities caused severe psychological distress to students and staff, as well as to citizens in the surrounding neighborhood.

1.3.2 Participants and data

Data collection
The trauma population examined in this book was Hong Kong residents originally from the Chinese Mainland. This ethnic group is one of the major ethnic groups in Hong Kong, representing about one-seventh of the total population[6] at the time of the research. During the social unrest, this ethnic group faced an elevated risk of trauma, as some radical protesters directed violence and abuse specifically toward them, leading to significant distress and safety concerns (Reuters 2019).

Before the commencement of this study, ethical approval was obtained from the Human Subjects Ethics Sub-Committee of the Hong Kong Polytechnic University (HSEARS20191211001). Assurances of anonymity, confidentiality, and the right to withdraw were ensured for all participants, and written informed consent was obtained.

Data collection began shortly after the previously mentioned traumatic event. In line with the criteria for diagnosing ASD (American Psychiatric Association 1994, 2013), the data collection period was restricted to one month since the end of the traumatic event, from Dec 12 to Dec 28, 2019. Given the tense social climate and the risks associated with outdoor activities, participants were recruited online using convenience sampling from social networking groups set up by the target population and snowball sampling among their acquaintances.

---

6 According to the statistics released by the Hong Kong Census and Statistics Department (https://www.censtatd.gov.hk/tc/scode600.html#section3, accessed on Jan 28, 2023), from 1997 to the end of 2021, about 1.12 million people immigrated from the mainland of China to Hong Kong, and the total population of Hong Kong was 7.413 million. Statistics of the 2021 Population Census showed that 134,845 non-permanent residents of Hong Kong, including people who hold student and working visa, were from the mainland https://www.censtatd.gov.hk/en/data/stat_report/product/B1120112/att/B11201122021XXXXB0100.pdf, accessed on Jan 28, 2023).

Data collection started with a briefing on the purpose and procedure of the research. After that, the participants were invited to a semi-structured interview to talk about their subjective experience during the social unrest. The interviews were later transcribed into written text and analyzed for the metaphors they contained. Shortly after the interview, the participants' traumatic experiences were assessed using a psychometric questionnaire. Owing to the unstable social situation and participants' concerns for personal safety, both the semi-interviews and questionnaires were conducted online. The audio interviews were conducted via WeChat, a popular social media platform among mainland Chinese, and the questionnaires were distributed via Wenjuanxing[7] ("问卷星"), an online Chinese questionnaire platform.

Participants

The impact of the social unrest was widespread. While some residents experienced psychosocial stressors like negative emotions triggered by social media and interpersonal tensions, they were not considered traumatized following the APA criteria, as the experience did not involve immediate life threats or physical injuries. This group of individuals were thus excluded from the recruitment.

After screening interviews, forty-six participants were deemed qualified and invited to this study. All participants met the DSM-V criteria for trauma exposure, which means they had either witnessed or experienced highly distressing events, such as physical assault, violence to others, and destruction of buildings and public transportation. The participants' demographic information is summarized in Table 1.1 below.

Table 1.1: The participants' demographic information.

Socio-demographic features of the 46 participants	
Gender	33 Females and 13 Males
National origin	The Chinese Mainland
Native language	Mandarin Chinese
Age	22 to 39 (Mean = 26.61, SD = 4.52)
Educational background	Undergraduate or above

---

7 The software can be accessed via https://www.wjx.cn/ (accessed on April 15, 2022).

The participants included thirty-three females and thirteen males. All participants were native Mandarin Chinese speakers. All were students or staff of the occupied university or local residents who work or live in the affected area. All participants had an undergraduate education or higher, with ages ranging from 22 to 39 (M = 26.61, SD = 4.52). Due to the intense social atmosphere, participants' political stances were not solicited. Nevertheless, all participants agreed that their lives and emotions had been greatly affected by the social unrest and identified themselves as victims of the event. None of the participants had a psychology or psychotherapy background, nor did they have experience in metaphor research. At the time of the study, none of them had sought mental health support for the traumatic event. Therefore, their descriptions of psychopathological experiences can be regarded as authentic reflections of spontaneous reactions toward trauma exposure.

As mentioned earlier, some radical protesters directed violence and abuse specifically toward mainland Chinese (Reuters 2019). A large proportion of participants reported experiences of verbal abuse, harassment, and malicious behaviors from radical "yellow" camp supporters. Given the social pressure and psychological burden, the participants experienced unprecedented challenges in maintaining interpersonal relationships, dealing with social situations, and even accomplishing necessary life-supporting tasks like food shopping and doctor's visits. Many participants reported psychological stress due to the rioters' acts of terror committed on public facilities, their malicious behaviors toward people with mainland Chinese characteristics, and criminal activists' fatal retaliation on government supporters (e.g., Wong 2020; South China Morning Post 2019). At the most violent stage of the social unrest, many decided to leave Hong Kong due to safety concerns.

Another possible cause of the significant psychological crisis among mainland Chinese might be their limited experience in dealing with political conflicts, such as protests, social unrest, and mass shootings. This lack of experience may have made it challenging for them to stay away from potentially traumatizing situations before actually encountering one. Consequently, this could have increased their chances of trauma exposure and led to a greater psychological impact. For the same reason, individuals traumatized by the social unrest may also face challenges in seeking emotional support from their family and friends from the same ethnic group. Insufficient self-care and social support might have further impeded the processing of traumatic memories, exacerbated the persistence of psychopathological symptoms, and heightened the risk of developing more severe mental health issues.

Furthermore, in the mainland of China, police are usually perceived as having a positive and prestigious image and a protective force that saves citizens from danger and threat of crime[8] (Chen 2016; Wang, Zhao & Zhang 2020). This perception stands in stark contrast to that in Hong Kong during the social unrest and in many Western societies. Therefore, it was both conceptually and emotionally difficult for mainland Chinese immigrants to understand some local residents' negative attitudes and the protesters' malicious acts toward the police. This clash of opinion was reported by several participants of the present study.

Linguistic data

Linguistic data were collected using semi-structured interviews with qualified participants. The aim was to probe into the participants' personal traumatic experiences, especially their subjective thoughts, emotions, and feelings. Interview questions and follow-up strategies were developed in close consultation with a professional psychologist and counseling supervisor, certified by the Chinese Psychological Association (CPA). All interviews were conducted by the author of this book, who had received professional training in psychotherapy and had 5 years of experience in conducting mental health interviews (refer to Appendix 1 for a reflexivity statement).

The interview questions were phrased in an emotionally neutral and open-ended way. Example questions include "What were the moments that impressed you the most?", "What were your immediate feelings", "Could you elaborate on your emotional experiences during that time?", and "How has your life changed since the traumatic event?". The interviewees were encouraged to describe their subjective experiences in as much detail as possible. As the interview aimed to elicit trauma victims' natural use of metaphors rather than extract a metaphorical model of their traumatic experiences, the interviewees were not guided or instructed to use metaphors or to elaborate on any specific aspects of their traumatic experiences (c.f. Gök & Kara 2022; Stanley et al. 2021). Metaphorical language was carefully avoided when phrasing the interview questions. Spontaneous clarifying questions were mostly open-ended questions, beginning with "how", "what", and "why". Deictic terms such as "this" and "that", along with general nouns and adjectives like "emotions", "thought", "negative", and "positive" were used instead of more specific expressions. To prevent potential interference from interviewer-generated metaphors, the questions were phrased mainly using the interviewee's own expressions.

---

8 Refer to Chen (2016) and Jiao (2001) for comparative analyses of police image and police-culture relationships in China and Western societies).

All interviews were conducted in Mandarin Chinese, which was the native language of both the interviewer and the interviewees. Considering the sensitive nature of the social unrest, the interviews were recorded with additional verbal consent from the interviewees. The total length of recordings was about 1,000 minutes (16.67 hours), and the average length per interview was 21.72 minutes. The recordings were transcribed into written text for further analysis. *Xunfei Tingjian* ("讯飞听见")[9] was used to assist transcription. Transcripts generated by the software were then proofread by the author while listening to the recordings and errors were corrected manually. As this study focuses exclusively on the interviewees' linguistic metaphors, intonation contours and paralinguistic cues such as laughter, cries, and sighs were not transcribed.

The 46 transcripts consisted of 207,959 Chinese characters, with 177,981 contributed by the interviewees (averaging 3,869 per interview, SD = 1,751). Each transcript was then examined for the use of metaphors following the discourse dynamics approach (Cameron & Maslen 2010). The metaphor identification procedure will be detailed later in Section 3.2.1 using authentic linguistic examples. The identified metaphors were then coded in terms of several therapeutically interesting variables. As each main body chapter (i.e., Chapters 3, 4, and 5) probes into different aspects of metaphors, the metaphor variables and descriptive data will be presented later in corresponding chapters.

Psychometric data

This book examines metaphor use associated with the potential incidence of ASD,[10] characterized by intense, unpleasant, and dysfunctional reactions within one month following trauma exposure (see Section 2.4.1 for more information). To ensure that the participants' accounts were not to be influenced by the questionnaire's symptom descriptions, psychometric data was collected after the interview.

The Chinese-translated version of the Stanford Acute Stress Reaction Questionnaire (SASRQ), designed by Cardeña and colleagues (2000) and translated by Hou (2008), was employed to measure the participants' experiences of Acute posttraumatic stress reactions. The questionnaire consists of five subscales that measure trauma victims' experiences of the five major ASD symptoms:

---

9 https://www.iflyrec.com/ (accessed on April 15, 2022).
10 The diagnosis of PTSD does not apply to the current research context, as it requires relevant symptoms to last for at least a month after trauma exposure (American Psychiatric Association 2013).

Dissociation: alterations in the perception and awareness of self, others, and the surrounding environment.

Re-experiencing: the extent to which the individual relives the memories and feelings related to the traumatic event.

Avoidance: the tendency to avoid traumatic-related stimuli, such as thoughts, activities, people, feelings, etc.

Anxiety and hyperarousal: experience of increased anxiety, sensitivity, and physiological arousal in response to external stimuli.

Impairment in functioning: the extent to which the individual's physical, cognitive, and social functioning are affected.

The five subscales consist of a total of 30 items, and each item is rated on a 6-point scale from 0 to 5, ranging from "not experienced" to "very often experienced". The ratings can be calculated continuously to measure the overall degrees of trauma and severities of more specific symptoms, or dichotomously to assess the clinical presence of ASD and symptoms. Psychopathological experiences of ASD and the diagnosis will be further introduced in Section 2.4.1. As Chapters 4 and 5 of this book examine the two dimensions of traumatic experiences in relation to different aspects of metaphor use, more details about the ratings and descriptive statistics will be presented later in Sections 4.2 and 5.2.

The SASRQ was developed based on the Diagnostic and Statistical Manual of Mental Disorders (4th edition, DSM-IV)[11] criteria for diagnosing ASD (American Psychology Association 1994). Both the original questionnaire and the Chinese translated version have demonstrated good reliability and validity in measuring acute stress reactions to various traumatizing events (Cardeña et al. 2000; Lötvall, Palmborg & Cardeña 2022; Luo et al. 2021). The questionnaire also has strong predictive power for later PTSD symptomatology, depression, anxiety, and other psychological and medical outcomes (Lötvall, Palmborg & Cardeña 2022).

1.4 Research aims

In line with the two major research gaps summarized earlier, this book proposes two major research aims:

The primary, linguistic aim is to investigate previously neglected contextual characteristics of trauma victims' metaphors. Chapter 3 sets out to explore the

---

[11] At the time of the research, the SASRQ has not yet been updated to conform with the DSM-V criteria. An updated version of the SASRQ is now available (refer to Lötvall, Palmborg & Cardeña 2022).

multifaceted nature of metaphor use by examining the systematic interactions among multiple presentational and semantic features. Chapters 4 and 5 examine how trauma victims' metaphor usage patterns vary with quantitative and qualitative differences in subjective experiences. In the present research context, the differences manifest as different severities and varieties of psychopathological experiences.

The secondary, clinical aim is to investigate the potential relevance of metaphorical language to psychopathological experiences of trauma. The findings are expected to reveal the value of metaphor-based analysis in investigating psychopathological experiences. The findings are also expected to provoke new thoughts on cross-disciplinary research that integrates linguistic insights and clinical observations.

This book intends to make several specific methodological points. Firstly, by combining quantitative methods with qualitative discourse analysis, this book will demonstrate how traditional semantic analysis of mental health metaphors can be extended. Secondly, this book aims to show how the incorporation of psychometric data and clinical observations can bring new insights into the contextualized nature of mental health metaphors. Most importantly, this book presents a *multi-level analysis* of trauma metaphors, which is composed of text-level, individual-level, and disorder/symptom-level analyses (refer to Section 1.5.2 for more details). A key methodological point is to illustrate how the multi-level analysis offers a convenient and feasible framework for integrating cross-disciplinary insights about mental health communication.

1.5 Structure of book

1.5.1 Outline of chapters

Chapter 1 provides an introduction to trauma, metaphors, and the current research context. It also presents an overview of the research aims, the research questions, and the methods to be used.

Chapter 2 sets the ground for this book by providing an overview of previous literature, identifying major research gaps, and suggesting feasible approaches to address the research gaps. Following a critical review of existing research on trauma metaphors, the chapter summarizes the two major research trends and gaps. Based on insights offered by clinical studies of trauma narratives and mental health metaphor research, I will suggest approaches for advancing research in the two directions. The approaches will be demonstrated later in Chapters 3, 4, and 5. An outline of the three main body chapters is presented in Figure 1.1.

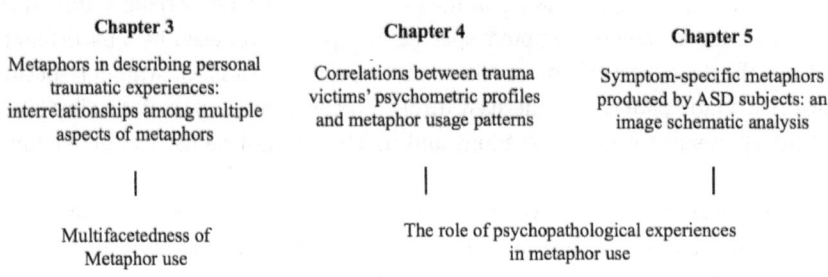

Figure 1.1: A diagram of the book outline.

Chapter 3 investigates the multifacetedness of metaphor use reflected by the interrelationships among multiple presentational and semantic features. A mixed-method analysis is designed to examine the instantiations of EMOTIONAL VALENCE and CONVENTIONALITY in 1) metaphors about eight therapeutically interesting TARGET CATEGORIES and 2) metaphors generated from two contrasting PSYCHOLOGICAL PERSPECTIVES. Categorical data analysis will be applied to investigate the interrelationships among these variables, and their interrelationships will be visualized using Multiple Correspondence Analysis (MCA) plots. Statistically significant patterns will then be illustrated using genuine linguistic examples and interpreted from a qualitative discourse analytic perspective. The patterns will be discussed in terms of their theoretical implications for metaphor research and practical implications for clinical practitioners' understanding of client-generated metaphors.

While Chapter 3 addresses typical metaphor theoretical questions at the level of language, without considering clinical input, Chapters 4 and 5 set out to explore the interactions between trauma victims' metaphor use and their psychopathological experiences measured using the SASRQ. Similar to Chapter 3, Chapter 4 follows a mixed-method approach that combines quantitative methods and qualitative discourse analysis. It focuses on how trauma victims with different overall degrees of trauma and different severities of symptoms use metaphors in contrasting ways. A series of correlation analyses will be performed to identify metaphor variables that are significantly related to the participants' SASRQ scores. The statistical analyses will be supplemented with discourse analytic interpretations of linguistic examples. The patterns will also be discussed based on tentative inferences drawn from previous research on trauma narratives.

In contrast to Chapter 4, which places greater emphasis on quantitative relationships between metaphor use and psychopathological experiences, Chapter 5 focuses on how psychopathological experiences of the five major ASD symptoms may prime specific conceptual elements into trauma victims' metaphors. To extract expressions that are sufficiently representative of the psychopathological experiences, this chapter focuses specifically on symptom-specific metaphors produced by 5 participants who met the diagnostic criteria of ASD as measured by the SASRQ. Symptom-specific image schematic patterns are derived through a correspondent analysis (Tay 2016) that juxtaposes linguistic observations and psychological insights. Trauma victims' metaphors will first be examined for their relevance to the five ASD symptoms, and those directly relevant to the symptoms will be analyzed for underlying image schemas. Implications for understanding corresponding symptoms, ASD, and client-generated metaphors in clinical scenarios will be discussed.

Chapter 6 concludes this book with a synthesized summary of the three studies. Following an overview of the major findings and implications, I will provide a critical reflection on key limitations in the research design. Future research avenues highlighted by the three studies will also be discussed.

1.5.2 Methodology and research design

This book follows a mixed-method, cross-disciplinary approach. Chapters 3 and 4 demonstrate how the combination of statistical methods and qualitative discourse analysis can yield new theoretical and practical insights. Chapters 4 and 5 showcase the strengths of incorporating linguistic and psychometric data in exploring mental health metaphors. In particular, Chapter 4 illustrates how the incorporation of quantitative psychometric data broadens the scope of quantitative metaphor analysis. Chapter 5 demonstrates how qualitative metaphor analysis can be extended by incorporating qualitative psychometric data and clinical observations.

The three main body chapters exhibit a gradual progression in specificity regarding the contextualization of metaphor use (see Figure 1.2). Chapter 3 examines trauma victims' metaphor use in describing their personal traumatic experiences, whereas Chapters 4 and 5 zoom in on more specialized clinical scenarios, i.e., trauma and symptom evaluation and ASD diagnosis.

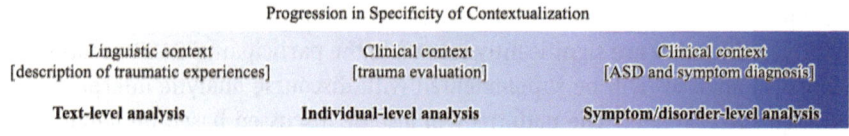

Figure 1.2: Structure of the multi-level analysis.

The three chapters work on distinct yet interrelated levels of metaphor use. Taking different metaphor variables as the units of analysis, Chapter 3 examines the contextualized instantiations of presentational and semantic features in describing personal traumatic experiences. As the study investigates trauma victims' choices and packaging of metaphors without considering clinical data, it can be regarded as a *text-level analysis*. Chapter 4 focuses on the relationships between each trauma victim's personal metaphor usage patterns and psychological profiles, it could therefore be seen as an *individual-level analysis*. Chapter 5 probes into symptom-specific metaphors by participants who met the diagnostic criteria of ASD; it is thus summarized as a *disorder/symptom-level analysis*. Together, the three analyses form a multi-level analysis that offers a comprehensive view of clinically interesting metaphor usage patterns. The structure of the multi-level analysis is also represented in Figure 1.2.

This research design is a response to recent calls for situating metaphor research, particularly the study of mental health metaphors, within more specialized contexts (e.g., Low et al. 2010; McMullen 2008; Steen 2011; Tay 2013; Zanotto, Cameron & Cavalcanti 2008). Through a case study of people's spontaneous use of metaphors in response to a traumatic event, this book aims to exemplify how large-scale crisis events situated in specific sociocultural contexts offer valuable opportunities for theoretical exploration of contextualized metaphors (Frank 2008; Geeraerts, Kristiansen & Peirsman 2010; Tay 2021).

2 Trauma metaphors: Beyond semantic features

2.1 Chapter introduction

As introduced in Chapter 1, trauma victims' metaphors often represent "deep internal states rooted in the complex, cognitive-emotional processing" of difficult life experiences (Wilson & Lindy 2013: 3), encoding meaningful information for clinical understanding, assessment, and treatment of trauma. Hence, the contextual features of trauma metaphors are of interest to both metaphor researchers and clinical psychologists. Following a critical review of the literature on trauma metaphors, this chapter summarizes the major research trends and gaps and proposes possible approaches to advance research in these areas.

Existing research has provided detailed descriptions of metaphors in trauma narratives. Numerous studies have analyzed how trauma victims use metaphors to articulate their subjective experiences, including emotional feelings, cognitive disturbances, and physical experiences, associated with the traumatic events. Other studies have focused specifically on metaphors in describing trauma victims' psychopathological experiences of mental health disorders like PTSD. The two strands of research will be introduced in Section 2.2. Based on the literature review, Sections 2.3 and 2.4 will discuss the two major research gaps summarized earlier in Chapter 1, i.e., the overlooked multifaceted nature of metaphor use, and the potential role of psychopathological experiences in shaping metaphor use. Finally, Section 2.5 concludes this chapter, summarizing the key arguments and elucidating the research aims.

2.2 Metaphors in describing trauma

2.2.1 Overview of previous studies

Metaphors in describing personal traumatic experiences
Numerous studies have investigated trauma victims' metaphorical conceptualizations of complex, nuanced subjective experiences during traumatic events. The experiences are frequently interpreted through more concrete, tangible, and "human-oriented" experiences (Reijnierese et al. 2018). Many studies suggest that intense, extraordinary physical experiences during traumatic events are often interpreted through basic, universally shared bodily experiences. The expressions help to translate abstract and vague traumatic feelings that are relatable within the speech community. Tay (2014: 91–93) observed that trauma victims of earth-

https://doi.org/10.1515/9783111346502-002

quakes draw upon the loss of physical control to interpret the uncertainties in their lives and the sense of frustration; typical examples are "the whole ground had shifted" and "it was that unknown in the dark". In a study of metaphors in describing traumatic experiences of natural disasters, Rechsteiner et al. (2019) found universal bodily experiences like BURDEN,[12] SHOCK, and WOUND to be key metaphor vehicle terms in describing the physical, emotional, and cognitive impacts of the disasters.

The centrality of bodily experiences is also found in accounts of taboo or stigmatized experiences, such as sexual assault, bereavement, and pregnancy loss. In a study of metaphors in describing pregnancy loss, Littlemore and Turner (2020: 51–54) found that the unusually painful physical experience of pregnancy loss and suddenly altered perceptions of the body are often interpreted in terms of more basic embodied experiences, such as in "have the rug pulled out from under", "part of me is missing", and a perceived sense of "emptiness". In studies examining metaphor use by female victims of sexual abuse, both Stroińska (2014) and Wilson and Lindy (2013) reported cases where victims used metaphors about CONFRONTATIONS and PARALYSIS to interpret their physical experiences and bodily mutilations. The expressions make trauma victims' inner experiences more accessible and interpretable. More importantly, they introduce alternative frames of reference, allowing difficult emotions and experiences that are not openly discussable to be expressed without re-experiencing the emotional afflictions (Busch 2020; Stroinska 2014).

Apart from adding transparency to personal and stigmatized experiences, metaphors serve as an important conceptual tool for individuals to understand and come to terms with their experiences. In other words, the expressions help to define experiences that are new and confusing even to trauma victims themselves. Littlemore and Turner (2019) provided in-depth analyses of metaphor usage patterns that characterize different stages of pregnancy loss, including receiving the diagnosis, decision-making on specific clinical issues, and the eventual funerals, rites, and rituals. Turner et al. (2020) studied how the bereaved and their families make meaning of the loss and its impact on self and time perception through metaphorical thinking. Their findings indicate that metaphor-based communication facilitates trauma victims' comprehension of the unprecedented crisis and assists in navigating through these distressing experiences. Among various metaphor vehicle terms, bodily experiences such as PHYSICAL LOCATION,

---

12 Following the conventions used by the discourse dynamics approach (Cameron & Maslen 2010), emergent themes of metaphor vehicle terms and target topics in English will be represented using capital letters throughout this book.

JOURNEY, and CONTAINER are particularly significant in conceptualizing be-reavement. Based on an analysis of metaphors produced by twenty bereaved family caregivers of COVID patients, Guité-Verret et al. (2021) found that the trau-matic experience of bereavement is often interpreted as the individual being physically CUT OFF from the world, the experience of being struck by WAVES of shocks, and the emotions being BLOCKED within the self or from their loved ones. Metaphors that draw on physical experiences reflect trauma victims' latent psychological needs for social connection, reconstruction of coherence in self-narratives, and social recognition of their bereavement and grief (Guité-Verret et al. 2021).

Metaphors and psychopathological experiences of trauma

In contrast to the strand of research on trauma victims' narration of personal expe-riences, a group of studies focused more narrowly on metaphors in describing sub-jective experiences of trauma-related mental health disorders and symptoms. Unlike personal traumatic experiences, which can vary across traumatic contexts and even individuals, psychopathological experiences of trauma-related disorders and symptoms capture emotional, cognitive, and physiological disturbances com-monly experienced by trauma victims. As previously mentioned in Chapter 1, typi-cal manifestations of post-traumatic symptoms include dissociation from reality, detachment from the normal sense of self, re-experiencing of trauma-related emo-tions and thoughts, anxiety, physiological hypervigilance, insomnia, etc. (American Psychiatric Association 2013). These experiences are elusive, complex, and deviate from ordinary sensations; therefore, trauma victims often resort to metaphors to bridge the gap between their subjective experiences and what they can express with words.

Similar to metaphors about personal traumatic experiences, metaphors about psychopathological experiences of trauma also draw heavily on fundamental, uni-versal embodied experiences. Wilson and Lindy (2013) discovered that metaphors rooted in universal bodily experiences such as CONTAINER/CONTAINMENT, BAL-ANCE, and MOVEMENT are crucial in conceptualizing PTSD. In a study of metaphor use by veterans who developed combat-induced PTSD, Foley (2015) observed that psychopathological experiences of trauma are often interpreted in terms of physi-cal and sensory experiences such as "breaking down", "suffocating", and "hiding". In a study of metaphor use in describing PTSD induced by traumatic childbirth, Beck (2016) identified that the psychopathological experiences are often metaphor-ized as physical and sensory experiences such as "falling into" a "bottomless abyss" and "a dangerous ocean", and being surrounded by "enveloping darkness". The role of these embodied experiences in describing PTSD symptoms was further confirmed by a follow-up study on metaphorical conceptualizations of long-lasting PTSD (Beck 2017).

PTSD clients' preferences for vehicle terms and topics can vary markedly throughout trauma recovery as traumatic stress gradually diminishes and positive insights develop. Through an in-depth analysis of interviews with seven individuals who had developed and recovered from PTSD, Costa and Steen (2014) discovered that the gradual shift from the trauma stage to the recovery stage can be discerned from the transformation of vehicle groupings and the metaphor scenarios they build. Their findings showed that both trauma and the subsequent recovery process can be metaphorized using four basic vehicle groupings: MOTION, MOVEMENT, CONTAINER, and SIGHT. However, the vehicle groupings that characterize the two clinical stages formed two contrasting metaphor scenarios: the traumatic stage was often characterized as a state of no MOTION or DOWNWARD MOVEMENT, a closed CONTAINER, and loss of SIGHT, whereas the recovery process was more frequently described as increased MOTION, UPWARD MOVEMENT, an open CONTAINER, and enhanced SIGHT. Foley (2015) reported similar dynamic transitions of metaphor vehicle groupings across different clinical stages. As the veterans gradually recovered from PTSD, their choices of vehicle terms shifted from the self being "controlled" or "dominated" by PTSD, to the self "surviving" PTSD, and eventually "embarking on a survivor's mission". The theme of "regaining agency and control" was also reported by Littlemore and Turner (2020) as a potential linguistic marker of recovery from traumatic pregnancy loss.

As post-traumatic stress reduces and positive insights develop, trauma victims' preferences for target topics also evolve. According to Wilson and Lindy's (2013) observations, during the recovery or treatment, the focus of client-generated metaphors gradually shifts from i) trauma-related physical and physiological experiences, emotional feelings, and thoughts to ii) problem-solving cognitive activities for managing trauma-related thoughts, and eventually to iii) re-establishing a continuous sense of self, reconnection to others, and re-integrating into the broader sociocultural context.

2.2.2 A summary of trauma-related metaphor usage patterns

Although previous studies focused on different traumatic events, we can still identify several recurrent vehicle groupings and topics in trauma victims' metaphors. Frequently observed vehicles include sensory information, war and threat, space and spatial relations, and physical activity, and recurrent topics include emotions and emotional processes, thinking and understanding, and self-references.

Vehicle groupings

SENSORY INFORMATION: A traumatic event usually triggers unusual bodily experiences and induces substantial changes in the perception of the surrounding environment. As the feelings often exceed ordinary life experiences, it can be difficult for trauma victims to describe them directly using everyday expressions. Instead, it is much easier to interpret their experiences in terms of more basic sensory impressions and physical sensations. According to existing research (e.g., Beck 2016, 2017; Berntsen, Willert & Rubin 2003; Costa & Steen 2014; Gušić et al. 2018; Nijenhuis, Van Der Hart & Steele 2010; Rechsteiner, Tol & Maercker 2019; Rechsteiner et al. 2020; Wilson & Lindy 2013), the psychological consequence of the traumatic event is often metaphorized as the impairment or loss of SIGHT, the experience of NUMBNESS and SUFFOCATION, and the perception of PHYSICAL PAIN.

WAR AND THREAT: Because traumatic events are often physically confrontational and even fatal (Ehlers, Ehring & Kleim 2012; Foa, Molnar & Cashman 1995), trauma victims often relate their perceptions and reactions with WAR and FIGHTING, and perceive the drastic changes in the environment as THREAT. Typical examples are expressions about "fight", "dying", "defeat", and "on guard". These vehicles have been identified in descriptions of traumatic combat experiences (Foley 2015; Witztum, Dasberg & Bleich 1986) as well as non-combat-related experiences such as pregnancy loss and rape (Beck 2016; Ehlers et al. 1998; Wilson & Lindy 2013).

SPACE AND SPATIAL RELATIONS: As the psychological impact of trauma can last for quite a long time, trauma victims may conceptualize themselves as being in a BOUNDED SPACE, and recovering from trauma may be interpreted as entering an OPEN SPACE (Beck 2016, 2017; Costa & Steen 2014; Guité-Verret et al. 2021; Littlemore & Turner 2020; Turner et al. 2020; Wilson & Lindy 2013). As the event also brings about unexpected and unprecedented changes to trauma victims' psychological worlds, the individual may interpret the perceived changes in the surrounding environment, the disruption of life order, and an alienated sense of time in terms of SPATIAL RELATIONS in the physical environment (Costa & Steen 2014; Littlemore & Turner 2020; Tay 2014; Wilson & Lindy 2013). The most commonly used vehicle terms are horizontal and vertical orientations like FORWARD/ BACKWARD and UP/DOWN, and expressions indicating locations such as "I am beside myself" and "all over the place".

PHYSICAL ACTIVITY: Universally shared physical activities such as PHYSICAL MOVEMENT, EXERTION OF FORCE, and CONTROL OF BODY constitute a rich source of trauma metaphors (Costa & Steen 2014; Foley 2015; Gušić et al. 2018; Littlemore & Turner 2019; Littlemore & Turner 2020; Meili, Heim & Maercker 2019; Tay 2014; Wilson & Lindy 2013). These vehicle terms play an especially active role in describing sudden changes in emotions and thoughts, perceived alterations in self-identity, and trauma victims' intellectual efforts to cope with their post-traumatic feelings.

Metaphor topics

EMOTIONS AND EMOTIONAL PROCESSES: Psychological trauma is character-ized by the experience of overwhelming negative emotions. One of the typical manifestations of trauma-related disorder is increased sensitivity toward trauma-related emotions such as depression, anxiety, anger, and shame (Berntsen, Willert & Rubin 2003; Ehlers & Clark 2000; Ehlers, Ehring & Kleim 2012; Foa, Molnar & Cashman 1995; Halligan et al. 2003; O'Kearney & Perrott 2006). Sometimes trauma victims may also experience greater difficulties in disengaging themselves from these negative feelings. Compared with milder emotions, the experience of in-tense emotions can create a more pressing need for the speakers to provide de-tailed and vivid descriptions of their subjective experiences (Fainsilber & Ortony 1987). This, in turn, may lead to an increased use of emotion-related metaphors, especially novel expressions.

THINKING AND UNDERSTANDING: The traumatic experience can be very dif-ferent from and even contradictory to trauma victims' previous knowledge of the world and established psychological schemas (Janoff-Bulman 1989), therefore, peo-ple may find themselves overwhelmed by new information and feel confused about what happened. They may also experience difficulties in organizing coherent accounts of the traumatic event (Ehlers, Ehring & Kleim 2012; Foa, Molnar & Cash-man 1995; Zoellner & Bittenger 2004). In the attempt to figure out "why did it hap-pen to me" (Ehlers, Ehring & Kleim 2012) and to make meaning of the traumatic events and the associated changes (Tedeschi & Calhoun 1995), trauma victims may pay more attention to abstract and subjective aspects of their experiences and pro-duce more metaphorical accounts of thinking and understanding. According to clin-ical research on trauma narratives, (Alvarez-Conrad, Zoellner & Foa 2001; Ehlers & Clark 2000; Ehlers, Ehring & Kleim 2012; Foa, Molnar & Cashman 1995; Jaeger et al. 2014; Manne 2002; O'Kearney & Perrott 2006), individuals with higher degrees of trauma are often troubled by obsessive thoughts about the traumatic details, such as the cause, processes and consequence of the event, and relevant individuals, ob-jects, and situations.

SELF-REFERENCES: Traumatic experiences can bring about unexpected changes to people's basic assumptions, beliefs, and expectations of the self, which can lead to a suddenly altered sense of the self. The alteration in self-perception can in turn trig-ger in-depth reflections on their state of being and perceived changes in self-identities (Berntsen, Willert & Rubin 2003; Janoff-Bulman 1989; Tedeschi & Calhoun

1995). Since issues regarding the self, self-identity, and self-changes are highly abstract and complex, individuals would naturally draw metaphorical connections between their internal experiences and external conceptual resources (Fullagar & O'Brien 2012; Kopp & Eckstein 2004; Kopp 1995; Lakoff 1990; Moser 2004; Moser 2007). According to the thematic dimensional analysis of PTSD patients' self-representation by Wilson and Lindy (2013), coherence, autonomy, vitality, and perceived continuity of the self are among the most frequent topics of self-related metaphors.

The two strands of research hold important practical implications for the clinical understanding of clients' subjective experiences, especially the links between metaphor use and psychopathological manifestations. First, the analyses deepen our understanding of how trauma victims make meaning of intensely painful, unspeakable experiences, and how they cope with emotionally and cognitively challenging issues. Second, the study of metaphor use across different clinical stages highlights the potential for metaphor vehicle terms and topics to encode clinically meaningful information. The body of research on metaphor use by PTSD clients, in particular, underscores trauma victims' psychopathological experiences as a crucial factor in shaping metaphor use. The findings point toward the possibility of integrating metaphor analysis into therapeutic practices as prompts for facilitating positive changes and post-traumatic growth.

The following sections discuss the two earlier mentioned research gaps in existing studies. Section 2.3 argues that trauma metaphor research could be advanced by taking multiple semantic and presentational features into consideration. Section 2.4 introduces how psychopathological experiences can be compared in quantitative and qualitative manners and discusses how these differences may manifest in different forms of metaphor variations.

2.3 From semantic features to the multifacetedness of metaphor use

We can see the scope of existing research was mostly restricted to two semantic features of metaphor use, i.e., vehicle terms and topics. Only scant attention has been paid to "presentational features" (Kövecses 2015: 187), which reflect how a specific metaphorical idea is "packaged" and conveyed. Examples of presentational features are *emotional valence* (the emotional tones or attitude expressed using metaphors), *conventionality* (whether a metaphorical idea is novel or conventional), *psychological perspectives* (the viewpoint adopted by the speaker in metaphorical meaning-making), *pragmatic functions* (the communicative purpose of using metaphors), *relevance to the key topic* (whether the metaphor is directly relevant or peripheral to the topic under discussion).

While semantic features offer an immediate view of what is being expressed using metaphors, presentational features reveal how the speakers organize and elucidate their personal experiences (Kövecses 2015). The features encode implicit information about the speakers' default emotional states and their preferred or characteristic ways of metaphorical meaning-making. The tendencies reflect the speakers' habitual ways of information processing, unexpressed emotional and cognitive states, operationalization of tacit knowledge, and understanding of complex knowledge and abstract processes (Moser 2000). Patterns extracted from large-scale data may reveal characteristics that are distinctive of a specific population. This section introduces three therapeutically interesting presentational features that have been neglected in trauma language studies: conventionality, emotional valence, and psychological perspectives. After introducing their definitions and contextual characteristics, I will argue for broadening the research scope from semantic features to the interrelationships among multiple semantic and presentational features, which reflect the multifaceted nature of metaphor use. The combination of categorical data analysis and qualitative analysis will be introduced as a viable approach for investigating the multifaceted nature of metaphor use.

2.3.1 Therapeutically interesting presentational features

Conventionality

One commonly discussed presentational feature of mental health metaphors is conventionality, which refers to the extent to which a metaphor is entrenched in everyday use by ordinary people for everyday communicative purposes (Kövecses 2010).

Conventional metaphors are expressions that have become socially established and are widely shared by members of a linguistic community (Kövecses 2010). For instance, the prepositional phrase "在我心里 (in my mind)" conceptualizes the mind as a CONTAINER of emotions and thoughts. This metaphor is highly conventionalized and systematically used in both Mandarin Chinese and English. In contrast, *novel metaphors* are less systematically used in a linguistic community. According to Gelo & Mergenthaler (2012), creative metaphors in mental health communication include both the modification of conventional metaphors (Lakoff & Turner 1989) and the creation of novel metaphorical ideas. "我的心被锁住了 (my heart has been locked)" is a typical example of novel metaphors in describing traumatic dissociation.

Both novel and conventional metaphors can provide valuable insights into the speakers' emotional inclinations, thought processes, or ways of interpretation, especially when making meaning of emotion-laden topics (Long & Lepper 2008; McMullen 1996). Previous studies have yielded interesting findings about the role of conventionality in expressing emotions and thoughts.

Novel metaphors have been found with an evident edge in expressing intense emotions and idiosyncratic thoughts (Barlow et al. 1977; Gelo & Mergenthaler 2012; Gibbs & Franks 2002; McMullen 1985; Pollio & Barlow 1975; Semino 2011; Turner et al. 2020). According to Turner et al. (2020), extremely painful and over-whelming experiences like pregnancy loss, and extraordinary feelings like altered perception of time, can trigger particularly active use of novel metaphors. Other studies also emphasize novel metaphors' strength in capturing nuanced thoughts and difficult emotional feelings, such as intimate characteristics of the self, troubling experiences, and physical pain (e.g., Barlow, Pollio & Fine 1977; Gibbs & Franks 2002; McMullen 1985; Pollio & Barlow 1975; Semino 2011). Fainsilber and Ortony's (1987) study on emotion metaphors showed that individuals experiencing intense emotional feelings are more inclined to use novel than conventional metaphors when describing their experiences. Gelo and Mergenthaler (2012) provide corroborative evidence for this argument. Their analysis, based on metaphors in 42 therapeutic sessions, showed that frequencies of novel metaphors are significantly related to the experience of emotion-laden and cognitively complex processes, such as the organization and modification of emotional feelings, the articulation of abstract thoughts, and therapeutic engagement; however, no apparent patterns were found for conventional metaphors.

Some studies have emphasized the capacity of conventional metaphors to capture the speaker's implicit emotions, thoughts, and information processing patterns (Long & Lepper 2008; McMullen 1996; Moser 2000, 2007). Their findings suggest that conventional metaphors bear no less personal and therapeutic significance than novel metaphors do. For example, Moser (2000: 4) argues that conventional metaphors, often used automatically and subconsciously, can capture the speaker's implicit knowledge of the self and world, latent psychological processes, and unconscious thoughts. The argument is supported by a subsequent empirical study (Moser 2007), which revealed significant correlations between the choices of conventional metaphors and the speakers' personality traits. In an intensive qualitative analysis of metaphors produced by four patients in 12 therapeutic sessions, Long and Lepper (2008) found both conventional and novel metaphors can be used to provide vivid and revealing accounts of therapeutically meaningful concepts like the self, others, relationships, mental states, and thought processes, and the metaphor usage patterns can provide clinical insights for the diagnosis and understanding the client's therapeutic improvements. McMullen's

(1989) comparative study of successful and unsuccessful cases of psychotherapy revealed that some novel metaphors can be less therapeutically relevant than others, and that conventional metaphors also play a crucial role in addressing complex mental health issues.

Emotional valence
Another feature of interest is the emotional valence carried by linguistic expressions. Emotional valence can be either rated as a continuous variable in terms of intensity (e.g., Bradley & Lang 1994; Rasmussen & Berntsen 2009), or identified as broader categories, such as negative, neutral, or positive, based on the nature of emotions or connotations of expressions (e.g., Espuny et al. 2018; Kauschke et al. 2019).

Preferences for specific emotional valences reflect the individual's default and even implicit emotional inclinations toward the issues under discussion. In the mental health context, the patterns can provide key clinical insights into the speakers' psychological states and therapeutic progress. Preference for negatively valenced expressions and/or the lack of positive expressions are often seen as indicators of poor mental health conditions or unsatisfactory therapeutic improvements, and vice versa (Levitt, Korman & Angus 2000; Pennebaker 1993; Pennebaker & Francis 1996). Nevertheless, some studies identified heightened use of positive emotion words as a defensive mechanism to conceal negative experiences (e.g., Borbely 2008), or a sign of higher levels of distress (e.g., Pennebaker, Mayne & Francis 1997).

A large number of clinically oriented studies identified the preference for negatively valenced expressions as significant predictors of trauma and more specific clinical symptoms such as re-experiencing (e.g., Cohn, Mehl & Pennebaker 2004; Halligan et al. 2003; Jaeger et al. 2014; Kleim et al. 2018; Luno, Louwerse & Beck 2013; Todorov et al. 2018; Wardecker et al. 2017). Some studies discovered significant correlations between more frequent use of positive emotion words and lower levels of post-traumatic stress (e.g., Frewen et al. 2011; Jaeger et al. 2014; Kleim et al. 2013; Kleim et al. 2018; Manne 2002; Wardecker et al. 2017). However, the patterns were mostly investigated by clinical researchers without differentiating between literal and metaphorical language, and the patterns are typically examined in relation to clinical factors rather than linguistic variables. How different emotional valences are instantiated in metaphorical language remains largely unexplored.

Research on emotion-laden metaphorical language showed that inclinations toward emotional valences can vary with presentational features such as conventionality and the ways of presenting evaluation. In a study of metaphor conventionality, emotional polarity, and explicitness in film reviews, Fuoli, Littlemore, and Turner (2022) found that both novel and conventional metaphors are more closely associated with negative rather than positive evaluations. While novel metaphors are more likely to convey evaluative meanings implicitly, conventional metaphors are often associated with explicit evaluations.

Psychological perspectives

Another variable of theoretical and clinical interest is the choice of psychological perspectives,[13] which is defined by Nigro and Neisser (1983) as the viewpoints adopted in describing or evaluating a specific event or experience. Two broad categories of psychological perspectives are identified by Nigro and Neisser (1983). In *the field perspective,* the individual experiences the scene in the way it is from her/his own perspective without seeing or feeling the self. In contrast, in *the observer perspective,* the individual adopts an external standpoint, observing the self in relation to the situation from an external viewpoint.[14]

Inclinations toward specific psychological perspectives reveal the speakers' dominant or habitual way of accessing the emotions, thoughts, and concrete details of the event. According to Nigro and Neisser (1983), narrations of personal experiences in different situations are often associated with distinct perspective preferences. For instance, situations with higher degrees of emotional self-awareness, such as escaping from a threatening situation, are often described using the observer perspective, while attempts to focus on feelings rather than objective or factual aspects of the situation (e.g., watching a horror movie) are more likely to elicit the field perspectives.

Choices of psychological perspectives are closely related to trauma psychopathology. Quite a few studies on trauma narratives have highlighted the observer perspective as a potential marker of traumatization. The study by McIssac and Eich (2004) on perspective-taking in traumatic memories showed that self-accounts from the field perspective contain richer details of the individual's affective reactions, somatic sensations, and psychological states during the traumatic event, as compared with narrations from the observer perspective. By contrast, recollections from the

---

13 The term used by Nigro and Neisser (1983) and subsequent psychology literature was "perspectives". In this book, the term "psychological perspectives" is used consistently to distinguish the concepts from the notions of "perspectival system" and "perspectives" in cognitive semantic studies (Talmy 2003).

14 Although the field and the observer perspectives have been extensively studied in cognitive, social, and clinical psychology (Radvansky & Svob 2019), they were not the viewpoints in narrative recollections. In one of the questionnaire-based studies reported by Nigro and Neisser (1983), about 12% of 200 responses indicated that neither perspective was appropriate, and 9.97 % of 291 responses belonged to neither perspective. While studies on narrative recollections focused mainly on the field-observer distinction or perspective shifts, only scant attention has been paid to the exceptional cases.

observer perspective are often accessed from a greater psychological distance and perceived with relatively lower degrees of emotional involvement (McIsaac & Eich 2002; McIsaac & Eich 2004; Nigro & Neisser 1983; Robinson & Swanson 1993). Therefore, the observer perspective is often adopted by the severely traumatized as a spontaneous strategy to keep the overwhelming memories and feelings at bay.

In other words, the field perspective enables the memories to be accessed in a self-immersed way, whereas the observer perspective allows the experience to be narrated in a self-detached manner. The contrast has been similarly observed in semantic studies of metaphor topics in psychotherapy. As noted by Kopp (1995), metaphorical expressions about mental health issues often revolve around six key dimensions. These dimensions include three basic elemental categories, i.e., SELF, OTHERS, and SITUATIONS, and their relationships with the self, i.e., SELF AND SELF, SELF AND OTHERS, and SELF AND SITUATION. In this book, the dimensions are referred to as *target categories* following Tay (2015). Metaphors in the basic elemental category focus on the speaker's mental image of the three major elements, while those in the relationship-focused category are the individual's reflections on how the self is related to the major elements (Kopp & Eckstein 2004). This dichotomy aligns with the division between the field and the observer perspectives: target categories experienced with the speaker "inside" themselves (i.e., SELF, OTHERS, and SITUATION) correspond to the field perspective, and those in which the self is both the subject and the object of the observation (i.e., SELF AND SELF, SELF AND OTHERS, and SELF AND SITUATION) can be seen as subcategories of the observer perspective. While target categories summarize the semantic meanings of the metaphor topics, the field and the observer perspectives capture more structural aspects of metaphor use (i.e., the speakers' standing point when metaphorizing their experiences). The relationship between the two psychological perspectives and the six target categories is shown in Figure 2.1.

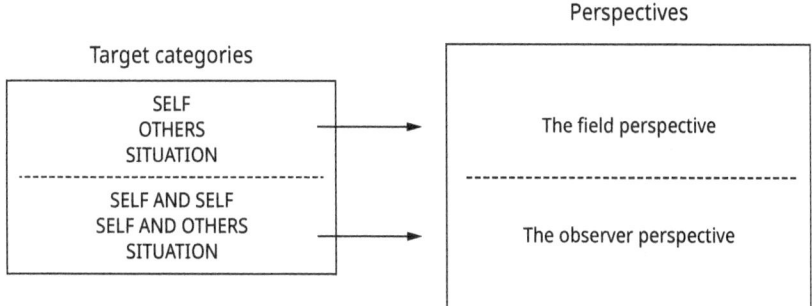

Figure 2.1: The field and observer perspectives and Kopp's (1995) taxonomy of target categories.

There has been extensive research on target categories in mental health metaphors (e.g., Eckstein et al. 2012; Rowat, De Stefano & Drapeau 2008; Tay 2015, 2017, 2018), however, no prior research has been found on psychological perspectives in metaphorical language. Previous efforts in distinguishing the two psychological perspectives mainly focused on trauma victims' narrations of concrete traumatic experiences (e.g., what had happened, the process and consequence of the event), which are typically described using literal rather than metaphorical language. The contextualized instantiations of psychological perspectives in metaphorical language, especially their interactions with other presentational features, remain intriguing questions for both metaphor researchers and clinical psychologists.

2.3.2 Exploring multifacetedness via a mixed-method approach

In existing mental health metaphor research, these presentational features were mostly studied in the context of psychotherapy in relation to psychometric measures or therapeutic outcomes (e.g., Barlow, Pollio & Fine 1977; Gelo & Mergenthaler 2012; McMullen 1985, 1989, 1996; Pollio & Barlow 1975; Pollio et al. 1977; Tay 2017, 2018, 2019). Limited attention has been given to the systematic interplay between these presentational features and their relationships with semantic features of metaphor use.

As demonstrated above, presentational features of metaphors can interact with each other in meaningful ways, for example, the associations between conventionality and emotional valence noted by Fuoli, Littlemore, and Turner (2022). Presentational features may also engage in systematic ways with different semantic features, so that the relationship between two metaphor aspects varies with the instantiation of other, for example, the interaction observed among psychological perspectives, emotional valence, and semantic features of metaphors (McIssac & Eich 2004). The potential for multiple variables and their sub-categories to engage in systematic, dynamic interactions is referred to as the multifacetedness of metaphor use

Compared with the study of vehicle-topic mappings and the instantiation of individual presentational aspects, multifacetedness of metaphor use abstracts even further from the idiosyncrasies of specific metaphorical expressions. It captures how multiple aspects of metaphors are interconnected with each other, and how the relationships between two variables and their subcategories may vary when other variables are taken into consideration. Patterns indexed by presentational features, in particular, could offer a complementary perspective on the speaker's implicit emotions, thought processes, and beliefs. In clinical diagnosis and treatment, the information may serve as informative references for the development of metaphor-based therapeutic protocols (e.g., Grove & Panzer 1989; Kopp 1995; Sims & Whynot 1997), where therapists guide their clients to elaborate on their metaphors by asking questions like "What do you feel" and "What does it (the emotional feeling) look like". The findings could also help therapists prepare for metaphor usage patterns that are characteristic of specific mental health contexts and patterns that are likely (or unlikely) to occur. Findings about specific variable categories could provide useful supplementary information for therapists' understanding and management of client-generated metaphors.

Despite the prospective theoretical and practical implications, the multifaceted nature of metaphor use has not been adequately addressed in the study of mental health metaphors. Tay (2017) noted that existing research on mental health metaphors exhibits a strong preference for qualitative analytic strategies over quantitative methods. In-depth qualitative analyses of emergent metaphor themes can capture nuanced patterns that are characteristic of the context and provide insights into questions of theoretical and practical concerns (Charteris-Black 2012; Tay 2013). However, this approach may be less effective in extracting systematic patterns across larger datasets and the relationships among multiple variables and their subcategories (Tay 2017). While some qualitative studies have considerably large sample sizes, the analyses often focus on a small number of examples and sometimes fragmented use of metaphors. Even though the studies reveal subtle, unexplored patterns of metaphor use and characteristics reflecting idiosyncrasies of personal experiences, they may not capture general tendencies typical of the given trauma population.

Compared to qualitative analysis, quantitative methods can be more efficient and reliable in capturing the multifaceted nature of metaphor use. A particularly useful group of methods is categorical data analytic methods (Moser 2000), which investigate quantitative relationships among clearly delineated variable categories.

Among categorical data analytic methods, log-linear analysis and chi-square tests of independence (hereafter "chi-square tests") are the most commonly used in the study of mental health metaphors. These methods examine the relationships between categorical variables based on the deviations of observed frequencies from expected frequencies. The log-linear analysis explores higher-order relationships, which refer to the interrelationships among three or more variables. An example is the study of metaphor use in psychotherapy by Tay (2017), which investigated the interactions among five theoretical and contextual variables (i.e., speaker, functions of metaphors, target topic, phase of therapy, and therapeutic dyad) of 2,893 metaphors in 29.5 hours of talk. For example, the significant three-way interaction among target topic, metaphor function, and speakers suggests that different target topics are associated with different communicative functions, and that the associations found in therapist and client language are different. The significant four-way interaction among therapeutic dyad, target topic, metaphor function, and therapeutic phase, suggests that the association between target topics and metaphor functions varies across therapeutic dyads, and the within-dyad patterns may vary further across different phases of therapy. As the relationships encompass multiple variables and subcategories, they may not be easily identified and interpreted using qualitative methods and descriptive statistics.

Another approach for examining multifacetedness is to examine the associations between two pre-determined variables. For example, Tay (2018) examined the presentational features of 512 MOVEMENT metaphors in 20 therapeutic sessions. Log-linear analysis was used to examine the relationships between TOPIC, DIRECTION OF MOVEMENT, and SPEAKER. Three significant bivariate associations were found, i.e., TOPIC*DIRECTION, DIRECTION*SPEAKER, and TOPIC-*SPEAKER. Contingency tables were generated to probe into the observed and expected frequencies for each category of the associated variables. For example, the DIRECTION*SPEAKER association shows that clients produced a significantly higher number of SIDEWAYS metaphors than expected, whereas therapists were less likely to draw on this aspect of MOVEMENT; a similar contrast in frequencies was identified for the two speakers' metaphors about uncertain directions.

Also utilizing categorical data analytic methods, Moser (2007) investigated the conceptual resources involved in 1,162 SELF metaphors. Configural frequency analysis, a statistical technique based on Chi-square tests, was used to examine the distribution of 22 vehicle terms across six specific aspects of the SELF, including actual self, ideal self, social self, negative self, ought self, and self changes. The six aspects were found to be associated with distinctive groups of vehicle terms. For instance, the actual self is significantly more likely to be described using WEIGHT and BALANCE metaphors, whereas the ideal self is significantly less likely to be represented using FIGHTING metaphors.

When the significant relationship contains more than two variables, the patterns can be intuitively difficult to conceive. A useful tool for visualizing higher-order relationships is the Multiple Correspondence Analysis (MCA) factor plot, which detects relationships between categorical variables. In MCA plots, different categories of the variables are represented as discrete points on a two-dimensional plot, and their interrelationships are visualized as positions of and distances between the points. By converting abstract statistical relationships among multiple variables into visualizable forms, MCA plots reduce the difficulty of understanding and interpreting complex interrelationships. In addition, the visualization could also pinpoint metaphor usage patterns of special theoretical or practical concerns and reveal potential directions for subsequent qualitative discussion.

As shown above, categorical data analytic methods serve as a useful tool for exploring the multifaceted nature of metaphor use.[15] However, we should be aware that quantitative methods alone are not sufficient for exploring contextualized metaphor use. Instead, as noted by Moser (2000), quantitative metaphor analysis reaches its full potential only when it is combined with qualitative discourse analysis. This integration allows overall tendencies of metaphor use to be interpreted in relation to situational, biographical, and social features characteristic of the given context. Supporting this view, Tay (2017), points out that patterns extracted with frequency-based quantitative methods (e.g., categorical data analytic methods and correlation analysis) do not necessarily entail thematic significance. In other words, quantitative methods could only be used as a complement rather than a substitute for qualitative discourse analysis. The combination of categorical data analysis and qualitative discourse analysis, therefore, is regarded as a more suitable approach for exploring the multifaceted nature of metaphor use. While categorical data analysis captures systematic, quantitative relationships among multiple variables, qualitative discourse analysis offers a context-informed view of how and why those patterns came into being.

2.4 The interaction between metaphor use and psychopathological experiences

The role of psychopathological experiences in metaphor use is under-explored in both metaphor research and clinical studies of trauma narratives. While clinical studies of trauma narratives take psychometric data as an important source of information, metaphorical language was seldom acknowledged as clinically relevant. In contrast, linguistic research on trauma metaphors takes the speaker's emotions, thoughts, and physiological experiences as crucial information for in-

---

15 While categorical data analytic methods offer a convenient way for modelling interrelationships among multiple metaphor variables, it should be noted that assigning metaphors to a finite number of mutually exclusive categories is only a simplified approach to understanding the phenomenon. Previous researchers have provided critical reflections on issues like whether metaphors can be defined by necessary and sufficient conditions that yield clear-cut category boundaries and whether a single instantiation of metaphor can be included in more than one category (e.g., Giora 2002; Cameron 1999; Cameron et al. 2009). Some have proposed tentative solutions for making consistent decisions over borderline cases and accounting for qualitative nuances of metaphors (e.g., Cameron 1999; Fuoli, Littlemore & Turner 2022; Kimmel 2010; Pragglejaz Group 2007). It is therefore important for researchers who apply category-based analyses to acknowledge the trade-off between analytic convenience and pursuing the truth about language use, and maintain sensitivity to real-life complexities.

terpreting emergent linguistic patterns. However, the subjective experiences were rarely assessed with structured and quantifiable measures, and their systematic relationships with metaphor use were not thoroughly examined.

In Section 2.4.1, I will provide a brief introduction to psychopathological experiences of ASD, with special attention to quantitative and qualitative differences as the two basic dimensions of variations. Section 2.4.2 will present a review of previous findings about the interactions between subjective experiences and metaphor/language use, and discuss how quantitative and qualitative differences in subjective experiences can be captured from metaphor use.

2.4.1 Psychopathological experiences of ASD: Two basic dimensions

In clinical settings, psychopathological experiences of trauma-related disorders like PTSD and ASD[16] are usually assessed against clearly defined diagnostic criteria, such as the DSM standards from the American Psychiatric Association and the International Classification of Diseases (ICD; World Health Organization 2019). Given this book's emphasis on metaphor use shortly after trauma exposure, psychopathological experiences of trauma will be introduced based on the diagnosis of ASD.[17] The introduction will draw from the DSM-IV criteria (American Psychiatric Association 1994), which is the basis for developing many existing ASD screening tools, including the SASRQ selected for this book. The diagnostic criteria are reproduced in Table 2.1.

In DSM-IV, eight criteria were specified for the diagnosis of ASD. Criterion A is a clinical definition of experiences that are considered traumatic. Criteria B to F delineate five specific symptoms that form the basis for diagnosing ASD, including dissociation, re-experiencing, avoidance, anxiety and hyperarousal, and impairment in functioning. Criterion G defines the duration of symptom persistence necessary for an ASD diagnosis. Criterion H lists exceptional cases that require special consideration in diagnosis. To obtain a diagnosis of ASD, the individual must meet Criteria A, G, and H; in addition, the individual must exhibit at least three indicators of dissociation as per Criterion B and at least one indicator for each of the remaining symp-

---

16 There is in fact extensive overlap between the diagnostic criteria proposed for ASD and PTSD. The most prominent differences are the clinical manifestations of specific symptoms and duration of symptom presence required for diagnosis (refer to Cahill & Pontoski 2005 for a comparison of ASD and PTSD symptomatology and diagnoses based on DSM-IV, and Perry 2021 for a comparison based on DSM-V).
17 The diagnostic criteria of ASD had been updated in the latest DSM-V published in 2013 (American Psychiatric Association 2013).

Table 2.1: The DSM-IV criteria for diagnosing ASD (American Psychiatric Association 1994).

A. The person has been exposed to a traumatic event in which both of the following were present: 1. The person experienced, witnessed, or was confronted with an event or events that involved actual or threatened death or serious injury, or a threat to the physical integrity of self or others. 2. The person's response involved intense fear, helplessness, or horror.
B. Either while experiencing or after experiencing the distressing event, the individual has three or more of the following dissociative symptoms: 1. a subjective sense of numbing, detachment, or absence of emotional responsiveness 2. a reduction in awareness of his or her surroundings 3. derealization 4. depersonalization 5. dissociative amnesia (i.e., inability to recall an important aspect of the trauma)
C. The traumatic event is persistently re-experienced in at least one of the following ways: recurrent images, thoughts, dreams, illusions, flashback episodes, or a sense of reliving the experience; or distress on exposure to reminders of the traumatic event.
D. Marked avoidance of stimuli that arouse recollections of the trauma (e.g., thoughts, feelings, conversations, activities, places, people).
E. Marked symptoms of anxiety or increased arousal (e.g., difficulty sleeping, irritability, poor concentration, hypervigilance, exaggerated startle response, motor restlessness).
F. The disturbance causes clinically significant distress or impairment in social, occupational, or other important areas of functioning or impairs the individual's ability to pursue some necessary tasks such as obtaining necessary assistance or mobilizing personal resources by telling family members about the traumatic experience.
G. The disturbance lasts for a minimum of 2 days and a maximum of 4 weeks and occurs within 4 weeks of the traumatic event.
H. The disturbance is not due to the direct physiological effects of a substance (e.g., a drug of abuse, a medication) or a general medical condition, is not better accounted for by brief psychotic disorder, and is not merely an exacerbation of a preexisting Axis I or Axis II disorder.

toms outlined in Criteria C to F (American Psychiatric Association 1994). Each of the five symptoms (described in Criterion B to F) features a cohesive cluster of emotional, cognitive, and physiological disturbances, highlighting a distinctive clinical feature of ASD. Together, the five symptoms distinguish ASD from other mental health disorders.

Trauma victims may not experience the symptoms in precisely the same way. For example, some individuals might be more affected by intrusive re-experiencing of their traumatic feelings, some may develop more severe avoidance behaviors and reluctance to talk and think about the traumatic event, whereas some may feel particularly disturbed by functional impairments and experience greater difficulties maintaining pre-trauma life routines and interpersonal relationships. It is also possible that trauma victims exhibit different symptom combinations and manifestations (Galatzer-Levy & Bryant 2013).

Several psychometric tools have been developed for diagnosing ASD, including clinician-rated scales like the Acute Stress Disorder Interview (ASDI; Bryant et al. 1998), and self-report measures such as the Acute Stress Disorder Scale (ASDS; Bryant, Moulds & Guthrie 2000), Trauma Symptom Inventory (TSI; Briere 1995), and the SASRQ (Cardeña et al. 2000) introduced earlier in Section 1.3.2. The psychometric tools could provide precise and consistent assessment of two broad dimensions of psychopathological experiences: 1) *quantitative differences* in the severity of traumatization (including overall degrees of trauma and severities of specific symptoms), and 2) *qualitative differences* in the clinical presence of symptoms.[18]

Overall degrees of trauma and *severities of specific symptoms* are quantified with Likert scales and represented using continuous scores. Higher scores suggest more severe traumatization and higher risks of developing ASD, and lower scores reflect less severe symptoms and a reduced likelihood of developing ASD. Due to a variety of factors (e.g., the nature and duration of traumatic events, individuals' coping capacities, social support, and various other risk factors), individuals may not experience trauma in precisely the same severity (Brewin, Andrews & Valentine 2000; Ozer et al. 2003; Shalev et al. 1996). Some may suffer from higher degrees of trauma, with more intense physiological, emotional, and cognitive disturbances, while others might be less affected by the traumatic event. According to Bryant et al. (2011), about 7 to 28% of those who had trauma exposure meet the diagnostic criteria of ASD; about half of those with ASD may progress to PTSD. Individuals with different severities of traumatization can be seen as showing quantitative differences in a given aspect of psychopathological experience.

The *clinical presence* of a symptom or disorder indicates whether the trauma victim's psychopathological experiences surpass the diagnostic threshold and require special clinical attention or intervention. This is usually evaluated based on the numbers and severities of specific clinical indicators. For example, following the SASRQ criteria, only ratings of three or higher on the 6-point scale count as evidence for clinical presence, and the numbers of valid indicators must conform to the DSM-IV criteria described earlier (i.e., three or more for dissociation and at least one for the other four symptoms). The evaluation of symptom presence consti-

---

18 The severity of traumatization and the clinical presence of symptoms are examined not only in trauma diagnosis but also in assessing other mental health disorders, like depression and anxiety.

tutes the principal basis of ASD diagnosis.[19] To be diagnosed with ASD, the individual needs to fulfill the clinical presence criteria for all five symptoms.[20] Meeting clinical presence criteria for fewer than five symptoms is considered below the threshold of ASD. Individuals with diverse clinically present symptoms can be seen as showing qualitative differences in clinical manifestations.

2.4.2 Psychopathological experiences and metaphor use

Previous studies have shown that both quantitative and qualitative differences in psychopathological experiences can manifest in trauma victims' language use. In a synthesized review of trauma narratives research, O'Kearney and Perrott (2006) found that individuals with higher degrees of traumatization exhibit increased focus on sensory and perceptual impressions, negative emotions, emotional and thought processes, self-identity, self-references, psychological perspectives, and temporal disruptions in describing their traumatic experiences. Several studies highlighted interesting correlations between symptom severity and linguistic preferences, including both presentational features like emotional valence and disorganization, and semantic aspects such as descriptions of threat, death, and self-references (e.g., Berntsen, Willert & Rubin 2003; Ehlers, Hackmann & Michael 2004; Ehlers, Ehring & Kleim 2012; Foa, Molnar & Cashman 1995; Harvey & Bryant 1999; Luno, Louwerse & Beck 2013).

Trauma victims with qualitatively different psychopathological experiences may highlight and downplay different aspects of their traumatic experiences. For example, individuals who suffer from dissociation in particular, often report a sense of disconnection or deviation from the normal sense of the self (Janoff-Bulman 1989; Gušić et al. 2018). The experience might lead the trauma victims to provide more detailed accounts of their perceived loss of integrity compared with those less disturbed by the symptom. In contrast, language use by trauma victims with more severe anxiety and hyperarousal, as compared with those less affected by the symptom, may contain more sensory and perceptual information, as the former diagnostic group is more alerted to changes in the external environment.

---

19 Some psychometric questionnaires (e.g., the Mississippi Scale for PTSD developed by Keane et al. 1988) and follow-up clinical research use clinical cutoff points for diagnosing trauma-related disorder and symptoms (Orsillo 2001).

20 High scorers of a psychometric questionnaire may not necessarily meet the diagnosis threshold and clinical presence criteria. A trauma victim may be profoundly affected by a symptom, yet not fulfill the clinical presence criterion if the number of reported symptom indicators fall below the DSM-IV threshold. Similarly, fulfilling the criterion for a particular symptom does not guarantee an ASD diagnosis if not all five symptoms are clinically present.

These findings provided convergent evidence that both quantitative and qualitative differences in psychopathological experiences can manifest in trauma victims' language use. However, many of the studies used dictionary-based computerized text analytic tools such as LIWC (Linguistic Inquiry Word Count; Pennebaker et al 2015) to identify clearly observable, quantifiable patterns. As a result, the analyses focused almost exclusively on literal markers of symptom-related emotions and thoughts (e.g., "sad", "worry", and "death") and grammatical words like first-person pronouns. Compared with these linguistic aspects, metaphorical expressions such as "my heart is sealed" are not apparently related to specific symptoms and are less quantifiable; therefore, they are often omitted from the analysis. This research trend might be a result of clinical diagnoses focusing almost exclusively on clearly observable and directly quantifiable aspects of trauma. As noted by Galatzer-Levy and Bryant (2013), to establish reliability and ensure the validity of diagnoses, clinical practitioners prioritize universally shared, reliably observable aspects of the traumatic experience, like the triggering event, the process and consequence of the event, and the duration of specific symptoms (refer to Table 2.1). Metaphorical accounts of subjective experiences are often regarded as ornamental, vague, and idiosyncratic. Therefore, they are seldom considered relevant in clinical diagnosis.

Contrary to clinically situated research, linguistic studies of trauma metaphors have focused more on specific forms of meaning-making than on the speakers' psychopathological experiences. Many studies recognized trauma victims' emotions, thoughts, and physical and physiological experiences as key factors in shaping metaphor use (e.g., Beck 2016, 2017; Costa & Steen 2014; Foley 2015; Littlemore & Turner 2019, 2020; Wilson & Lindy 2013). However, the findings were mainly derived from qualitative analyses of trauma victims' language use, without relating to psychometric outcomes. In the few studies that combined linguistic data and therapeutic observations (i.e., Costa & Steen 2014; Foley 2015; Wilson & Lindy 2013), only chronologically delineated and broadly defined therapeutic stages (e.g., before and after recovery) were taken as the basis for categorizing and comparing metaphor usage patterns; structured and quantifiable measures like psychometric questionnaires were not employed.

Despite the lack of prior research, metaphor use is by no means irrelevant or peripheral to psychopathological experiences. As we can see from Table 2.1, psychopathological experiences of mental health disorders are in essence emotions, thoughts, and physiological experiences categorized in clinically meaningful ways. Although not many studies have directly related psychopathological experiences to metaphor use, extensive research has identified nuanced differences in emotions, thoughts, and physiological experiences as key factors in shaping metaphor variations (e.g., Cameron & Maslen 2010; Johnson 1987; Kövecses 2000, 2010, 2015, 2020; Lakoff 1987; Lakoff & Johnson 1980, 1999; Littlemore 2019; Semino 2010; Tay 2013).

Recent studies in other mental health contexts have also highlighted quantitative and qualitative differences in psychological and psychiatric states as potential triggers of metaphor variations. Their findings are summarized below.

Quantitative differences in subjective experiences and metaphor use

According to Kövecses (2010, 2015, 2020), different subjective experiences like emotions, ways of thinking, and physical sensations may lead the speakers to present their metaphorical ideas in particular ways, and/or highlight or downplay specific aspects of their personal experiences. Quantitative differences in a given subjective experience, such as different intensities of emotions, reliance on certain ways of thinking, and salience of physical sensations, may assign different salience to the related conceptual resources, or result in varying degrees of reliance on the associated way of thinking. In terms of metaphorical meaning-making, the differences may manifest as more or less frequent occurrences of certain presentational features or semantic themes.

Quantitative differences in subjective experiences, captured by psychometric measures, can be distinguished from the speakers' metaphor use. A study that incorporated psychometric data into metaphor analysis, conducted by Moser (2007), revealed the potential for metaphor use to display continuous, quantitative variations across diverse psychometric outcomes. A correlation analysis was conducted on 63 individuals' SELF conceptualizations and their ratings on the Big Five dimensions of personality traits, including agreeableness, openness, extraversion, neuroticism, and conscientiousness (John, Donahue, & KENTLE 1991). Results showed that the participants' personality trait scores are significantly correlated with their preferences for certain metaphor vehicle terms and topics. For example, openness to experience is positively and significantly correlated with vehicle terms like CONTAINER, PATH, and topics such as ACTUAL SELF, SELF CHANGE, and SOCIAL SELF; agreeableness is positively and significantly correlated with metaphors about SCIENCE, TECHNOLOGY, and ACTUAL SELF; as extraversion score goes up, metaphors about PLAY AND SPORTS, OUGHT SELF, and SOCIAL SELF also increase (Moser 2007).

Varying intensities of emotional disturbances may prompt individuals to accentuate different aspects of metaphor vehicle terms or topics. Demjén et al. (2019) compared metaphor use by 10 schizophrenic patients with different stress levels. Frequencies of POWER metaphors are examined in relation to psychometric outcomes yielded by the Depression Anxiety Stress Scale (DASS-21; Lovibond & Lovibond 1995). It was found that patients with high and low levels showed different preferences in metaphor use: those with higher levels of distress were more likely to describe the voices as agentive aggressors and themselves in a disempowered position, whereas those with lower levels of distress were more inclined to conceptualize themselves as empowered agents (Demjén et al. 2019). In a study of COVID-related metaphor use, Gök and Kara (2022) investigated how the experience of different health-related stressors and stress levels influenced individuals' choices of vehicle terms and topics. It was found that people with different stress levels had contrasting preferences for vehicle terms: individuals with higher stress levels showed stronger preferences for RESTLESSNESS metaphors than expressions about BEING RESTRICTED, whereas those with lower stress levels exhibited the reverse trend. Fainsilber and Ortony (1987) compared speakers' preferences for metaphor topics when describing intense and mild emotions. Their study revealed that intense emotions led to more frequent use of FEELING-related metaphors compared to milder emotions, but this pattern did not extend to metaphors about emotion-related ACTIONS.

According to Boers (1999), when a specific experience becomes particularly prominent, people naturally get attuned to the experience and make more extensive references to it in metaphorical meaning-making. Findings reported by the abovementioned studies suggest quantitative differences in mental health and psychiatric disturbances can be clearly identified from the individuals' metaphor usage profiles. However, these analyses were based on binary categories (e.g., high and low stress levels, intense and mild emotions) rather than continuous data yielded by psychometric measures. The contrast between metaphor usage patterns associated with different types of psychopathological experiences, such as different clinical symptoms, is also underexplored. While psychometric tools like the SASRQ allow for a more detailed and precise depiction of quantitative differences in various clinical aspects, how these differences manifest in trauma victims' metaphor use remains an intriguing question. Based on trauma victims' psychometric data (i.e., overall degrees of trauma and severities of symptoms) and their metaphor usage profiles summarized based on trauma-related variables (introduced in Section 2.3.1), Chapter 4 of this book explores how quantitative differences in psychopathological experiences can be distinguished from the systematic use of metaphors.

Qualitative differences in subjective experiences and metaphor use
Qualitative differences in subjective experiences might prompt the speakers to focus on different aspects of their emotions and thoughts, and therefore, draw on diverse conceptual resources in metaphorical meaning-making (Kövecses 2020).

Yu and Tay (2020) explored the relationships between three key emotional themes (i.e., ANGER, DEPRESSION, and ANXIETY) and four types of image schemas in 964 metaphors. While certain image schemas like CONTAINMENT, FORCE, PATH, and VERTICAL ORIENTATION were common to all three emotions, the frequency of their use differed significantly. For example, ANGER is significantly more likely described using CONTAINMENT metaphors and less likely represented as PATH and VERTICAL ORIENTATION. In contrast, DEPRESSION was significantly more likely to be interpreted in terms of FORCE and VERTICAL ORIENTATION but less likely represented as CONTAINMENT. The analysis highlights distinct metaphor usage patterns for the three emotions, which can provide useful information for understanding and dealing with the emotions. Apart from different varieties of emotions, different stages of a specific emotion may also be discerned from metaphor use. The study of ANGER metaphors by Lakoff and Kövecses (1987) showed that different developmental stages of ANGER, such as perception of anger, attempt to control anger, and restoration of equilibrium, are often conceptualized using different types of embodied experiences and different aspects of FORCE RELATIONS.

Different clinical manifestations and stages of a given psychiatric or mental health disorder, which have differential emotional, cognitive, and physiological experiences, are also likely to be metaphorized using distinct sets of conceptual resources. In a study of metaphor use by patients with different types of seizure, Plug, Sharrack & Reuber (2009) discovered that patients with epileptic seizure tend to metaphorize seizure as an AGENT/FORCE or EVENT/SITUATION, while those in the non-epileptic group are more inclined to conceptualize their subjective experience as being in a SPACE or PLACE. In a study of metaphors in describing Obsessive-compulsive Disorder (OCD), Knapton (2016) observed that the conceptualization of THREAT varies across different subtypes of OCD. Clients who are particularly concerned with self-identity prefer to describe THREAT as something trapped inside the CONTAINER of the self, those who are particularly attentive to the negative outcomes of activity tend to conceptualize THREAT as dynamic, unpredictable, and constantly moving along the trajectory of SOURCE-PATH-GOAL, and those who are more concerned about the effects of objects were more inclined to perceive the SELF as a CONTAINER and THREAT as external to the SELF. Moreover, the clients' metaphorical conceptualizations of threat vary as different OCD episodes (e.g., trigger, distressing thought, response) unfold. Among all, metaphors about MOVEMENT OF THREAT are most pertinent to the experience of fear and distress. The studies summarized in Section 2.2 (Beck 2016, 2017; Foley 2015; Littlemore & Turner 2019, 2020; Wilson & Lindy 2013) also showed that qualitatively different aspects of trauma, such as different emotional disturbances and different recovery or treatment stages, are often metaphorized with distinct vehicle groupings and topics.

Compared with metaphors about different emotions (e.g., anger and happiness) and psychopathological disorders (e.g., depression and anxiety), the conceptualization of different symptoms of a given psychopathological disorder has received much less attention. However, findings about trauma victims' accounts of psychopathological experiences have provided interesting, albeit fragmented, insights that different post-traumatic symptoms may be perceived and interpreted in terms of different embodied experiences. As noted in Section 2.4.1, psychopathological experiences of ASD can be categorized into five dominant symptoms, each marked by a distinct cluster of emotional, cognitive, and physiological disturbances. A case study of a PTSD client's metaphor use presented by Wilson & Lindy (2013: 95) suggests that dissociative symptoms are often interpreted in terms of physical experiences of SPLITTING (e.g., "I am split apart" and "I am diffused and unglued"). Gušic et al. (2018: 546–547) also reported similar expressions in a study of war-traumatized refugees' experiences of PTSD, for example, "My thoughts split" and "I don't feel present sometimes, thoughts are not here". Unlike dissociative symptoms, trauma victims' experience of hypervigilance is often described as EXPLOSION, for example, "I was about to explode" (Wilson & Lindy 2013: 69) and "being set off" (Foley 2015: 141).

The interesting convergence offers preliminary evidence that different symptoms of the same mental disorder may be metaphorized using distinct types of embodied experiences. Nonetheless, the conceptualization of specific clinical symptoms has not yet been investigated systematically in empirical metaphor research due to the general lack of attention to clinically validated psychopathological experiences.

To study symptom-specific metaphors, an important aim would be to classify infinite types of clinically interesting bodily experiences into a finite number of categories. Given this objective, a top-down analysis based on a predetermined coding scheme is favored over a bottom-up approach that focuses on emergent themes, as the former allows for more consistent and replicable coding of metaphor patterns across various datasets and clinical settings. A feasible way of doing top-down analysis is to code the expressions based on an established inventory of *image schemas*.

According to Lakoff (1987) and Johnson (1987), image schemas are meaningful cognitive structures that arise from discrete, universally shared embodied experiences. Metaphors structured by image schemas are commonly observed in the representation of abstract knowledge, emotions, and thoughts, as seen in trauma victims' narratives. As noted by Wilson and Lindy (2013: 45), the metaphor "I am empty inside" highlights the CONTAINER-like properties of the HEART and its capacity to be filled or emptied. The schema is motivated by the physical act of getting in and out of clearly delineated spaces like architectures and cabinets, and the experience of using body parts like the stomach and mouth as containers of food, water, and air. By contrast, "No one can get close to me" instantiates the CONTACT schema, which arises from the experience of physical interactions between different individuals or tactile experiences of the surface of an object. Several cognitive semanticists have proposed tentative lists of image schemas to categorize recurrent, universal bodily experiences[21] (e.g., Clausner & Croft 1999; Hampe 2005; Lakoff 1987; Lakoff & Turner 1989; Johnson 1987). The list proposed by Johnson (1987) was chosen as the coding scheme for Chapter 5 (see Table 2.2; refer to Section 5.3 for more details about the methods).

Table 2.2: Johnson's (1987) list of image schemas.

CONTAINER	BALANCE	COMPULSION
BLOCKAGE	COUNTERFORCE	RESTRAINT REMOVAL
ENABLEMENT	ATTRACTION	MASS-COUNT
PATH	LINK	CENTRAL-PERIPHERY
CYCLE	NEAR-FAR	SCALE
PART-WHOLE	MERGING	SPLITTING
FULL-EMPTY	MATCHING	SUPERIMPOSITION
ITERATION	CONTACT	PROCESS
SURFACE	OBJECT	COLLECTION

Apart from providing a finite number of categories, coding metaphors based on established image schemas also enables the identification of potentially generalizable patterns and features that can be easily tracked by clinical practitioners. While metaphor analyses based on emergent vehicle terms focus on the speakers' embodied experiences, cultural knowledge, and individual-specific experiences (e.g., Cameron & Maslen 2010; Kövecses 2005, 2010, 2015, 2020; Lakoff 1987; Lakoff & Johnson 1980, 1999; Johnson 1987), the study of image schemas concentrates on basic, universal embodied experiences that structure human cognition and thinking. This approach downplays individual and cultural differences and underscores the universal and comparatively constant elements of human experiences (Pritzker 2007; Yu 2008). This aligns with the aim of clinical diagnosis, which is to identify clearly observable and universal patterns in subjective experiences. The strength of image schematic analysis in the study of symptom-specific metaphors will be illustrated in Chapter 5. Through a combination of psychometric data, therapeutic observations, and linguistic data, the study extracts underlying patterns in trauma victims' conceptualizations of the five major ASD symptoms.

---

21 Image schemas proposed by linguists have never been a closed set (Hampe 2005). As noticed in the main text, numerous cognitive linguists, with different theoretical and practical considerations, have made subsequent additions to the inventories proposed by Lakoff (1987) and Johnson (1987).

2.5 Chapter conclusion

This chapter identifies two significant research gaps in the current literature. Firstly, there has been limited attention to presentational features like conventionality, emotional valence, and psychological perspectives, which reveal the speakers' implicit emotions and thinking patterns. Studies from other mental health contexts have shown that these features can interact systematically with each other and with key semantic features, highlighting the multifaceted nature of metaphor use as an understudied yet important research area. This research avenue will be addressed in Chapter 3 by combining categorical data analysis and qualitative discourse analysis.

There is also a lack of research on the role of psychopathological experiences in shaping metaphor use. This chapter introduced two basic dimensions of psychopathological experiences that are likely to interact with metaphor use. Quantitative differences in the severity of symptoms may be reflected by the speakers' preferences for certain presentational and semantic features. Qualitative differences in the varieties of symptoms may be distinguished from the speakers' choices of conceptual resources in metaphorical meaning-making. These two forms of metaphor variations will be investigated in Chapters 4 and 5 by incorporating different types of psychometric data into metaphor analysis.

Before moving on to the next chapter, it should be noted that studies presented in this book do not intend to pinpoint the particularities of trauma metaphors compared to their literal counterparts or metaphors about other mental health disorders. Neither the sampling of participants nor the selection of variables permits the drawing of such conclusions (refer to Section 6.3 for a more detailed reflection on limitations). Instead, the aim is to highlight the relevance of metaphorical language to diagnostic practices and to enhance mental health practitioners' awareness of the interplay between metaphor and psychopathological experiences.

Another caveat is that the analyses of trauma- and symptom-related metaphor usage patterns in Chapters 4 and 5 do not establish causal links between metaphor use and psychopathological experience, nor do they attempt to propose metaphor analysis as a replacement or alternative to existing psychometric measures of trauma and symptoms. Rather, to reiterate from Section 1.4, the primary linguistic aims are to probe into the contextual characteristics, especially the quantitative dynamics underlying trauma metaphors, and exploit the interactions between psychological/psychopathological experiences and the use of therapeutically interesting metaphor variables. The clinical aim is to identify potentially trauma-related metaphor usage patterns that could be used to assist the prediagnostic screening, clinical evaluations, and subsequent therapeutic treatment and set the stage for future diagnostic applications.

It is also noteworthy that the linguistic examples selected for discourse analysis are not necessarily representative of typical clinical manifestations of trauma. Instead, the purpose is to provide clinical practitioners with an intuitive view of how trauma- and symptom-related metaphor usage patterns are played out in the local communicative context. While metaphor analysis usually concentrates on the associations between an abstract topic and more concrete vehicle terms, the interpretations of metaphorical mappings should not be awarded any special "truth status" in clinical practices. Rather, they should be evaluated in terms of their "usefulness" (Spong 2010: 72) in uncovering speakers' implicit ways of thinking and enhancing our understanding of metaphor use in clinical situations and mental health communication in general.

3 The multifaceteness of trauma metaphors

3.1 Chapter introduction

In the attempt to document qualitative, contextual nuances of trauma metaphors, existing mental health metaphor research, including trauma studies, mainly focused on the semantic features of metaphors. While presentational features of metaphors like CONVENTIONALITY, EMOTIONAL VALENCE, and PSYCHOLOGICAL PERSPECTIVES encode important information about trauma victims' implicit emotional and cognitive inclinations, their systematic instantiations have rarely been investigated in large-scale data (refer to Section 2.3). As a result, the bivariate relationships between metaphor vehicles and topics received much more attention than the multifaceted nature of metaphor use, which is characterized by the dynamic interrelationships among multiple variables and categories.

This chapter addresses this research gap through a text-level analysis of 1,634 metaphors identified from 46 trauma interviews.[22] The multifaceted nature of trauma metaphors will be explored by examining the contextualized instantiations among multiple presentational and semantic variables. A mixed-method analysis that combines categorical data analysis and qualitative discourse analysis will be conducted to investigate the interrelationships among the variables and their subcategories. Log-linear analysis with chi-square decompositions will be used to examine how CONVENTIONALITY and EMOTIONAL VALENCE are instantiated 1) in discussing therapeutically TARGET CATEGORIES and 2) when taking up different PSYCHOLOGICAL PERSPECTIVES. The first analysis focuses on the interactions between presentational features and semantic features, and the second examines how different presentational features are interrelated with one another when the semantic distinctions among metaphor topics are blurred.

The metaphor identification procedure and metaphor variables are introduced in Section 3.2. The research methods and research questions are presented in Section 3.3. Statistically significant metaphor usage patterns identified in the two analyses will be addressed in Sections 3.4.1 and 3.4.2, respectively. The patterns will be visualized, illustrated, and interpreted based on linguistic examples from a discourse analytic perspective. Lastly, Section 3.5 will discuss the implica-

---

[22] Section 3.4.1 of this chapter was previously published as Qiu, Han & Dennis Tay. 2022. The interaction between metaphor use and psychological states: a mix-method analysis of trauma talk in the Chinese context. In Dennis Tay & Xie Pan (eds.), *Data analytics in cognitive linguistics: methods and insights*, 197–228. Berlin/Boston: De Gruyter Mouton. The content has been substantially revised.

https://doi.org/10.1515/9783111346502-003

tions for understanding trauma victims' metaphor use, as well as the limitations and future directions of this study.

3.2 Data and variables

3.2.1 Metaphor identification

In mental health communication, metaphors are usually used to describe the speakers' nuanced and complex emotions and thoughts. These expressions do not occur exclusively at the level of the lexical unit (Fainsilber & Ortony 1987; Tay 2017); rather, they are often instantiated in large chunks of language that contain multiple words, phrases, sentences, and even paragraphs. To identify trauma victims' metaphors in expressing emotions, thoughts, and physiological experiences,[23] this study follows the discourse dynamics approach proposed by Cameron and Maslen (2010).

According to Cameron and Maslen (2010), the discourse dynamics approach focuses on the interconnections between language and multiple contextual factors such as embodied experience, ongoing emotions and thoughts, and sociocultural knowledge. This approach identifies metaphor vehicle terms and topics from single lexical units to larger chunks of language like phrases, sentences, and paragraphs. As a clearly operationalized and reliable method for identifying metaphors in mental health communication (Mathieson et al. 2018), this approach has been successfully applied to the study of metaphors in various mental health contexts (e.g., Mathieson et al. 2015; Mathieson et al. 2018; Mathieson, Jordan & Stubbe 2020; Tay 2016, 2017, 2018; Knapton & Rundblad 2018).

The discourse dynamics approach goes through each word or phrase in the data to see whether "there is a contrast or incongruity between the meaning of the word or phrase in its discourse context and another meaning; together with a transfer of meaning that enables that contextual meaning to be understood in terms of basic meaning" (Cameron & Maslen 2010: 105). In other words, metaphoricity is determined based on the contrast and transfer between the basic meaning and the contextual meaning of the vehicle term. The definition of basic and contextual meaning used by the discourse dynamics approach is borrowed from the Pragglejaz Group (2007: 3): the basic meaning refers to the contemporary mean-

---

23 In contrast, some methods identify metaphors at the level of lexical unit, for example, Metaphor Identification Procedure (MIP; Pragglejaz Group 2007) and Metaphor Identification Procedure VU University Amsterdam (MIPVU; Steen et al. 2010).

ing of the word or phrase in other contexts, which is "more concrete, related to bodily action, more precise, [and/or] historically older", and the contextual meaning refers to how the word or phrase "applies to an entity, relation, or attribute in the situation evoked by the text", with the surrounding text taken into consideration. If a more basic contemporary meaning does exist, the contextual meaning needs to be checked to see whether it "contrasts with the basic meaning but can be understood in comparison with it" (Pragglejaz Group 2007: 3). Stretches of language that are potentially metaphorical are referred to as "metaphor vehicle terms", and referents of vehicle terms are called "topics" of metaphors.

The discourse dynamics approach embraces indeterminate boundaries for metaphor vehicle terms as a theoretical assumption. Because a metaphor vehicle term may stretch beyond a single lexical unit to its surrounding phrases and sentences, and the topic is often blended into the vehicle rather than being independent of it, it is suggested that researchers first identify "the most clearly incongruous or contrasting word", and then "work outwards" to determine where a vehicle term begins and ends (Cameron & Maslen 2010: 108). Instead of yielding clearly delineated analytical units as MIP or MIPVU, decision-making on metaphor boundaries following the discourse dynamics approach was guided by the principle of "includ(ing) all that appears relevant" (Cameron et al. 2009: 72; c.f. Fuoli, Littlemore & Turner 2022). Stretches of language that express internally consistent or coherent meanings are identified as a single metaphor, and those that express conceptually distinct ideas or incoherent meanings are coded separately.

Metaphor identification for this project was accomplished by a researcher who received professional training in both cognitive linguistics and psychotherapy. As the discourse dynamics approach accepts indeterminate, it would be impractical to use quantitative methods to measure the interrater reliability of metaphor identification. Following Cameron et al. (2009), two strategies were adopted by the current study to maximize the trustworthiness of metaphor coding:

(1) the Contemporary Chinese Dictionary (《现代汉语词典》, the 7th edition) (henceforth "the CCD7") was chosen for this study to assist in the identification of basic and contextual meanings. As one of the most authoritative Chinese language dictionaries, the CCD series provides a comprehensive inclusion of contemporary meanings of single characters, phrases, and idiomatic expressions in Mandarin Chinese. More importantly, in the CCD series, distinctions between the entries' literal and figurative meanings were clearly indicated (Zhao 2015); this provides convenience for the identification of metaphors. Given all that, the CCD7 is particularly suitable for examining metaphor use in the current dataset. "The most clearly incongruent or contrasting word" (Cameron & Maslen 2010: 108) in the metaphor was chosen as the search term.

(2) Ambiguous cases were resolved consistently through discussion with several metaphor researchers who are experienced in the study of mental health metaphors. The decisions were recorded in the project notes for reference during the remaining coding.

The process of metaphor identification is illustrated by the examples below.[24] Metaphor vehicle terms are in bold type. While a sentence may contain more than one metaphor vehicle terms, only those directly related to the metaphor variable or methodological points under examination are marked (the same hereafter).

(1) 可能在我的二十多年人生里面, 应该是没有试过在短短的时间内情绪或者是心理状态会经历**那么大的起伏**。

'More than 20 years have passed in my life, I have never experienced **such great rises and falls** in emotions or psychological states within a short period of time.'

(2) 以前觉得还可以, 就是我们不谈, 我们不说, 我们置身事外, 但是现在就发现不行, 就是政治已经**糊在你脸上了**, 就是你**跑都跑不掉了**。

'I thought it was ok, as long as we don't talk about it, if we don't say anything about it, we could stay out of it. But now I find it's not like this. Politics has been **pasted to your face** now, you **can't run away from it** anyway.'

(3) 突然有一群人在那里喊口号的时候, 我们下意识的都在那愣住了, 全都停下来了, 然后就立马转头, 然后再下一秒就想着该怎么逃跑。

'When a group of people suddenly began to shout their slogan, we were subconsciously stunned, all of us stopped, turned around immediately, and then the next second, I began to think how to escape.'

In example (1), the most clearly incongruent word is "起伏 (rises and falls)". According to the CCD7, the basic meaning of "起伏" is "changes in vertical height". The contextual meaning is the emotional ups and downs experienced by the speaker. We can see there is an obvious meaning contrast between the basic and the contextual meanings, and the latter could be understood in comparison with the former; therefore, the word is identified as a metaphor vehicle term. Working outwards from "起伏", we can find that "那么大的" (such great) also contributes to the basic meaning of "起伏" by specifying the magnitude of the rises and falls.

---

24 In this book, translations of linguistic examples aim to retain the original metaphorical meaning in Mandarin Chinese, therefore, metaphor vehicle terms in the original text may not always correspond to consecutive stretches of language in the English translations.

As the two meanings are coherent with each other, "那么大的起伏" was underlined as one metaphor vehicle term rather than two separate metaphors.

Similarly, in example (2), both "糊在你脸上" (have something slimy pasted to your face) and "跑都跑不掉" (cannot run away) contain a clearly incongruent word whose basic meaning contrasts with and enables the understanding of its contextual meaning (i.e., "糊" and "跑"). In the first metaphor vehicle term, the experience of being involuntarily involved in the social unrest is interpreted as having something slimy "pasted" to the speaker's face. In the second, the inability to keep her study and future development unaffected by the social unrest is described as the speaker being physically unable to "run away" from a place. As their contextual meanings are obviously different, they are identified as two metaphor vehicle terms. However, the boundary of the second vehicle term is not as clear as that in example (1): whether the aspect marker "了 (le)" at the end of example (1) should be identified as a part of "跑都跑不掉" or an independent lexical unit can be debatable. As the inclusion of "了" does not introduce substantive changes to the metaphorical meaning, the principle of "includ(ing) all that appears relevant" was applied.

Example (3), by contrast, is a case where no obvious meaning contrast and transfer is found. While "逃跑" (run away) also describes a physical activity, its contextual meaning overlapped with the basic meaning, therefore it was not identified as metaphorical.

In Mandarin Chinese, some conventionalized expressions, such as "心里" (in my heart), "给" (give), and "东西" (things) are potentially metaphorical, as their basic meanings involve physically concrete entities or actions that contrast with and contribute to the understanding of their contextual meanings. However, the metaphorical meanings are highly conventionalized and do not bear much relevance to the topic under discussion. Following Cameron and Maslen (2010), these expressions were excluded from the analysis unless the metaphorical meanings were explicitly foregrounded and exploited by the speaker. The following examples are illustrative:

(4) 关注那些东西会让你自己非常焦虑, 非常痛苦, 非常无助。
'Paying attention to those things will make you very anxious, very miserable, and very helpless.'

(5) 生活中仿佛那些**五彩斑斓的东西不见了**。
'It's like all those **colorful and splendid things** in my life **disappeared from sight**.'

In example (4), the interviewee uses "东西" (things) to describe the anxiety-arousing news on social media. Although the phrase has a more concrete meaning, i.e., "concrete entities" and the basic meaning is clearly incongruent with its contextual meaning ("social media messages"), the meaning transfer is not directly relevant to the speaker's description of the traumatic experience; therefore, it was not included in the analysis. Example (5) presents a contrasting case. The interviewee deliberately exploits the metaphorical meaning of "东西" by elaborating on the abstract issues' ontological features: enjoyable moments of life are interpreted as visually colorful and splendid things ("五彩斑斓"). Given its direct relevance to the speakers' subjective experience, "东西" was identified as part of the metaphor vehicle term.

Following the above criteria, 1,634 metaphor vehicle terms were identified from the 46 interviews. The average number of vehicle terms per interview is 35.52 (SD=25.62), and the average density is 8.92 (SD=3.59) per thousand Chinese characters.

3.2.2 Metaphor variables

To provide a more comprehensive account of trauma victims' metaphor use, the 1,634 metaphors were further identified in terms of several finer metaphor variables that hold theoretical and clinical significance for the study of trauma metaphors. The variables include conventionality, emotional valence, psychological perspectives, and target categories. This section offers the operational definitions, linguistic examples, and descriptive statistics for each variable and their sub-categories. As this chapter adopts categorical data analysis (refer to Agresti 2002 for a comprehensive introduction), each metaphor was assigned to only one variable category.

Conventionality
According to Steen et al. (2010), the conventionality of metaphorically used lexical units can be identified as a binary construct[25] using a dictionary based on their linguistic definitional properties provided by dictionaries. If the metaphor's contextual meaning is included as one of the standard senses of the word, then it can be identified as a conventional metaphor; if not, it can be coded as a novel metaphor (Steen et al. 2010).

---

25 There are also researchers who places more emphasis on the perception properties of metaphors (i.e., how it sounds to the readers) and examine conventional and novel metaphor as different points on a scale or continuum (e.g., Giora 2002; Littlemore et al. 2018).

As mentioned earlier, emotions and thoughts in mental health communication are not always expressed with single lexical units (Mathieson et al. 2016; Tay 2017). Instead, speakers in mental health contexts may modify conventional metaphors in creative ways or extend the metaphor into phrases, sentences, and longer stretches of language (Cirillo & Crider 1995; Ferrara 1994; Gelo & Mergenthaler 2012). Similar cases were also identified in the present dataset. To take all lexical units in the vehicle term into account, the vehicle term was broken down to the most clearly incongruent word and the surrounding expressions that build upon the core metaphorical meaning. Firstly, the most clearly incongruent word was checked in terms of conventionality using the CCD7. If the word was identified as novel, then the whole metaphor vehicle was coded as novel without checking the remaining parts. If the mostly clearly incongruent word was identified as conventional, we then worked outward from the most incongruent word and checked the surrounding expressions one by one. Following Gelo and Mergenthaler's (2012) guidelines for identifying mental health metaphors, if any of the surrounding expressions built upon or extended the core conventional metaphor in a creative way, the whole vehicle term was identified as novel (e.g., "五彩斑斓的东西, colorful and splendid things"). If the expressions merely elaborated on or repeated the core conventional metaphor without introducing new conceptual resources, the whole vehicle term was identified as conventional. If two conventional expressions that do not usually work together were combined to express one coherent metaphorical idea (e.g., 媒体 "添油加醋"的"描绘", media "portrays" that "added oil and put in vinegar"), the whole metaphor vehicle was coded as novel.

Following this approach, 716 novel metaphors and 918 conventional metaphors were identified. Linguistic examples are provided in Table 3.1 below.

Table 3.1: Frequencies and examples of conventional and novel metaphors.

Conventionality	Example
Conventional (918)	可能在我的二十多年人生里面, 应该是没有试过在短短的时间内情绪或者是心理状态会经历**那么大的起伏**。'More than 20 years have passed in my life, I have never experienced **such great rises and falls** in emotions or psychological states within a short period of time.'
Novel (716)	以前觉得还可以, 就是我们不谈, 我们不说, 我们置身事外, 但是现在就发现不行, 就是政治已经**糊在你脸上了**, 就是你**跑都跑不掉了**。'I thought it was ok, as long as we don't talk about it, if we don't say anything about it, we could stay out of it. But now I find it's not like this. Politics has been **pasted to your face** now, you **can't run away from it** anyway.'

Emotional valence

Emotional valence refers to the emotion or attitude conveyed by a specific metaphorical expression. For the present study, metaphors that indicate a pessimistic, passive, or disapproving attitude were labeled as *"negative"*, those that reflect an optimistic, active, or approving attitude were identified as *"positive"*, and those indicating calmness and rational thinking were rated as *"neutral"*.

For the sake of consistency, several key points were established before the coding. Firstly, emotional valence was identified based on the speakers' expressed or intended meaning in the interview rather than the expression's semantic connotations. For example, if a metaphor with a positive connotation was negated or rephrased to express negative attitudes or emotions (e.g., "不再觉得温暖, not feeling warm anymore"), it was identified as negative. Secondly, emotionally valenced literal expressions outside the boundary of the metaphor vehicle term were not taken into account. Thirdly, metaphors associated with psychopathological experiences or non-adaptive ways of coping, such as "numbness (麻木)" and "detachment (抽离)", were identified as "negative" rather than "neutral" given their psychopathological significance. Lastly, cases where different valences were juxtaposed (e.g., "喜忧各半, half joy, half worry"), where one emotion was embedded in another one of different valence (e.g., "担忧中夹杂着激动, excitement is mixed inside of worry"), and where no apparent emotional valence can be discerned (e.g., "有新鲜血液输入社会, new blood is being transfused into the society") were identified as "neutral".

In the present dataset, 826, 711, and 97 metaphors were identified for the three valences, respectively. Frequencies and examples for the three categories are provided in Table 3.2.

Table 3.2: Frequencies and examples of the three emotional valences.

Valence	Example
Negative (826)	我自己甚至都可能会意识到我是不是**就像(进入)一个黑洞一样, 被负面情绪吸进去了**。 'Even I myself realized, if I was, **just like (entered) a black hole, if I was absorbed by the negative emotions**.'
Neutral (711)	这个事情, 我感觉啊,**就是个小小插曲**。 'This event, I feel, is **just a small, small episode**.'
Positive (97)	突然间就会觉得好像感受到了**希望之火慢慢燃烧起来**。 'Suddenly I felt that **the fire of hope, slowly, started to burn**.'

Psychological perspectives and target categories

As introduced earlier in Section 2.3.1, the field and the observer perspectives (Nigro & Neisser 1983) are two vantage points adopted by the speaker in narration. In the field perspective, the speaker experiences the surrounding world and her/his emotions and thoughts in a self-immersed way, without noticing the existence of the self, whereas in the observer perspective, the self becomes detached yet closely related to the scene, or an object under inspection. The distinction between the two psychological perspectives coincides with the elemental and relational features of target categories proposed by Kopp (1995), with the former being a less substantive abstraction of the latter. Therefore, in the present study, codings of target categories, which contain richer semantic information, are used as the basis for coding psychological perspectives.

The original taxonomy of target topics proposed by Kopp (1995) includes six categories: SELF, OTHERS, SITUATIONS, SELF AND SELF, SELF AND OTHERS, and SELF AND SITUATION. The six categories capture the metaphoric structure of an individual's subjective reality, or one's way of being in the social world (Kopp 1995). While the original taxonomy is largely coherent with the topics covered in the interview data, a close reading of the data suggests trauma victims of the social unrest often experience obvious incongruence between their personal lives and the larger social environment. Their daily routines were greatly disrupted by mass vandalism, and many suffered from severe psychological distress due to unexpected property damage, concerns for personal safety (Ng 2020), and interpersonal conflicts (Shek 2020). This would lead trauma victims to conceptualize their personal lives and the broader social and political environment as incongruent and even conflicting. For example, when talking about crime events caused by the protests, an interviewee mentioned that "你就会想这些东西离你最好远一点 (you would think these things should better stay far away from you)". Example (5) provided earlier is also typical: the speaker's leisure time before the social unrest is conceptualized as having many "colorful and splendid things" ("五彩斑斓的东西"), and a result of the social unrest is described as these things "disappear from sight (不见了)". These expressions drew clear delineations between the surrounding social situation and the speaker's personal life.

To better capture the complexities of the current research context, an extended taxonomy with finer distinctions of SITUATION-related categories was proposed (see Figure 3.1). "Situation" in the original taxonomy was divided into "personal situation" and "social situation", and "self and situation" was split into "self and personal situation" and "self and social situation" accordingly. This makes a total of eight categories.

During the coding, some borderline cases were identified, for example, when the speakers focused on the relationship between OTHERS and a PERSONAL or a

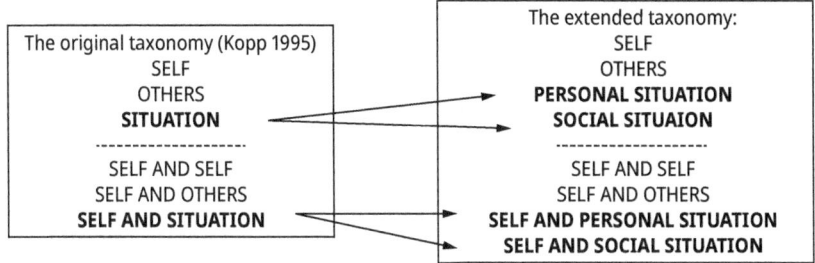

Figure 3.1: An extended taxonomy of target categories.

SOCIAL SITUATION, or the relationship between a PERSONAL SITUATION and a SOCIAL SITUATION. These cases were rare in the current dataset; therefore, they were not singled out as separate categories for the convenience of subsequent quantitative analyses. Instead, they were coded as OTHERS, PERSONAL SITUATION, or SOCIAL SITUATION according to which category was foregrounded as the primary topic or focus of the metaphor.

As Kopp's work did not provide explicit criteria for making distinctions between SELF and SELF AND SELF, Lakoff's (1992) framework of "multiple selves" was incorporated to guide the coding. According to Lakoff (1992: 9), people's cognitive activities are often metaphorically conceptualized as the interaction between two different facets of the person, i.e., the "subject" as the center of consciousness, will, and judgment, and the "self", including the person's beliefs, emotions, feelings, etc. The self is constantly under the inspection of the subject; it could be perceived as consistent with, separated from, or even incompatible with the subject. An example of the subject being totally conscious and consistent with the self is "I'm very happy to see you". In contrast, expressions like "I keep telling myself to leave" and "I wasn't myself yesterday" capture situations where the subject does not have control over all aspects of the self or when the subject is partly unconscious (Lakoff 1992). For the present study, cases where the speaker's subject is conscious, compatible with the self, or has normal control over the self were labeled as SELF, those in which the two are incompatible, or either is unconscious or uncontrollable, were labeled as SELF AND SELF. Those depicting the self's interactions with others, personal life, and social situation were labeled accordingly.

In the present study, psychological perspectives in trauma victims' metaphorical meaning-making were coded based on codings of target categories. Metaphor topics described with speakers "inside" themselves (i.e., SELF, OTHERS, PERSONAL SITUATION, and SOCIAL SITUATION) were categorized as the field perspective, and those in which the speaker was both the observer and the subject of the observation (i.e., the SELF AND X categories) were labeled as the observer perspective. The relationship between the two psychological perspectives and the eight target categories in the extended taxonomy is shown in Figure 3.2. Frequencies and linguistic examples of the subcategories are provided in Table 3.3.

To recap, this chapter examines how metaphors about eight therapeutically interesting TARGET CATEGORIES and two PSYCHOLOGICLA PERSPECTIVES are instantiated in terms of CONVENTIONALITY and EMOTIONAL VALENCE. A cross-tabulation of the four variables is presented in Table 3.4.

All metaphor variables entered into the analysis were coded in an Excel spreadsheet, with each metaphor vehicle term listed in a single row and each metaphor variable in a separate column. A screenshot of the Excel spreadsheet, which shows a randomly selected set of metaphors, is presented in Figure 3.3.

Target categories   Perspectives

SELF OTHERS PERSONAL SITUATION SOCIAL SITUATION	The field perspective
SELF AND SELF SELF AND OTHERS SELF AND PERSONAL SITUATION SELF AND SOCIAL SITUATION	The observer perspective

Figure 3.2: Psychological perspectives and the extended taxonomy of target categories.

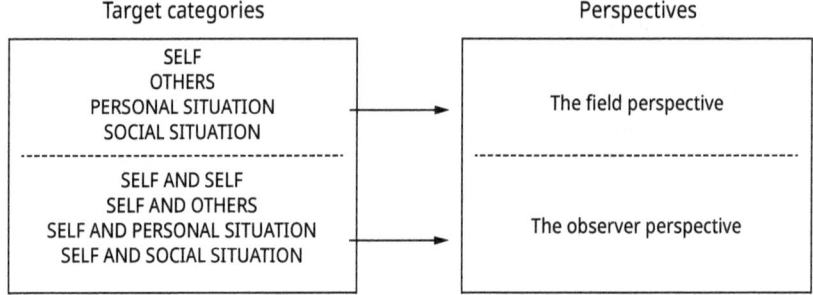

Figure 3.3: A screenshot of the Excel spreadsheet for categorical data analyses.

Table 3.3: Frequencies and examples of target categories and psychological perspectives.

Target category	Perspective	Example
SELF (341)	The field perspective (987)	我觉得可能就是一种比较无奈或者说**无力**的感觉。'What I felt was probably helplessness, or say, **lack of strength**.'
OTHERS (255)		学校毕竟是个挺净土的一个地方，**之前愤怒也是因为你怎么把手伸到学校这块地方来了**。'The university is, after all, like a pure land. The reason why I felt angry is how can you **lay your hands on this place**.'
PERSONAL SITUATION (181)		生活中仿佛**那些五彩斑斓的东西不见了**。'It's like all those **colorful and splendid things** in my life **disappeared from sight**.'
SOCIAL SITUATION (210)		那会儿(学校)已经就成**战场**了，然后失控状态。'At that time (the university) has become **a battlefield**, it lost control.'
SELF AND SELF (175)	The observer perspective (647)	**我仿佛身体里面有两个小人，然后一个小人喊着说**："你要冷静的看一看这边啊，你看一看这些民主社会"之类的，**另外一边就在说**："你是在这读一年书而已，可是这一年已经被损失了这么多"。'**It feels like there are two little persons in my body, and one is shouting**: "You should be calm and see what happened here, you should see the democratic society" and the like. **The one on the other side says**: "You are just doing a master here for one year, but just in one year you have lost so much".'
SELF AND OTHERS (90)		我也不冒犯你，但我就**远离**你们就好。'I don't want to offend you, but I will just **stay away from** you.'
SELF AND PERSONAL SITUATION (104)		我应该是一个很理性的人，但是你还是控制不住那个状态，控制不住自己会去被这种关照啊什么的，**被它温暖到**就这种样子。'I think I am a rational person, but still can't control that state of mind. You can't control yourself from **being warmed** by other people's kindness and care, or something like that.'
SELF AND SOCIAL SITUATION (278)		(2)以前觉得还可以，就是我们不说，我们不谈，我们置身事外，但是现在就发现不行，就是政治已经**糊在你脸上了**，就是你**跑都跑不掉了**。'I thought it was ok, as long as we don't talk about it, if we don't say anything about it, we could stay out of it. But now I find it's not like this. Politics has been **pasted to your face** now, you **can't run away from it** anyway.'

Table 3.4: A crosstabulation of CONVENTIONALITY, TARGET CATEGORY, PSYCHOLOGICAL PERSPECTIVE, and EMOTIONAL VALENCE.

Psychological perspective	Conventionality	Target category	Valence			Total
			Negative	Neutral	Positive	
Field	Conventional	Self	143	75	23	241
		Others	71	56	7	134
		Personal situation	64	45	4	113
		Social situation	62	66	5	133
	Novel	Self	61	31	8	100
		Others	62	52	7	121
		Personal situation	43	22	3	68
		Social situation	38	34	5	77
Observer	Conventional	Self and self	26	60	7	93
		Self and others	15	25	2	42
		Self and personal situation	19	32	7	58
		Self and social situation	47	55	2	104
	Novel	Self and self	35	43	4	82
		Self and others	27	15	6	48
		Self and personal situation	14	25	7	46
		Self and social situation	99	75	0	174
Total			826	711	97	1634

3.2.3 Inter-rater reliability

Metaphors in the interview data were coded by the author of this book. As mentioned earlier, inter-rater reliability of metaphor identification was maximized by 1) using the CCD7 for identifying basic and contextual meanings and 2) discussion with experienced metaphor researchers.

Since determining metaphor variable categories involves making categorical decisions on fixed analytical units, the reliability of coding could be systematically checked using quantitative interrater reliability measures. According to Bolognesi, Pilgram & Van Den Heerik (2017), a linguistic coding scheme has a greater degree of replicability if the codings provided by a trained rater are comparable to the work by a novice rater who has a different academic background and/or no prior experience in metaphor identification. As this book addresses the interests of mental health practitioners, who may not be experienced in metaphor identification, this approach was considered more suitable than relying solely on metaphor researchers.

A novice rater with a non-linguistic background was recruited and trained for interrater reliability checks. The training included repeated rounds of definition explanation and example discussion. Considering the novice rater's lack of prior experience in metaphor identification, the pre-coding training was dissected into four 2-hour sessions arranged on four consecutive days. The two coders discussed the theoretical and operational definitions of metaphor, the variables under examination, and their subcategories. Linguistic examples and interpretations provided by earlier mentioned metaphor studies and psychology studies were used as training materials. The two coders then read through the interviews and reviewed the metaphor variables to calibrate their understanding of metaphor use in the current research context. To add to the consistency of coding, project notes on recurrent metaphors and patterns were created based on the two coders' discussion. Based on the project notes, the two coders worked independently on 15% of all metaphors, which were randomly selected from the dataset using the RAND function of Excel.

Krippendorff's alpha[26] (Krippendorff 1970) was used to measure the agreement between the two coders' judgments. Compared with other reliability measures that are commonly used in content analysis, such as Cohen's kappa and Fleiss'K, Krippendorff's alpha has greater flexibility in that it can be applied on all measurement scales (i.e., nominal, ordinal, interval, and ratio) and codings provided by multiple coders; it can also handle codings with missing values (Zapf et al. 2016). The alpha values calculated for EMOTIONAL VALENCE and TARGET CATEGORY, were 0.741 and 0.865, respectively. Both values were greater than the smallest acceptable reliability (i.e., $\alpha=0.667$) suggested by Krippendorff (2004) for qualitative content analysis. Because conventionality was coded based on dictionary meanings and psychological perspectives were categorized based on target categories, no additional checks were needed.

---

26 Statistics for the present study were calculated using ReCal2, an online utility that computes interrater reliability coefficients for data coded by two or more coders (http://dfreelon.org/utils/recalfront/recal2/).

After the interrater reliability tests, the two coders discussed inconsistent coding results. Decisions about ambiguous and borderline cases were added to the project notes so that consistent decisions could be made in the remaining dataset. The author of the book then finished coding the rest of the dataset. Ambiguous cases were coded based on discussions with other metaphor researchers.

3.3 Research methods and questions

To recap, this chapter probes into the multifaceted nature of trauma metaphors by examining systematic interrelationships among two sets of metaphor variables. The first set includes both presentational features and semantic features, and the second includes presentational features only. The research questions are as follows:

(1) How do the eight TARGET CATEGORIES interact with the two presentational aspects of trauma metaphors, i.e., CONVENTIONALITY and EMOTIONAL VALENCE?

(2) How do metaphors generated from different PSYCHOLOGICAL PERSPECTIVES interact with CONVENTIONALITY and EMOTIONAL VALENCE?

A diagram of variable relationships under examination is shown in Figure 3.4.

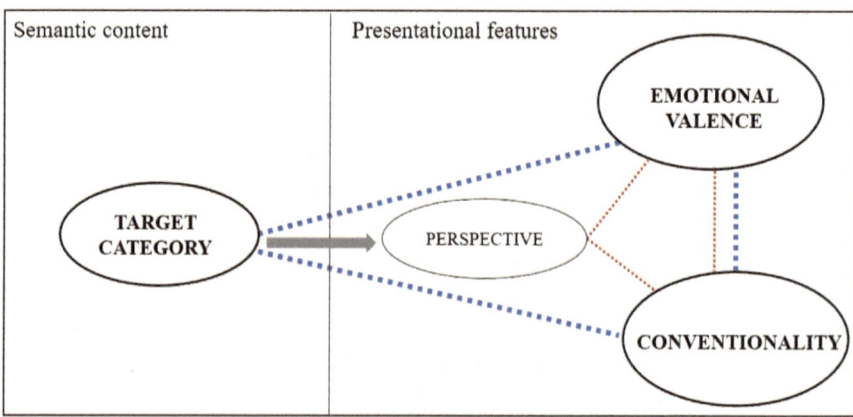

Figure 3.4: A diagram of variable relationships under examination.

Categorical data analytic methods were chosen to extract the interrelationships between the two sets of variables. As introduced earlier in Section 2.3.2, the methods take each variable category identified for each metaphor as the unit of analysis.

The relationships between multiple variables are investigated as the likelihood of one variable co-occurring with one or more variables. A relationship is considered statistically significant if the observed frequency of co-occurrence deviates far enough from its expected frequency, either in the positive or negative direction. In the present study, separate log-linear analyses were performed to investigate potential higher-order interactions, where the frequencies of three or more variables vary together, and bi-variate associations among the two sets of variables, where frequencies of two variables vary with each other.

Two strategies were adopted to visualize and interpret the significant statistical patterns. Firstly, the interrelationships among multiple variable categories were visualized using factor plots generated using Multiple Correspondence Analysis (MCA), a statistical technique that detects the relationships between multiple variable categories.[27] In MCA plots, different categories of the variables are represented as discrete points on a two-dimensional plot, and their interrelationships are visualized as positions of and distances between the points. Secondly, following Tay (2017), chi-square decompositions were used to probe into the bi-variate associations. Contingency tables that show the distribution of metaphors across all variable categories were generated. Chi-square statistics were used to interpret the relationships: adjusted residuals were calculated to examine the magnitude of differences between the observed and the expected frequencies, and Cramer's V coefficients were used to measure the strengths of associations. The log-linear analyses and chi-square tests were performed using Jamovi 2.0.0.0.[28] The contingency tables (including adjusted residuals) and the MCA plots were generated using IBM SPSS Statistics 22.0.[29]

Statistically significant relationships among the variable categories were then illustrated using genuine linguistic examples and interpreted from a discourse analytic perspective, so that the patterns can be understood in relation to the situated features of metaphor use in the current research context. The multifaceted presentational features of trauma metaphors reflected by the interactions among TARGET CATEGORY, CONVENTIONALITY, and EMOTIONAL VALENCE will be discussed in Section 3.4.1, and those distinguished from the interrelationships among PSYCHOLOGICAL PERSPECTIVE, CONVENTIONALITY, and EMOTIONAL VALENCE will be examined in Section 3.4.2.

---

27 Both MCA and log-linear analysis are methods for computing associations. In this chapter, MCA plot is only used for visualization purpose.

28 Retrieved from https://www.jamovi.org.

29 Retrieved from https://www.ibm.com/products/spss-statistics.

3.4 Results and discussion

3.4.1 TARGET CATEGORY, CONVENTIONALITY, and EMOTIONAL VALENCE

Results of categorical data analysis

A log-linear analysis was performed to examine the interactions among TARGET CATEGORY, CONVENTIONALITY, and EMOTIONAL VALENCE, which reflect how therapeutically interesting target topics are packaged using conventional/novel and emotion-laden metaphors. The final model included two significant bi-variate associations: TARGET CATEGORY * CONVENTIONALITY and TARGET CATEGORY * EMOTIONAL VALENCE. The highest three-way interaction was not retained (p = .338). This suggests that trauma victims tended to metaphorize the eight target categories with different levels of conventionality, and that the target categories were often metaphorized with different emotional valences. The relationship between CONVENTIONALITY and EMOTIONAL VALENCE was not statistically significant, χ^2 (2) = 2.903, p = .234, Cramer's V = .042. This suggests that the frequencies of conventional and novel metaphors did not vary substantially across negative, neutral, and positive metaphors.

A two-dimensional MCA factor plot was generated to visualize the interrelationships among the eight categories of the three variables (see Figure 3.5). As noted by Greenacre and Blasius (2006), the directions of associations between variable categories can be interpreted based on the location of one category in relation to another. Positively correlated categories are clustered at the same side of the origin, and negatively correlated ones are distributed on opposite sides. The strengths of associations can be discerned from (1) the distance of the category from the origin, with stronger ones denoted by longer distances, and (2) the magnitude of the angle, with sharper angles indicating stronger associations.

In Figure 3.5, the two dimensions captured a substantial proportion of variance: dimension 1 accounted for 41.68% of the total variance, and dimension 2 explained an additional 39.21%, making a total of 80.89%. The eight target categories are scattered at different sides of the origin along dimension 1, conventional and novel metaphors are distributed at different sides along dimension 2, and the three emotional valences are disseminated at different parts of the plot, far away and approximately equidistant from the origin. This suggests CONVENTIONALITY and EMOTIONAL VALENCE were good discriminators between the eight TARGET CATEGORIES. A closer reading of the category locations and distances suggests that SELF, SELF AND SOCIAL SITUATION, and positive metaphors are the furthest away along dimension 1, and SELF AND SELF, PERSONAL SITUATION, SELF AND PERSONAL SITUATION, and negative metaphors are the furthest along dimension 2. This means these variable categories had particularly strong associations with each other. Those distributed on the same side of the origin were positively associated with each other (e.g., SELF and negative metaphors, SOCIAL SITUATION and conventional metaphors), while those on different sides of the origin were negatively associated (e.g., SOCIAL SITUATION and novel metaphors, SELF AND SELF and positive metaphors).

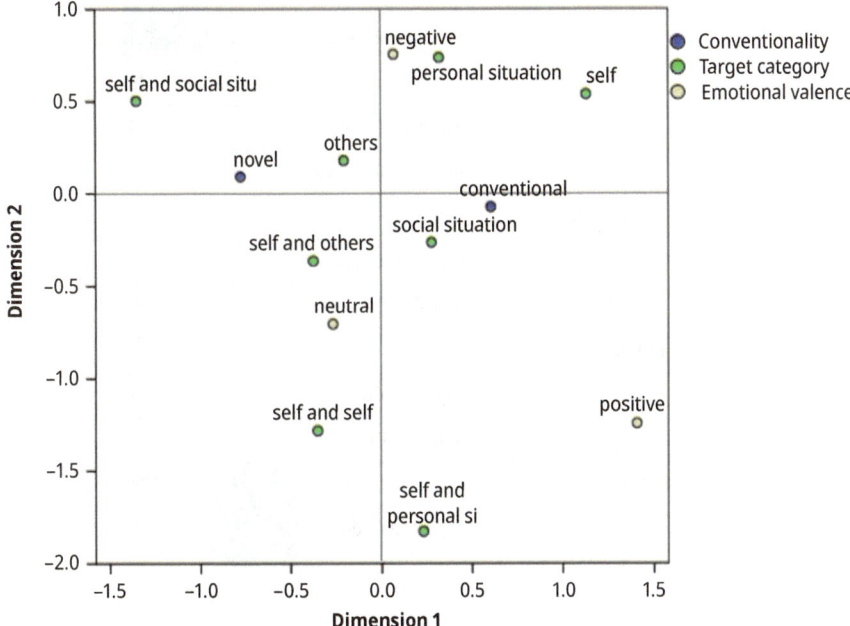

Figure 3.5: An MCA factor plot for the interrelationships among TARGET CATEGORY, CONVENTIONALITY, and EMOTIONAL VALENCE.

Chi-square decompositions were then used to identify the relationships among more specific variable categories. The requirement for minimal sample size in chi-square tests (Tabachnick & Fidell 2007) was met, with all cells having an expected frequency larger than one and more than 80% having a value larger than five. Chi-square statistics revealed a significant and moderate association between TARGET CATEGORY and EMOTIONAL VALENCE $\chi^2(14) = 84.79$, p < .001, Cramer's V = .161. The TARGET CATEGORY * CONVENTIONALITY association was also significant and moderate $\chi^2(7) = 81.46$, $p < .001$, and the strength was stronger than that between TARGET CATEGORY and EMOTIONAL VALENCE (Cramer's V = .223).

Cross-tabulations of the eight target categories across the three emotional valences and the two conventionality levels are shown in Tables 3.5 and 3.6.

Table 3.5: Crosstabulation of TARGET CATEGORY and EMOTIONAL VALENCE.

			Emotional Valence		
			Negative	Neutral	Positive
Target category	Self	Count	204	106	31
		Expected Count	172.4	148.4	20.2
		Adjusted Residual	3.9	−5.2	2.8
	Others	Count	133	108	14
		Expected Count	128.9	111.0	15.1
		Adjusted Residual	.6	−.4	−.3
	Personal situation	Count	107	67	7
		Expected Count	91.5	78.8	10.7
		Adjusted Residual	2.4	−1.9	−1.2
	Social situation	Count	100	100	10
		Expected Count	106.2	91.4	12.5
		Adjusted Residual	−.9	1.3	−.8
	Self and self	Count	61	103	11
		Expected Count	88.5	76.1	10.4
		Adjusted Residual	−4.4	4.3	.2
	Self and others	Count	42	40	8
		Expected Count	45.5	39.2	5.3
		Adjusted Residual	−.8	.2	1.2
	Self and personal situation	Count	33	57	14
		Expected Count	52.6	45.3	6.2
		Adjusted Residual	−4.0	2.4	3.4
	Self and social situation	Count	146	130	2
		Expected Count	140.5	121.0	16.5
		Adjusted Residual	.7	1.2	−4.0
Total		Count	826	711	97
		Expected Count	826.0	711.0	97.0

Table 3.6: Crosstabulation of TARGET CATEGORY and CONVENTIONALITY.

			Conventionality	
			Conventional	Novel
Target category	Self	Count	241	100
		Expected Count	191.6	149.4
		Adjusted Residual	6.1	−6.1
	Others	Count	134	121
		Expected Count	143.3	111.7
		Adjusted Residual	−1.3	1.3
	Personal situation	Count	113	68
		Expected Count	101.7	79.3
		Adjusted Residual	1.8	−1.8
	Social situation	Count	133	77
		Expected Count	118.0	92.0
		Adjusted Residual	2.2	−2.2
	Self and self	Count	93	82
		Expected Count	98.3	76.7
		Adjusted Residual	−.9	.9
	Self and others	Count	42	48
		Expected Count	50.6	39.4
		Adjusted Residual	−1.9	1.9
	Self and personal situation	Count	58	46
		Expected Count	58.4	45.6
		Adjusted Residual	−.1	.1
	Self and social situation	Count	104	174
		Expected Count	156.2	121.8
		Adjusted Residual	−6.9	6.9
Total		Count	918	716
		Expected Count	918.0	716.0

The deviation of the observed frequency from expectation was reflected by statistics of adjusted residuals. An adjusted residual with a positive value suggests the category's observed frequency is higher than its expected frequency, and one with a negative value suggests the observed frequency is significantly lower than its expected frequency. Adjusted residuals with absolute values greater than 2.0 but smaller than 2.6 suggest that the deviations are statistically significant at the level of .05, and those with absolute values greater than 2.6 mean the frequency deviations are significant at the level of .01. In Tables 3.5 and 3.6, variable categories that occurred significantly more and less frequently than by chance were colored in blue and yellow, and frequency deviations significant at the .05 level and the .01 level were marked in light and dark colors. The expected frequency of a variable category was calculated based on the frequencies of other categories (refer to Gilbert 1993 for the calculation principles). This means even a category with a relatively high observed frequency may occur at a less frequent rate than expected, and a category with a particularly low observed frequency may occur more frequently than expected. In other words, the value of adjusted residuals should be interpreted as how (un)common, or "uniquely motivated" the association is in the statistical sense, rather than its prevalence in the dataset (Tay 2018: 5).

Table 3.5 shows that the participants described the eight target categories with different emotional valences. SELF was presented with significantly higher numbers of negative and positive metaphors, and lower numbers of neutral metaphors as compared with the expected frequencies (all $ps < .01$). Metaphors about PERSONAL SITUATION were presented with significantly more negative metaphors ($p < .05$). SELF AND SELF was described with significantly fewer negative metaphors ($p < .01$) and significantly more neutral metaphors than expected ($p < .01$). SELF AND PERSONAL SITUATION was significantly less likely to be described using negative metaphors ($p < .01$) but significantly more likely to be interpreted in the neutral and positive valence than by chance alone ($p < .05$ and $p < .01$, respectively). SELF AND SOCIAL SITUATION was significantly less likely to be interpreted in the positive light than by chance alone ($p < .01$). The associations between other target-valence pairs were not significant, which suggests that the observed frequencies did not deviate much from their expected frequencies.

Table 3.6 shows that significantly more conventional and fewer novel metaphors were found in descriptions of SELF ($p < .01$) and SOCIAL SITUATION ($p < .05$), and more novel and thus fewer conventional metaphors were observed for SELF AND SOCIAL SITUATION ($p < .01$). Other target categories (e.g., OTHERS, PERSONAL SITUATION, and SELF AND SELF) also had noticeable differences in the distribution of conventional and novel metaphors, but the relationships were not statistically significant (all adjusted residuals between ±2). This suggests that the observed frequencies of conventional and novel metaphors in describing other categories did not differ remarkably from their expected frequencies.

In what follows, the bi-variate associations between TARGET CATEGORY and EMOTIONAL VALENCE and that between TARGET CATEGORY and CONVENTION-ALITY will be discussed in turn.

Discussion

The TARGET CATEGORY * EMOTIONAL VALENCE association

Although trauma is often characterized by a mixture of overwhelmingly negative emotions (Badour, Resnick & Kilpatrick 2017), the target categories were not exclusively metaphorized in the negative valence. The significant association between TARGET CATEGORY and EMOTIONAL VALENCE suggests that the participants' metaphors about the eight target topics expressed diversified emotions.

Trauma victims' metaphorical conceptualizations of the SELF focused mainly on personal emotions, thoughts, and physical/physiological experiences. Their metaphors were characterized by the dominance of both negative and positive emotions; the frequency of neutral metaphors was significantly less frequent than expected.

As negative emotional experience is one of the most typical reactions to a traumatic event (American Psychiatric Association 2013), it is unsurprising that trauma victims' descriptions of personal thoughts and feelings (i.e., SELF) contained significantly more negative metaphors than by chance alone. Example (6) below is an instance of negative SELF metaphor:

(6) [SELF * negative metaphor] 我觉得可能就是一种比较无奈或者说**无力**的感觉。
     'What I felt was probably helplessness, or say, **lack of strength**.'

This example describes the speaker's feelings of helplessness and frustration during the peak of the traumatic event, which is a typical acute stress reaction commonly reported by individuals exposed to various types of traumatic events (American Psychiatric Association 2013). These abstract and elusive emotional feelings are interpreted as the lack of physical strength ("无力"), which is an undesirable condition inherently linked to unpleasant feelings and the loss of physical control.

Besides the preference for negative metaphors, the participants generated significantly more positive metaphors than expected when describing their emotions and thoughts. A close examination of the interview data suggests a large proportion of positive metaphors described the emotional support provided by the trauma victims' family and friends. Some participants also produced metaphors about the unwavering hope they had for Hong Kong and the positive insights they gained from their traumatic experiences. Example (7) illustrates the former case, which was more dominant in the dataset:

(7)　[SELF * positive metaphor] 突然间就会觉得好像感受到了**希望之火慢慢燃烧起来**。
　　'Suddenly I felt that **the fire of hope, slowly, started to burn**.'

In this example, the speaker describes the positive emotions conveyed by her friends, which had been long absent in the speaker's life due to the social unrest. Kindness and support received from a close friend are conceptualized as a tangible and experiential phenomenon, i.e., "the fire of hope (希望之火)", with the gradual intensification of positive emotions interpreted as the fire "slowly, started to burn (慢慢燃烧起来)".

While SELF metaphors often expressed polarized emotions, SELF AND SELF, which describes the speaker's internal conflicts, was presented with significantly more neutral metaphors and fewer negative metaphors than expected. Example (8) is an instance of neutral SELF AND SELF metaphors:

(8)　[SELF AND SELF * neutral metaphor] 通过那段经历来学会一些辩证思考，然后重新去反省自己过往的那些认知，然后把自己从当时的环境脱离开来，**作为一个旁观者**去分析。
　　'Through my experience during the social unrest, I learned to think in a dialectical way. I learned to reflect upon my past ways of thinking, get myself detached from that environment, and analyze all these thoughts **as an onlooker**.'

Here the speaker is reflecting on her coping strategies. The SELF AND SELF metaphor describes her attempts to eliminate her negative emotions and habitual ways of thinking. The speaker metaphorizes herself as an "onlooker (旁观者)" who is detached from the traumatic event, standing beside the traumatized self, observing the social situation in a rational way.

Another notable contrast is found between PERSONAL SITUATION and SELF AND PERSONAL SITUATION metaphors. While PERSONAL SITUATION was described by a significantly higher number of negative metaphors than by chance alone, SELF AND PERSONAL SITUATION featured a predominance of neutral and positive metaphors and correspondingly, a scarcity of negative metaphors. This contrast is illustrated by example (5) presented earlier (reproduced below) and example (9):

(5)   [PERSONAL SITUATION * negative metaphor] 生活中仿佛那些**五彩斑斓的东西不见了**。
       'It's like all those **colorful and splendid things** in my life **disappeared from sight**.'

(9)   [SELF AND PERSONAL SITUATION * positive metaphor] 我应该是一个很理性的人，但是你还是控制不住那个状态，控制不住自己会去被这种关照啊什么的,被它温暖到，就这**种**样子。
       'I think I am a rational person, but still can't control that state of mind. You can't control yourself from **feeling warm** because of other people's kindness and care, or something like that.'

Example (5) contrasts the speaker's perceptions of the surrounding environment before and after the social unrest. Enjoyable interpersonal and leisure activities before the traumatic event are reified as colorful and splendid entities ("五彩斑斓的东西"), and the sudden loss of positive feelings, due to the growing sense of fear and distrust among individuals, is interpreted as the colorful entities disappearing from sight ("不见了").

Example (9) is a positive SELF AND PERSONAL SITUATION metaphor, following the "fire of hope" metaphor presented earlier as example (7). Building upon the POSITIVE EMOTION IS HEAT metaphor, friendly gestures from the speaker's colleagues are conceptualized as something emitting comforting heat, and feelings of being moved by kindness are interpreted as sensing physical warmth ("被它温暖到").

In sum, the eight target categories differed substantially in the relative proportions of emotional valences. Some target categories carried more negative emotions (e.g., SELF and PERSONAL SITUATION), whereas some were more likely described in a neutral or positive tone due to self-regulatory or self-persuasive purposes (e.g., SELF AND SELF and SELF AND PERSONAL SITUATION). Some target categories were presented with mixed and even conflicting emotions. For example, SELF was significantly and positively associated with both negative and positive emotions. More interestingly, contrary to the common expectation that traumatic experiences are laden with intense negative emotions, target categories that are directly relevant to the social situation were often metaphorized with neutral or mixed emotions. SELF AND SOCIAL SITUATION, as a key theme of the traumatic event, was not so much associated with negative metaphors, but instead, featured a proportional lack of positive metaphors. SOCIAL SITUATION, which is the counterpart of SELF AND SOCIAL SITUATION in the field perspective, was not explicitly marked by any specific valence but had a relatively balanced blend of all three valences.

The diversified emotional focuses identified for the eight target categories suggest that trauma victims' conceptualizations of their personal experiences were not all negative. Rather, different aspects of the traumatic event were experienced and metaphorized with distinct emotional nuances. The findings provide new insights into the relationship between emotional expression and psychological well-being. Although extensive research has probed into the associations between the frequencies of emotion words and the speaker's psychological states or therapeutic outcomes (e.g., Batten et al. 2002; Cohn, Mehl & Pennebaker 2004; Jaeger et al. 2014), the findings have been inconsistent (Wardecker et al. 2017). As noted by Wardecker et al. (2017), these inconsistencies may arise because the linguistic constructs under examination were not further distinguished in terms of topics. The findings yielded by this analysis provide supporting evidence for this argument. Although metaphors only cover part of language use in trauma narratives, the patterns still highlight topics as an important factor interacting with emotional expression, underlining the need for future research on topic-valence associations to zoom in on more nuanced classifications of topics.

The TARGET CATEGORY*CONVENTIONALITY association

The eight target categories also showed interesting contrasts in conventionality. Some target categories, for example, SELF and SOCIAL SITUATION, were more frequently described with conventional metaphors that are common to the whole community and less likely described using novel metaphors. Examples (1) and (10) presented earlier are illustrative (reproduced below).

(1)　　[SELF＊conventional metaphor] 可能在我的二十多年人生里面, 应该是没有试过在短短的时间内情绪或者是心理状态会经历**那么大的起伏**。
'More than 20 years have passed in my life, I have never experienced **such great rises and falls** in emotions within such a short period of time.'

(10)　[SOCIAL SITUATION＊conventional metaphor] 这个事情, 我感觉啊, 就是个**小小插曲**。
'This event, I feel, is **just a small, small episode**.'

In example (1), the speaker's psychological states during the traumatic event are described as "rises and falls" ("起伏") of a tangible object, which is included in the OCD7 as a highly conventionalized metaphor for describing changes in emotion and relationships. In example (10), the occurrence of the traumatic event is conceptualized as a "small, small episode" ("小小插曲") within a longer story or play, which is a conventional way of metaphorizing unforeseen yet minor events in a long period of time or a broad social backdrop.

In contrast, SELF AND SOCIAL SITUATION, the alternative of SOCIAL SITUATION from the observer perspective, was significantly more likely to be interpreted using novel metaphors and less likely described with conventional metaphors than expected. Example (2), discussed earlier in Section 3.2.1, presents two novel metaphors about the speaker's understanding of her relationship with the social unrest:

(2)   [SELF AND SOCIAL SITUATION * novel metaphor] 以前觉得还可以, 就是我们不谈, 我们不说, 我们置身事外, 但是现在就发现不行, 就是政治已经**糊在你脸上了**, 就是你**跑都跑不掉了**。
      'I used to think that it was ok, we could stay out of it as long as we don't talk about it. But now this doesn't work anymore. Politics has been **pasted to your face** now; you **can't run away from it** anyway.'

This example describes how the speaker was involuntarily connected to and affected by the social unrest. The speaker's university being occupied and vandalized by radical protesters is interpreted as the sensory experience of having something "pasted" to the speaker's face ("糊在你脸上"). The speaker being unable to keep her study and future development unaffected by the rioters' acts of terror is metaphorized as the physical inability to run away from a place ("跑都跑不掉"). Different from the "起伏" and "插曲" metaphors presented above, which are commonly shared by native Mandarin Chinese speakers, the two metaphors in example (2) convey the speakers' idiosyncratic understanding of herself in relation to the social situation and are thus less likely to be shared by other speakers in the same linguistic community.

The difference in metaphor choices at the target category level might be explained by these topics having different degrees of salience in everyday communication. As naturally occurring thoughts and feelings, interpersonal interactions, and social situations are common topics in everyday communication and media, speakers may find it easier to cite from conventional expressions than create their own metaphors. By contrast, issues such as emotional and cognitive conflicts, perceived changes in personal life, and personal evaluations of the broader social context are unlikely to be experienced by the whole linguistic community in precisely the same manner. Instead, people may have idiosyncratic understandings and interpretations of these issues, which then lead them to metaphorize their emotions and thoughts with novel expressions. This is particularly evident in descriptions of SELF AND SOCIAL SITUATION, which is probably the least familiar target category for trauma victims of the present study. As the social and political environment in the Chinese mainland is relatively stable and peaceful, Mandarin Chinese speakers may not share many entrenched expressions about how one's life quality, psychological state, and future development could be affected by unexpected, large-scale social events. The scarcity of conventional metaphors and the pressing need to articulate their idiosyncratic subjective experiences may have together contributed to the active use of novel metaphors.

The relationship between CONVENTIONALITY and EMOTIONAL VALENCE

Previous studies on the relationship between CONVENTIONALIT and EMOTIONAL VALENCE have yielded inconsistent findings. The use of novel metaphors in mental health communication is often associated with the expression and regulation of stress (Borbely 1998; Gelo & Mergenthaler 2012), which is the major reason why these expressions are often prioritized in therapeutic interpretation over conventional metaphors. Previous research on the relationship between metaphor conventionality and emotional valences (e.g., Barlow, Pollio & Fine 1977; Gibbs & Franks 2002; McMullen 1985; Pollio & Barlow 1975; Semino 2011; Turner et al. 2020) has shown that negative emotions, as compared with positive or milder ones, are more likely to elicit novel metaphors. However, there is counterevidence as well. In a study of evaluative metaphors in film reviews, Fuoli, Littlemore, and Turner (2022) showed that the frequencies of conventional and novel metaphors did not differ significantly in positive and negative evaluations, which means both types of metaphors undertook important evaluative functions.

When considered alongside the significant link between TARGET CATEGORY and CONVENTIONALITY, the non-significant correlation between CONVENTIONALITY and EMOTIONAL VALENCE indicates that trauma victims' choices over conventional or novel metaphors were more topic-driven than emotion-oriented. While some target categories elicited proportionately higher numbers of novel metaphors, some were more likely to be described using conventional metaphors. This finding supports the view that not only novel metaphors are used as a crucial tool for expressing personal subjective experiences, but conventional metaphors also play an important role in articulating traumatic experiences (Long & Lepper 2008; McMullen 1989; Moser 2000, 2007).

3.4.2 PSYCHOLOGICAL PERSPECTIVE, EMOTIONAL VALENCE, and CONVENTIONALITY

The eight TARGET CATEGORIES, which reflect different semantic contents of trauma metaphors, could be further abstracted as the field and the observer PER-SPECTIVE based on the relationship between the SELF and the topic under discussion. An overview of the statistical results presented earlier in Section 3.4.1 suggests that metaphors from different PSYCHOLOGICAL PERSPECTIVES seem to have different preferences for EMOTIONAL VALENCE and CONVENTIONALITY. Table 3.5 showed that the four target categories from the field perspective (i.e., SELF, OTHERS, PERSONAL SITUATION, and SOCIAL SITUATION) were closely associated with the negative and the positive valence, whereas their counterparts from the observer perspective (i.e., SELF AND SELF, SELF AND OTHERS, SELF AND PERSONAL SITUATION, and SELF AND SOCIAL SITUATION) were closely related to the neutral valence. Table 3.6 showed that target categories from the field perspective were generally more likely to be presented with conventional metaphors, and those belonging to the observer perspective were more likely expressed using novel metaphors. The contrast between the two groups of target categories could also be discerned from the MCA plot presented in Figure 3.5.

Although the findings of Section 3.4.1 enable an intuitive view of how metaphors from the two PSYCHOLOGICAL PERSPECTIVES may be related to EMO-TIONAL VALENCE and CONVENTIONALITY, they do not indicate the statistical significance and strengths of the relationships. It is also impossible to infer potential three-way interactions based on the results of Chi-square tests. To obtain a more accurate understanding of trauma victims' metaphorical meaning-making from the two psychological perspectives, a separate log-linear analysis was performed to investigate the interrelationships among PSYCHOLOGICAL PERSPEC-TIVE, EMOTIONAL VALENCE, and CONVENTIONALITY.

Results of categorical data analysis

The presentational features of trauma metaphors identified at the PSYCHOLOGI-CAL PERSPECTIVES level turned out to be more complex than those at the TAR-GET CATEGORY level. The eventual best model comprised a three-way interaction and two bi-variate associations:

PSYCHOLOGICAL PERSPECTIVE * CONVENTIONALITY * EMOTIONAL VALENCE, $\chi^2(2)$ = 6.52, p = .038
PSYCHOLOGICAL PERSPECTIVE * CONVENTIONALITY, $\chi^2(2)$ = 30.62, $p < .001$
PERSPECTIVE * EMOTIONAL VALENCE, $\chi^2(2)$ = 45.32, $p < .001$

The three-way interaction suggests that metaphors generated from the field and the observer perspectives were presented with different emotional valences, and that the relationships between PSYCHOLOGICAL PERSPECTIVES and EMOTIONAL VALENCES varied further across conventional and novel metaphors. Consistent with the findings of the first log-linear analysis, the bi-variate association between EMOTIONAL VALENCE and CONVENTIONALITY was not statistically significant $\chi^2(2) = 0.223$, $p = .859$. This suggests the association between the two variables was only significant when the metaphors were categorized into the two PSYCHOLOGICAL PERSPECTIVES.

An MCA plot that visualizes the interrelationships among the three variables is shown in Figure 3.6. Dimension 1 explained 39.72% of the total variance, and dimension 2 captured an additional 34.63%; the two dimensions together accounted for 74.35% of the total variance in the data.

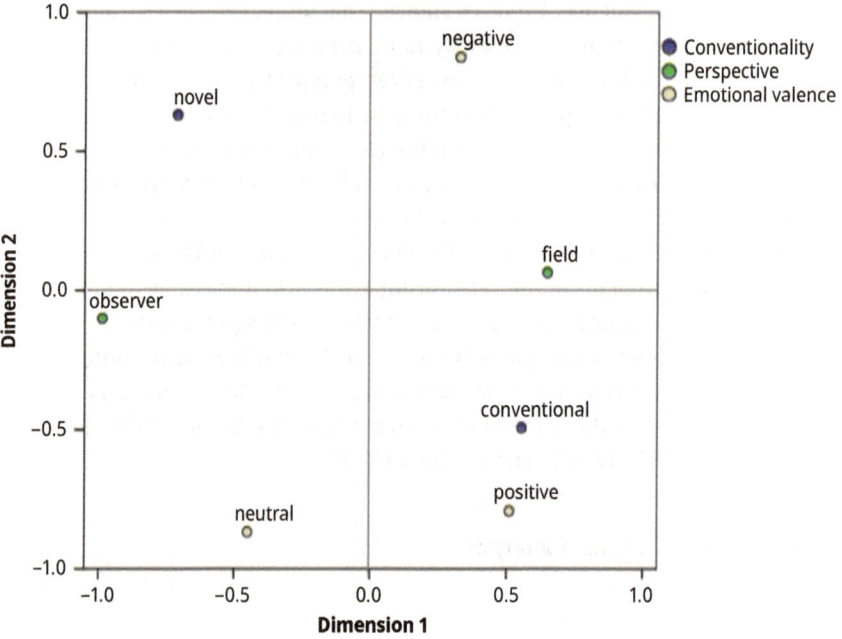

Figure 3.6: An MCA factor plot for the interrelationships among PSYCHOLOGICAL PERSPECTIVE, CONVENTIONALITY, and EMOTIONAL VALENCE.

The seven variable categories are disseminated in different parts of the plot and far away from the origin, which suggests close and dynamic associations among the variable categories. The observer perspective, novel metaphors, and the neutral valence are clustered on the left side of the origin along dimension 1, which suggests the three variable categories are positively associated with each other and negatively associated with those on the other side. The field perspective is located on the right side of the origin, together with conventional metaphors, the negative valence, and the positive valence. This suggests that the four variable categories are positively associated with each other and negatively associated with those on the left side of the plot.

Following Elliot (1988), a contingency table of frequencies that distinguishes between focus and contingency variables was used to assist in interpreting three-way interactions. Focus variables refer to variables of major analytical interest, and contingency variables are those that "elaborate the interaction pattern in which the focus variables are involved" (Elliott 1988: 123–124). For this log-linear model, PSYCHOLOGICAL PERSPECTIVE and EMOTIONAL VALENCE were selected as the focus variables, as they capture more substantively meaningful features of metaphors and are presumably more easily captured by therapeutic practitioners. CONVENTIONALITY was chosen as the contingency variable, as it carries less semantic meaning and therefore can be less easily noticed by therapists. A cross-tabulation of PERSPECTIVE and EMOTIONAL VALENCE across two different levels of CONVENTIONALITY is presented in Table 3.7.

We can see that metaphors generated from the field perspective, which depict the speaker's traumatic experiences from a self-immersed, first-person perspective, were significantly more likely to be negative than expected. Metaphors from this perspective were also significantly less likely to be presented in a neutral way. In contrast, metaphors generated from the observer perspective, which describe the speaker's traumatic experience from an external perspective, were significantly more likely to be neutral and less likely to be negative. The absolute values of all four adjusted residuals were greater than 2.6, which suggests all associations are statistically significant at the .01 level. The adjusted residuals of positive metaphors for both psychological perspectives were within ±2.0, which suggests the observed frequencies did not deviate much from their expected frequencies. The patterns are generally consistent with what can be roughly inferred from the first statistical model and the patterns identified from the MCA plot.

The general patterns identified above apply to both conventional and novel metaphors: the field perspective was more strongly associated with negative metaphors and less so with neutral ones, while the field perspective was more closely associated with neutral metaphors and less so with neutral ones. However, the associations were only statistically significant among conventional metaphors (p=.000, all adjusted residuals had absolute values larger than 2.6). When it comes to novel metaphors, the relationships became non-significant (p=.137, all adjusted residuals within ±2.0), although the ones involving neutral metaphors approached signifi-

Table 3.7: Crosstabulation of PSYCHOLOGICAL PERSPECTIVE and EMOTIONAL VALENCE across different levels of CONVENTIONALITY.

Conventionality	Psychological Perspective		Emotional Valence			Statistics
			Negative	Neutral	Positive	
Conventional	Field	Count	340	242	39	χ^2(2,
		Expected Count	302.4	280.1	38.6	N = 918)
		Adjusted Residual	5.3	−5.4	0.1	= 30.467,
	Observer	Count	107	172	18	p = .000,
		Expected Count	144.6	133.9	18.4	Cramer's
		Adjusted Residual	−5.3	5.4	−0.1	V = 0.182
Novel	Field	Count	204	139	23	χ^2(2,
		Expected Count	193.7	151.8	20.4	N = 716)
		Adjusted Residual	1.5	−1.9	0.8	= 3.979,
	Observer	Count	175	158	17	p = .137,
		Expected Count	185.3	145.2	19.6	Cramer's
		Adjusted Residual	−1.5	1.9	−0.8	V = 0.075
Total	Field	Count	544	381	62	/
		Expected Count	498.9	429.5	58.6	
		Adjusted Residual	4.6	−4.9	0.7	
	Observer	Count	282	330	35	
		Expected Count	327.1	281.5	38.4	
		Adjusted Residual	−4.6	4.9	−0.7	
	Total	Count	826	711	97	
		Expected Count	826.0	711.0	97.0	

cance (adjusted residuals = ±1.9). The effect size of the association was moderate within conventional metaphors (Cramer's V = 0.182) but much weaker in novel metaphors (Cramer's V = 0.075). The relationships between the two psychological perspectives and the positive valence were not significant among both conventional and novel metaphors (all adjusted residuals within ±2.0). In other words, metaphors generated from the field and the observer perspectives were found with distinct emotional patterns, characterized by contrasting distributions of the negative and the neutral valences. The distributions of the two valences were more unequal among conventional metaphors than among novel metaphors.

In what follows, the three-way interaction will be discussed in greater detail with linguistic examples.

Discussion

Metaphors from the two psychological perspectives differ remarkably in the distribution of emotional valences. Those from the field perspective were significantly more likely to be negative than expected. According to previous research on linguistic accounts of autobiographical memories, speakers who take up the field perspective access the experience in a self-immersed manner (Wallace-Hadrill & Kamboj 2016) and are more likely to focus on the subjective and emotional aspects of their experience (Nigro & Neisser 1983). In contrast, the observer perspective elicited significantly more neutral metaphors and fewer negative metaphors than expected. This is because the observer perspective enables trauma victims to access the painful and overwhelming emotional experiences with a greater psychological distance, lower degrees of self-involvement (Kenny & Bryant 2007; Kross, Ayduk & Mischel 2005; Metcalfe & Mischel 1999; Williams & Moulds 2007), and lower levels of negative emotions (Wallace-Hadrill & Kamboj 2016).

The contrast in emotional valences was noted for both conventional and novel metaphors, however, the associations were only significant for conventional metaphors, but not for novel metaphors. Conventional metaphors produced from the field perspective were significantly more likely to be negative, and those generated from the observer perspective were significantly more likely to be neutral. By contrast, novel metaphors from the field and the observer perspectives had quite balanced emotional valences.

Examples (1) and (5) discussed earlier in Section 3.4.1.1 (reproduced below) are conventional and novel metaphors that express negative emotions from the field perspective:

(1) [conventional metaphor * negative metaphor * the field perspective] 可能在我的二十多年人生里面，应该是没有试过在短短的时间内情绪或者是心理状态会经历**那么大的起伏**。
'More than 20 years have passed in my life, I have never experienced **such great rises and falls** in emotions or psychological states within a short period of time.'

(5) [novel metaphor * negative metaphor * the field perspective] 生活中仿佛那些**五彩斑斓的东西不见了**。

'It's like all those **colorful and splendid things** in my life **disappeared from sight.**'

As mentioned earlier, the conceptualization of drastic emotional changes as "rises and falls" in example (1) is a conventional metaphor in Mandarin Chinese. The speaker's emotional feelings are accessed directly from "within" the self and metaphorized in a self-immersed way. By contrast, example (5), illustrates how trauma-related emotions accessed from the first-person perspective are explicated using novel metaphors. Different from example (1), which is widely shared by Mandarin Chinese speakers, example (5) reflects the speaker's unique way of experiencing and conceptualizing trauma-related emotions.

Conventional and novel metaphors that express neutral emotions from the observer perspective are illustrated the two metaphors in example (8) (reproduced below):

(8) [the observer perspective*neutral metaphor] 通过那段经历来学会一些辩证思考, 然后重新去反省自己过往的那些认知, 然后把自己从当时的环境**脱离开来, 作为一个旁观者**去分析。

'Through my experience during the social unrest, I learned to think in a dialectical way. I learned to reflect upon my past ways of thinking, **get** myself **detached** from that environment, and analyze all these thoughts **as an onlooker.**'

In this example, the speakers' emotions and thought activities are evaluated from an externally situated perspective, with the self disconnected from the traumatic scene. The first vehicle term ("脱离") is a conventional metaphor that interprets psychological dissociation in terms of physical disconnection, and the second vehicle term ("旁观者") is a novel expression that describes the speaker as an "onlooker" who is watching the self and the traumatic event from an external standing point.

As noted earlier, the two perspectives often come along with different emotions: the field perspective is often associated with negative accounts, and the observer perspective is more compatible with neutral accounts. The results of loglinear analysis show that the distinction was better captured by conventional metaphors than novel ones. Compared with conventional metaphors, novel metaphors are more likely to be produced in a deliberate and conscious way[30] (Steen

---

30 It is important to note that the novel/conventional distinction should not be conflated with the deliberate/non-deliberate distinction: novel and conventional metaphors are distinguished at the conceptual level, whereas deliberate and non-deliberate metaphors are identified at the level of communication (refer to Steen 2011 for a review). While novel metaphors are typically used in

2008, 2011), requiring greater cognitive efforts (Bowdle & Gentner 2005; Gentner, Falkenhainer & Skorstad 1988; Gentner et al. 2001). It is possible that the incongruence between the perspective adopted and the emotions to be express prompted the speakers to exert more cognitive efforts to work out a novel metaphor that can best describe their feelings. It could also be that the idea to be metaphorized is complicated and requires extra cognitive work. The extra cognitive work might provide the speakers with more opportunities to explore the ideas and greater freedom to deviate from the typical perspective-emotion configuration.

Previous research on the field and the observer perspectives mainly concentrated on the speakers' recollection of autobiographical memories, which are more likely to be narrated in literal than metaphorical language. This study adds a new dimension to our understanding by examining metaphorical meaning-making from the two psychological perspectives. The findings provide empirical evidence that metaphorical meaning-making from the two psychological perspectives exhibits contrasting patterns, and that the two perspectives may engage in dynamic interactions with other linguistic variables. While interpreting and extending client-generated metaphors have been widely acknowledged as an effective strategy for facilitating positive therapeutic insights (Cirillo & Crider 1995; Kopp & Craw 1998; Kopp 1995; Sims & Whynot 1997; Sims 2003; Wagener 2017), instructed perspective shift (Wallace-Hadrill & Kamboj 2016), in which the therapist strategically guides the client to adopt an alternative psychological perspective when recalling an experience, may be used as an effective therapeutic tool for eliciting contrasting or alternative metaphors (Stott et al. 2010; Wilson & Lindy 2013; Witztum, Dasberg & Bleich 1986; Witztum, Van Der Hart & Friedman 1988).

It should be noted that although novel metaphors and those generated from the observer perspective were less closely associated with the negative valence, the two types of metaphors are not necessarily more psychologically adaptive or more therapeutically desirable than others. Lower levels of emotionality and preference for the observer perspective are not always signs of adaptive post-traumatic reactions or therapeutically desirable psychological states. As mentioned earlier in Section 2.3, quite a few empirical studies conducted in different mental health contexts have identified positive correlations between the observer perspective and higher levels of psychological distress and avoidance (e.g., Berntsen, Willert & Rubin 2003; McIsaac & Eich 2002, 2004; Nigro & Neisser 1983; Robinson & Swanson 1993). While the categorical data analyses presented in this chapter only reveal emotional valences

---

a deliberate way due to their creative nature, conventional metaphors can also be used deliberately (Steen 2008).

that are likely associated with the two psychological perspectives, the relationships between the two perspectives and psychopathological experiences of trauma will be examined later in Chapter 4 through a correlation analysis that juxtaposes the participants' personal metaphor usage patterns with their psychometric profiles.

3.4.3 Summary of findings

To summarize, this chapter investigated the multifaceted nature of trauma metaphors by examining the interrelationships among multiple variables and their subcategories. Presentational features, which were often neglected in previous mental health metaphor research, can engage in systematic, dynamic interactions with semantic features of metaphors and with other presentational features. The patterns can provide valuable information about the speakers' general tendency in packaging and presenting metaphorical ideas and the contextual features of the variables involved. Significant relationships identified in the two analyses are summarized in Figure 3.7.

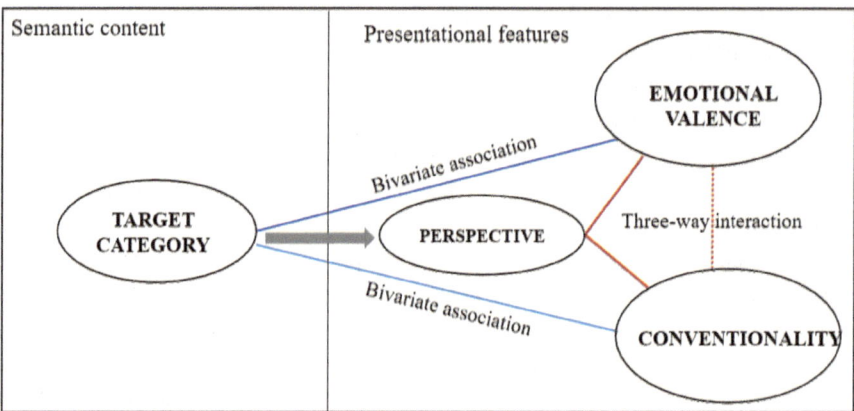

Figure 3.7: Significant relationships identified with categorical data analytic methods.

Section 3.4.1 investigated the multifaceted nature of trauma metaphors by examining the interrelationships among thirteen variable categories of two presentational features (i.e., CONVENTIONALITY and EMOTIONAL VALENCE) and one semantic feature (i.e., TARGET CATEGORY). Trauma victims' metaphors about the eight TARGET CATEGORIES exhibited therapeutically interesting interactions with the three EMOTIONAL VALENCES and the two levels of CONVENTIONALITY.

Section 3.4.2 explored the multifaceted nature of metaphor use reflected by the interrelationships among seven categories of three presentational variables: CONVENTIONALITY, EMOTIONAL VALENCE, and PSYCHOLOGICAL PERSPECTIVES. The two PSYCHOLOGICAL PERSPECTIVES exhibited robust associations with different EMOTIONAL VALENCES, and the relationship between the two variables varied further across different levels of CONVENTIONALITY. The findings suggest that not only different semantic features but also different ways of information processing may elicit distinct ways of metaphorical meaning-making.

A particularly interesting observation is that the relationship between two presentational features varied at different levels of semantic specificity. The two analyses offered interesting insights into the interaction between CONVENTIONALITY and EMOTIONAL VALENCE. In metaphors about different target categories, which contain rich semantic information, the distribution of the three emotional valences showed no remarkable difference across conventional and novel metaphors. This suggests that neither conventional nor novel metaphors leaned towards a particular emotional valence. However, when the metaphors were examined through the lens of psychological perspectives, which downplays the semantic distinctions between the target categories but highlight the difference in information processing, we saw a clear contrast in valence distributions across conventional and novel metaphors. This reveals the potential for semantic and presentational features to capture different contextual characteristics, highlighting the theoretical and practical value of studying metaphor multifacetedness.

3.5 Chapter conclusion

The present study extends the scope of existing literature from semantic analyses to the multifaceted nature of metaphor use, reflected by systematic, interrelationships among multiple variables and their subcategories. In terms of methodology, this study showcased how mixed-method analyses can uncover patterns that are not evident to qualitative observations. Categorical data analyses showed clear advantages in extracting systematic and context-sensitive patterns and capturing different facets of metaphor variable interactions. The use of MCA factor plots demonstrated how the multifaceted nature of metaphor use can be converted to visually distinguishable forms that are informative for subsequent qualitative analyses (Tay & Pan 2022). Discourse analysis highlighted the irreplaceable advantage of qualitative methods in substantiating statistically significant patterns with contextual features.

The findings underscore the potential for presentational features to capture the speakers' general tendency in "packaging" and presenting metaphorical ideas. The second analysis, in particular, adds to our empirical knowledge about the instantiation of the field and observer perspectives in metaphorical language. As mentioned in the discussion sections, some of the findings align with and reinforce previous research findings, while some offer a novel perspective that challenges prevailing therapeutic and linguistic assumptions.

This study holds therapeutic implications. The significant patterns highlighted by categorical data analysis provide insights into metaphor usage patterns that are more (or less) likely to occur in authentic therapeutic talk. The patterns can serve as useful guidance for applying metaphor-based therapeutic protocol (e.g., Grove & Panzer 1989; Kopp & Craw 1998; Kopp 1995; Sims 2003; Sims & Whynot 1997; Witztum, Van Der Hart & Friedman 1988) and techniques like instructed perspective shift (Wallace-Hadrill & Kamboj 2016).

However, the present study is limited in three major aspects. Firstly, as this book aims to identify therapeutically interesting metaphor usage patterns, vehicle terms and target topics in the present dataset were coded in a top-down manner using pre-established categories of therapeutic significance. In the absence of a systematic top-down coding scheme, vehicle terms were not included in this analysis. Future research could adopt bottom-up coding procedures (refer to Ahrens & Jiang 2020 for a dictionary- and corpus-based method of source domain verification) to obtain a more holistic view of contextually motivated metaphor usage patterns. Systematic metaphors (Cameron 1999) in trauma narratives, especially when and where they are used, and how they are presented, would also provide insights into trauma victims' implicit ideas, attitudes, and beliefs.

Secondly, only a limited number of metaphor variables were examined in this study. Future research could extend the study of metaphor multifacetedness by including vehicle terms and a broader range of presentational variables, such as the function of metaphors and relevance to the key topic. It would also be interesting to examine multifacetedness based on more finely coded variable categories, for instance, scaler codings of conventionality and five-scale coding for emotional valence.

Thirdly, this study took statistically significant patterns revealed by quantitative analyses as the starting points of qualitative analysis (see Creswell 2014 for an introduction to different configurations of qualitative and quantitative methods in mixed-method research). As noted by Tay (2017), patterns identified with frequency-based quantitative methods only reveal quantitative relationships among the variables but do not entail thematic significance. Instead of following a quantitatively oriented approach, future research could begin with qualitative discourse analysis, identify thematically salient or interesting patterns, and then use quantitative methods to assess the statistical significance and strengths of these patterns (c.f. McMullen 1989; Tay 2019). It is also worth mentioning that categorical data analytic methods, such as loglinear analysis and Chi-square tests, explore multifacetedness in a top-down manner by examining a prespecified set of variables or categories. A contrasting approach is to investigate the natural clustering of the data points, for example, through cluster analysis and association rule mining (see Section 6.4.2 for more details).

4 Correlations between trauma victims' metaphor use and severities of traumatization

4.1 Chapter introduction

In Chapter 3, we examined the multifaceted presentational features of trauma metaphors. While the study provided detailed accounts of how trauma victims organize and present their metaphorical ideas in quantitatively systematic ways, the focus was limited to contextual characteristics of linguistic variables. In Chapters 4 and 5, we will shift our focus from the interrelationships among metaphor variables to the interface between metaphor use and psychopathological experiences.

Chapter 4 presents an individual-level analysis of the correlations between trauma victims' metaphor use and their severities of traumatization. As introduced earlier in Chapters 1 and 2, trauma victims may experience various acute stress symptoms, which can be seen as a mixture of emotional, cognitive, and physiological disturbances. Owing to numerous objective and subjective risk factors, trauma victims may not develop the same degrees of trauma, nor would they experience all symptoms in precisely the same severities (Amir, Kaplan & Kotler 1996). Although numerous studies have revealed the possibility for contrasting intensities of emotions and psychiatric disturbances to be distinguished from the speakers' inclinations toward specific aspects of metaphors (e.g., Costa & Steen 2014; Demjén et al. 2019; Fainsilber & Ortony 1987; Gök & Kara 2022; Wilson & Lindy 2013), the patterns were mostly examined in relation to broadly defined psychopathological conditions such as different therapeutic or recovery stages. The variation of metaphor use across more subtle differences, such as the severity of psychopathological experiences and that of more specific symptoms, remains unexplored.

Combining linguistic and psychometric data, this chapter investigates whether and how trauma victims' personal metaphor usage patterns tend to vary with their overall degrees of trauma and severities of five major ASD symptoms as measured by the SASRQ.[31] In Section 4.2, I will provide an overview of the metaphor variables and psychometric data. The research methods and research questions are summa-

---

[31] Section 4.4.1 of this chapter was previously published as Qiu, Han & Dennis Tay. 2022. The interaction between metaphor use and psychological states: a mix-method analysis of trauma talk in the Chinese context. In Dennis Tay & Xie Pan (eds.), *Data analytics in cognitive linguistics: methods and insights*, 197–228. Berlin/Boston: De Gruyter Mouton. Section 4.4.2 has been accepted as Qiu, Han, Dennis Tay & Bernadette Watson. 2024. Metaphorical Language and Psychopathological Symptoms: A Case Study of Trauma Victims' Metaphor Use. *BMC Psychology.* The content has been substantially revised.

https://doi.org/10.1515/9783111346502-004

rized in Section 4.3. Section 4.4 presents the results of statistical analyses, illustrates the patterns using genuine linguistic examples from a qualitative discourse analytic perspective, and provides tentative interpretations based on findings of previous metaphor and trauma research. Implications, limitations, and future directions will be summarized in Section 4.5.

4.2 Data and variables

4.2.1 Linguistic data

Metaphor variables

Two sets of metaphor variables will be investigated in this chapter. The first includes conventionality, emotional valence, target categories, and psychological perspectives (refer to Section 2.3 for introductions, see Section 3.2 for operational definitions, linguistic examples, and descriptive statistics). As psychological perspectives can be inferred based on the coding results of target categories (see Section 2.3.1), they will not be included in the statistical analysis to reduce data redundancy. Instead, they will serve as reference points in the subsequent discussion where relevant target categories are involved.

The second set of variables are trauma-related vehicle groupings and discourse topics that are thematically salient in the present dataset (referred to from now on as "trauma-related vehicle groupings and target topics"). The vehicle groupings include SENSORY INFORMATION, PHYSICAL ACTIVITY, WAR AND THREAT, and SPACE AND SPATIAL RELATIONS. The discourse topics include EMOTIONS AND EMOTIONAL PROCESSES, SELF-REFERENCES, and THINKING AND UNDERSTANDING. An introduction to the variables and their relevance to trauma psychopathology was provided earlier in Section 2.2.2. Among the 1,634 metaphors identified in the present dataset, 936 instantiated the four trauma-related vehicle groupings, and 813 were coded under the three discourse topics.[32] Frequencies and examples are presented in Table 4.1.

---

32 As the categories do not cover all metaphors in the present dataset, they were not included in the categorical data analysis conducted in Chapter 3. While the associations between trauma-related metaphors and other metaphor variables can be examined by building two subsamples that exclude non-relevant vehicle groupings and target topics, the approach is at odds with the aim of context-based analysis, which is to extract patterns of metaphors from naturally occurring discourse (rather than from fragmented examples or selected excerpts). Therefore, this approach was not adopted in this book.

Table 4.1: Frequencies and examples of trauma-related vehicle groupings and discourse topics.

Category		Example
Potentially trauma-related vehicle groupings (936)	Sensory information (331)	有点烦躁, 有点焦躁, 也有点像是有点**透不过气的感觉**。 'I felt a bit agitated, irritated, and **difficult to breathe**.'
	War and threat (112)	但是作为**第一线**、在**主战场**来说, 我觉得主要令我感觉很不爽、很愤怒的点, 可能还是对个人的影响。 'Speaking of being **at the frontline, at the main battlefield,** what makes me very uncomfortable and angry is probably how the impact on my personal life.'
	Space relations (140)	但是我觉得我情绪**起起伏伏**的, 可能自己偷偷有担心过, 会不会影响我实际的健康这种。 'But I feel that my emotions are always **getting up and down**, sometimes I feel worried, I don't know if this will affect my health.'
	Physical activity (353)	一开始有情绪波动的时候, 我很快就**调整**过来, 但是后面就是一种**挥之不去**的感觉。 'At the beginning, when I felt the emotional fluctuations, I could **adjust** myself very quickly, but later it became very **difficult to dispel**.'
Clinically interesting discourse topics (813)	Emotional feelings and processes (517)	我自己甚至都可能会意识到我是不是**就像(进入)一个黑洞一样, 被负面情绪吸进去了**。 'Even I myself realized, if I was, **just like (entered) a black hole, if I was absorbed by the negative emotions**.'
	Thinking and Understanding (215)	就是试图**抛掉我所处的环境, 把这个事情放到更大的格局上来看**。 'I was trying to **separate myself from the environment I am now in, and look at this event in a bigger backdrop**.'
	Self-references (81)	当时就会有一些很焦虑的心理状态, 第二个就是暴躁, 因为会觉得自己是无辜的, 自己是**受了无妄之灾**的。 'At that time I often felt a lot of anxieties, and the second feeling was anger, because I think I am innocent, I am **a victim of an unexpected disaster**.'

Although categorical data analysis requires that the data be coded in terms of mutually exclusive categories, the boundaries between semantic categories are not always clear-cut. Sometimes the meaning expressed by one metaphor can fall into two different categories (Fuoli, Littlemore & Turner 2022; Kimmel 2010). For example, expressions about bodily movements like "fight and flee" may be coded as WAR AND THREAT or as specific forms of PHYSICAL ACTIVITY. A considerable number of self-referential metaphors may also be regarded as the speaker's reflections on personal emotions or thoughts. In this study, these expressions were coded based on the more specific meanings, which can better reflect the speakers' intended meanings. In some cases, the speakers' emotions were juxtaposed with, or embedded in, thinking processes. These expressions were coded according to which topic was given more attention or emphasis.

Frequencies of all metaphor variables were sorted by individuals and summarized in terms of their absolute frequencies in the interview. As the interviews varied substantially in length and the frequency of metaphor vehicle terms was positively correlated with the length of interviews (r = .076, p < .001), the absolute frequencies were converted to standardized frequencies per thousand Chinese characters to control for the differences in lengths. The metaphor variables and descriptive statistics are summarized in Table 4.2.

Table 4.2: An overview of all metaphor variables and descriptive statistics.

Metaphor variables		Mean of density
Conventionality	Novel	3.82 (SD = 2.09)
	Conventional	5.10 (SD = 2.41)
Emotional valence	Negative	4.47 (SD = 1.98)
	Neutral	3.89 (SD = 2.33)
	Positive	0.56 (SD = 0.64)
Target categories	SELF	1.93 (SD = 1.31)
	OTHERS	1.31 (SD = 1.64)
	PERSONAL SITUATION	1.02 (SD = 1.02)
	SOCIAL SITUATION	1.06 (SD = 0.98)
	SELF AND SELF	0.98 (SD = 1.25)
	SELF AND OTHERS	0.44 (SD = 0.67)
	SELF AND PERSONAL SITUATION	0.61 (SD = 0.53)
	SELF AND SOCIAL SITUATION	1.56 (SD = 1.24)
Trauma-related vehicle groupings	SENSORY INFORMATION	1.93 (SD = 1.14)
	PHYSICAL ACTIVITY	2.02 (SD = 1.28)
	WAR AND THREAT	0.48 (SD = 0.63)
	SPACE AND SPATIAL RELATIONS	0.76 (SD = 0.65)
Trauma-related discourse topics	EMOTIONAL FEELINGS AND PROCESSES	3.10 (SD = 1.89)
	SELF-REFERENCES	0.46 (SD = 0.73)
	THINKING AND UNDERSTANDING	1.49 (SD = 1.28)

Different from the long Excel spreadsheet used for Chapter 3 (see Figure 3.3), the linguistic data examined in this chapter was organized in a shorter form. Each participant's personal metaphor usage profile is summarized in terms of the 20 variable categories and represented using a series of data points. A partial screenshot of the Excel spreadsheet is shown in Figure 4.1. The participants were numbered from 1 to 46. Each row displays the metaphor usage profiles of a specific participant, and each column shows the standardized frequency of a specific metaphor variable.

	No	Novel metaphor	Conventional metaphor	Negative metaphor	Neutral metaphor	Positive metaphor	SELF	OTHERS	PERSONAL SITUATION	SOCIAL SITAUTION	SELF AND SELF	SELF AND OTHERS	SELF AND PERSONAL SITUATION	SELF AND SOCIAL SITUATION
2	1	5.43	4.83	3.02	4.52	2.71	2.11	1.21	0.90	1.81	1.51	1.21	0.00	1.51
3	2	3.72	5.08	7.11	1.69	0.00	0.68	1.52	0.00	2.37	0.17	1.02	0.51	2.54
4	3	4.43	1.58	3.16	2.53	0.32	0.47	0.47	0.63	0.79	0.63	0.00	0.00	3.00
5	4	0.84	8.37	3.77	5.02	0.42	1.67	3.35	2.09	0.00	0.00	0.00	0.84	1.26
6	5	6.10	6.10	6.98	3.78	1.45	2.62	0.58	1.45	2.62	1.16	0.00	0.58	3.20
7	6	6.32	10.92	7.66	8.24	1.34	5.75	0.96	0.77	0.57	4.60	0.38	1.15	3.07
8	7	6.01	4.37	6.97	3.14	0.27	3.01	0.00	2.05	0.41	1.37	0.27	0.55	2.73
9	8	0.87	5.78	2.02	3.76	0.87	1.73	0.29	0.29	0.00	0.29	2.60	1.16	0.29
10	9	6.94	5.95	10.17	2.73	0.00	2.23	0.99	0.74	1.98	0.50	1.98	0.25	4.22
11	10	1.55	3.87	4.26	1.16	0.00	1.94	0.39	0.39	0.77	0.39	0.00	1.55	0.00
12	11	2.58	5.16	4.79	2.95	0.00	1.84	1.11	0.00	0.74	0.74	0.74	0.37	2.21
13	12	4.28	6.12	4.90	5.51	0.00	2.45	3.67	0.00	0.61	0.61	0.00	0.61	2.45
14	13	7.08	7.60	6.82	6.55	1.31	1.05	5.50	2.88	0.52	0.26	0.52	1.83	2.10
15	14	6.01	4.60	6.01	3.18	1.41	1.06	3.53	0.00	1.06	1.77	0.00	0.00	3.18
16	15	6.74	2.59	3.63	4.66	1.04	0.52	1.04	0.52	1.55	3.11	0.52	0.52	1.55
17	16	4.14	5.69	6.73	3.10	0.00	2.07	0.52	5.17	0.00	0.00	0.00	1.03	1.03
18	17	3.91	5.87	7.18	2.61	0.00	4.24	0.00	0.65	0.65	1.30	0.98	0.65	1.30
19	18	9.33	10.18	5.94	11.87	1.70	1.98	8.06	0.42	4.52	2.26	0.57	0.28	1.41
20	19	1.72	2.70	1.72	2.21	0.49	0.49	3.20	0.25	0.00	0.00	0.00	0.00	0.49

Figure 4.1: A partial screenshot of the Excel spreadsheet for correlation analyses.

Interrater reliability

Interrater reliability in coding trauma-related variable categories was measured based on 15% of randomly selected data provided by the same two coders (refer to Section 3.2.3). The two coders went over the clinical significance of the categories and calibrated their understanding of the categories by discussing examples provided in relevant trauma and metaphor literature and in transcripts. They then worked independently to determine whether the metaphors fell into the four trauma-related vehicle groupings and three discourse topics; expressions that did not belong to any of the categories were coded as "others".

Krippendorff's alphas for trauma-related vehicle groupings and discourse topics were 0.697 and 0.721, respectively. Both values were greater than the smallest acceptable reliability for qualitative analysis suggested by Krippendorff (2004), i.e., α = 0.667. After the interrater reliability tests and the after-test discussion, the author of this book finished coding the rest of the dataset. Ambiguous cases were settled through discussion with other experienced metaphor researchers.

4.2.2 Psychometric data

Questionnaire items

Shortly after the interview, the participants had their degrees of trauma measured using the Chinese-translated version of the SASRQ (Cardeña et al. 2000), which is a 30-item self-report questionnaire developed following the DSM-IV diagnostic criteria (American Psychiatric Association 1994). It measures the participant's experience of five specific symptoms, including dissociation, re-experiencing, avoidance, anxiety and hyperarousal, and impairment in functioning. The symptoms' clinical manifestation and the corresponding questionnaire item numbers are summarized in Table 4.3.

Table 4.3: Clinical features of the five ASD symptoms measured by the SASRQ.

Symptom	Clinical manifestations	SASRQ item numbers
Dissociation	Alteration in perception and awareness of self, others, and the surrounding environment	5 diagnostic criteria, 10 items: Numbing: 20, 28; Reduction in awareness of surroundings: 4, 24; Derealization: 3, 18; Depersonalization: 10, 13; Dissociative amnesia: 16, 25.
Re-experiencing	Recurrence of trauma-related memories, thoughts, feelings, dreams, etc.	1 diagnostic criterion, 6 items: 6, 7, 15, 19, 23, 29
Avoidance	The tendency to avoid traumatic-related stimuli, such as places, people, thoughts, and feelings	1 diagnostic criterion, 6 items: 5, 11, 14, 17, 22, 30
Anxiety and hyperarousal	Increased anxiety, sensitivity, and physiological arousal to external stimuli	1 diagnostic criterion, 6 items: 1, 2, 8, 12, 21, 27
Impairment in functioning	Difficulty in engaging in social or interpersonal interactions, or in performing everyday actions	1 diagnostic criterion, 2 items: 9, 26

To recap, each questionnaire item is rated on a 6-point scale from 0 to 5 (0 = not experienced, 5 = very often experienced). The whole questionnaire can be rated either continuously or dichotomously (Cardeña et al. 2000; refer to Orsillo 2001 for a more detailed introduction). We can either calculate the total score to assess the individual's overall degrees of trauma or extract the symptom scores to examine the severities of specific symptoms.

· The total SASRQ score is the sum of all 30 items under all five symptoms. It reflects the individual's overall degree of traumatization: the higher the total score, the more traumatized the individual is. The symptom score is the sum of all item scores that measure the same symptom. Getting a high score on a specific symptom suggests that the participant is particularly disturbed by that symptom. The scores can provide the clinical practitioner with an immediate sense of the individual's severity of acute stress reactions and whether special clinical intervention is needed. Alternatively, the ratings can also be converted to dichotomous data to account for the clinical presence of specific ASD symptoms. The relationships between trauma metaphors and the clinical presence of symptoms will be explored in Chapter 5.

Descriptive statistics

In this chapter, the participants' metaphor use is examined in relation to their ratings on the full SASRQ scale and the five subscales. Each participant's psychological profile is summarized using six psychometric variables. Descriptive statistics of the overall SASRQ scores and the five symptom scores are summarized in Table 4.4. Internal consistencies of the ratings are also included.

Table 4.4: Descriptive statistics and internal consistencies of SASRQ ratings.

Variable	Number of items	Descriptive Statistics		Internal Consistency (Cronbach's α)
		Mean/total score	Standard deviation	
Overall degrees of trauma	30	39.09/150	23.75	.946
Dissociation	10	9.91/50	7.07	.837
Re-experiencing	6	5.98/30	4.57	.773
Avoidance	6	9.70/30	7.38	.886
Anxiety and hyperarousal	6	10.37/30	5.78	.826
Impairment in functioning	2	3.13/10	2.37	.635

The 46 participants' overall SASRQ scores averaged 39.09 out of a possible total of 150 points. Although the mean overall score was not intuitively high, the standard deviation (SD = 23.75) was quite large, indicating substantial variation among the participants. The dissociation scores, summed up from ten items scores with a possible total of 50 points, had an average of 9.91 (SD = 7.07). Ratings on re-experiencing, avoidance, and anxiety and hyperarousal averaged 5.98 (SD = 4.57), 9.70 (SD = 7.38), and 10.37 (SD = 5.78), respectively. Each of the symptoms was measured by six items with a possible total of 30 points. The mean impairment in functioning score was 3.13 (SD = 2.37) out of a total of 10 points. There were no missing data in the dataset.

Cronbach's α of the full-scale ratings indicated excellent internal consistency, and ratings on the five subscales demonstrated acceptable to good internal consistency (Cronbach 1951). Cronbach's α for impairment in functioning scores was relatively lower than those for other symptoms, which is probably because the symptom was measured by only two items, as smaller numbers of items are often correlated with lower reliability. The same issue was also reported by SASRQ-based studies of other traumatic contexts (e.g., Kweon et al. 2013; Pedersen & Zachariae 2010).

Table 4.5 summarizes SASRQ statistics reported by previous studies on different traumatic events. Because different traumatic events vary remarkably in substantive details, demographic features, and sociocultural backgrounds, it may not be clinically meaningful to make quantitative comparisons across psychometric outcomes yielded from different contexts. Nevertheless, psychometric data collected from different traumatic events can still provide an intuitive understanding of the current research context.

Table 4.5: Overall SASRQ scores reported by studies on other traumatic events.

Traumatic event	Overall SASRQ scores	Citation
The 1994 USAir 427 airplane crash	M = 26.37, SD = 25.52	Cardeña et al. (2000)
The 2008 Wenchuan Earthquake	M = 33, SD = 26	Tao et al. (2008)
The 2013 Boston Marathon bombings	M = 43.41, SE = 0.40	Holman et al. (2014)
Premature birth	M = 45.1, SD = 33.4	Jubinville et al. (2012)
Work-induced trauma among nurses during the COVID-19 pandemic	M = 33.15, SD = 25.55	Liao et al. (2021)

The statistics suggest that the overall degrees of traumatization induced by the Hong Kong social unrest did not differ substantially from the impact of other traumatic events. The mean overall score of the current sample is slightly higher than what was reported for the 1995 USAir 427 airplane crash (Cardeña et al. 2000), the 2008 Wenchuan Earthquake (Tao et al. 2008), and the psychological impact of Covid-19 on nurses in Wuhan, China (Liao et al. 2021). The mean score of the current sample is relatively lower than the mean score reported for the 2013 Boston Marathon bombings (Holman, Garfin & Silver 2014) and the experience of premature birth (Jubinville et al. 2012).

4.3 Research questions and methods

This study presents an individual-level analysis of the correlations between trauma victims' metaphor use and psychopathological experiences. Research questions to be addressed in this chapter are as follows:

(1) How are trauma victims' metaphor use correlated with their overall degrees of trauma? (See Section 4.4.1)

(2) How are trauma victims' metaphor use correlated with the severities of the five ASD symptoms? (See Section 4.4.2)

Correlation analysis was adopted to examine the relationships between the selected metaphor variables and the participants' psychometric scores (i.e., overall SASRQ scores and the five symptom scores). According to the Central Limit Theorem, sampling distribution in a sample of 30 or above tends to be normal, regardless of the actual distribution of data. In this case, parametric tests, which make no assumptions about data distribution, tend to have higher statistical power than their non-parametric alternatives. Therefore, the parametric measure of correlation, i.e., Pearson's r, was chosen. Following previous research on trauma language (e.g., Jaeger et al. 2014; Kaplow et al. 2018; Wardecker et al. 2017), $p = .05$ was used as the threshold for statistical significance. The analyses were conducted using Jamovi 2.0.0.0.

It is important to mention that psychometric ratings on the full-scale and the subscale scores are usually positively and significantly correlated, as the latter are by design subcomponents of the former. In the present dataset, the 46 participants' overall SASRQ scores and their ratings on the five subscales have strong and positive correlations (all r-values are larger than .70; statistics are summarized in Table 4.6). This means if we correlate the two sets of ratings with the same set of linguistic variables, we are very likely to see overlap in the results they elicit.

Table 4.6: Correlations between overall SASRQ scores and symptom scores.

Psychometric Variables	Overall SASRQ scores
Dissociation scores	$r = 0.89$ $p<.001$**
Re-experiencing scores	$r = 0.92$ $p<.001$**
Avoidance scores	$r = 0.88$ $p<.001$**

Table 4.6 (continued)

Psychometric Variables	Overall SASRQ scores
Anxiety and hyperarousal scores	$r = 0.86$ $p<.001**$
Impairment in functioning scores	$r = 0.77$ $p<.001**$

(Note: *p*-values less than .05 are indicated as * and those less than .01 as **).

Despite the issue of data redundancy, studying metaphor usage patterns associated with different psychometric indicators can provide valuable theoretical and practical insights. Examining metaphor usage patterns associated with different psychopathological constructs enables a more precise understanding of the roles played by different emotional, thought, and physiological experiences in metaphor variations. The findings can further open a unique perspective on the experiential and cognitive dynamics underlying mental health metaphors. From the clinical perspective, metaphor usage patterns associated with different psychopathological experiences can also help clinical practitioners derive a deeper understanding of client-generated metaphors. Furthermore, the patterns can offer useful supplementary information for the evaluation and treatment of trauma. Given all that, both the participants' overall SASRQ scores and their ratings on the five subscales were entered into the analyses.

A simplified version of the Excel spreadsheet used for correlation analyses is shown in Figure 4.2.

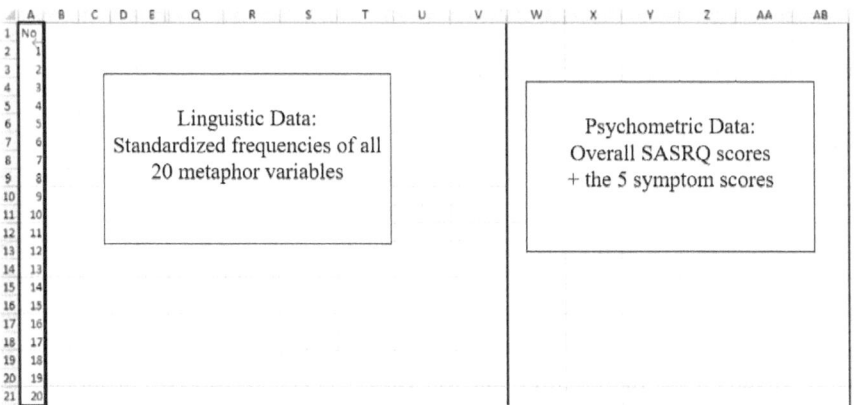

Figure 4.2: A simplified version of the Excel spreadsheet used (for correlation analyses).

Before we proceed with the results and discussion part, it is crucial to note that correlation analysis only detects the strengths and directions of relationships between two variables but is insufficient to infer causal relationships. In other words, significant patterns identified by this study only represent individual-level metaphor variations, i.e., how trauma victims' metaphor usage patterns vary across different overall degrees of trauma and different severities of symptoms. The patterns do not imply that the metaphor usage patterns led to higher or lower degrees of trauma or vice versa.

It is also crucial to reiterate that the examples are not necessarily descriptions of the symptoms (refer to Chapter 5 for an analysis of symptom-specific metaphors). Instead, the examples demonstrate how different psychopathological experiences may prompt trauma victims to highlight or downplay certain aspects of their experiences in metaphorical meaning-making. As the study is based on only one traumatic context and the sample is quite homogenous, the findings should be interpreted with caution.

4.4 Results and discussion

The correlations between trauma victims' metaphor usage patterns and their overall degrees of trauma will be reported in Section 4.4.1, and metaphor variations across different severities of specific symptoms will be discussed in Section 4.4.2. Each of the sections will first provide an overview of the statistical results and then illustrate the significant metaphor usage patterns using genuine linguistic examples. The findings will be summarized in Section 4.4.3.

4.4.1 Correlations between metaphor use and overall degrees of trauma

Results of correlation analysis
Three metaphor variables were positively and significantly correlated with the participants' overall SASRQ scores, including negative metaphors (r = .318, p = .031), SELF AND SELF (r = .339, p = .021), and self-reference (r = .311, p = .036). All r-values were greater than .30 and less than .50, indicating moderate correlations between the three metaphor variables and overall degrees of trauma. This suggests that compared with the less traumatized, individuals with higher degrees of trauma produced more metaphors in the negative valence. They also generated more metaphors in describing the incongruence between or within their emotional feelings and rational thinking and the perceived changes in their self-identity. The significant correlations are summarized in Table 4.7 (refer to Appendix 2 for the full correlation matrix).

Table 4.7: Significant correlations between metaphor use and overall SASRQ scores.

Metaphor variables	Posttraumatic variable: Overall degrees of trauma
Negative metaphors	$r = .318^*$ $p = .031$
SELF AND SELF	$r = .339^*$ $p = .021$
Self-references	$r = .311^*$ $p = .036$

(Note: p-values less than .05 are indicated as * and those less than .01 as **)

Discussion

Traumatization is characterized by the experience of various negative emotions like anger, shame, and fear, thought processes such as guilt and self-blame, and negative expectations of self and world (American Psychiatric Association 2013). Among others, negative interpretations of the self and the traumatic event have been identified as particularly strong predictors of persistent trauma (Bryant & Guthrie 2007; Dunmore, Clark & Ehlers 1999; Ehlers & Clark 2000). As the degree of trauma increases, people become more likely to engage in rumination (Ehlers & Clark 2000; Michael et al. 2007; Szabo et al. 2017), which is characterized by "repetitive and recurrent, self-related negative thinking about past negative experiences and/or negative mood" (Michael et al. 2007: 307). In the current research context, the increase in negative metaphors was identified as a significant indicator of high degrees of traumatization.

Compared with literal emotion words, metaphorical accounts of emotions capture larger chunks of information and reveal more differentiated and substantial details about the speaker's emotional feelings (Fainsilber & Ortony 1987). The positive and significant correlation between overall degrees of trauma and frequencies of negative metaphors suggests that individuals with higher degrees of trauma were more likely to produce more "granular" (Feldman Barrett et al. 2001) accounts of their subjective experiences than the less traumatized. Example (11) is a negative metaphor produced by a highly traumatized participant who scored 84 on the SASRQ (i.e., about 1.9 standard deviations above the sample mean of 39.09):

(11) 我自己甚至都可能会意识到我是不是**就像(进入)一个黑洞一样，被负面情
      绪吸进去了**。
      'Even I myself realized, if I was, **just like (entered) a black hole, if I was
      absorbed by the negative emotions**'

The metaphor describes how the participant strives to resolve the discrepancies
between post-traumatic life and her ideal way of living, exemplifying a typical response of trauma victims in making meaning of the traumatic event. The speaker's traumatic feelings are interpreted in terms of a "black hole (黑洞)" that sucks
in everything in the vicinity. The irresistible and overwhelming nature of trauma
is interpreted as an enormous attracting force, and the speaker being overwhelmed by negative emotions is conceptualized as the speaker being physically
absorbed by the "black hole".

Some previous studies on general trauma language showed that lower levels
of post-traumatic stress may also be discerned from more frequent use of positive
words (e.g., Jaeger et al. 2014; Kleim et al. 2018; Wardecker et al. 2017). Some studies showed that the preference for negative emotion words is sometimes accom-
panied by the decrease of positive emotion words such as "happy", "good", and
"well" (e.g., Frewen et al. 2011; Wardecker et al. 2017). However, these tendencies
were not observed in metaphor use extracted from the present dataset. Neither
the correlation between negative metaphors and positive metaphors (r = .105, p =
.487) nor the relationship between overall SASRQ scores and positive metaphors
(r = .235, p = .116) was statistically significant.

In addition to the apparent negative bias, high scorers on the SASRQ also
used more SELF AND SELF and self-referential metaphors than the low scorers.
Different from other semantic features, in these two types of metaphors, the self
is not just the subject who is experiencing the traumatic event but also the object
that is being observed by the self. While SELF AND SELF metaphors highlight the
incongruence or confrontations between the speakers' emotions and thoughts,
self-referential metaphors focus more on the identity and characteristics of the
self as an integral whole. Examples of the two types of metaphors produced by
severely traumatized participants are given below. Example (12) is a SELF AND
SELF metaphor produced by one of the most traumatized participants, who got
101 points on the full-scale (2.61 standard deviations above the sample mean). Example (13) is a self-referential metaphor generated by an interviewee who also
scored high above average.

(12) **我仿佛身体里面有两个小人，**然后一个小人喊着说："你要冷静的看一看这边
      啊，你看一看这些民主社会"之类的，**另外一边就在说**："你是在这读一年书而
      已，可是这一年已经被损失了这么多"。

'**It feels like there are two little persons in my body, and one is shouting**: "You should be calm and see what happened here, you should see the democratic society" and the like. **The one on the other side says**: "You are just doing a master here for one year, but just in one year you have lost so much".'

(13) 当时就会有一些很焦虑的心理状态, 第二个就是暴躁, 因为会觉得自己是无辜的, 自己是**受了无妄之灾**的。
    'At that time I often felt a lot of anxieties, and the second feeling was anger, because I think I am innocent, I am **a victim of an unexpected disaster**.'

In example (12), a metaphor scenario involving "two little persons (两个小人)" was constructed to describe the confrontations between rational thinking and emotional feelings. Under non-traumatic conditions, the self is usually perceived as an integral whole. This example shows how trauma victims may perceive themselves as being split into two pieces. In this example, the experience is interpreted as two little persons holding diametrically opposing opinions about the social unrest: one person represents the interviewee's rational thinking as a mature social being, and the other expresses her concerns over her life and studies as an emotional being. The metaphor describes how the individual strives to resolve the discrepancies between the post-traumatic life and her ideal way of living. The metaphor is also an instance of metaphors generated from the observer perspective. We can see the speaker adopts an external, detached vantage point in describing her feelings; she is both the experiencer of the conflict and a witness who is watching herself from the outside.

Different from example (12), which focuses on the opposition between the rational subject and the emotional self, example (13) describes how the self, as a unified entity, experienced a sudden and unexpected change in identity. The impact of the traumatic event is conceptualized as an integral part of the self. Based on the conceptualization of the traumatic event as an unforeseen natural disaster ("无妄之灾"), the speaker under the influence of trauma perceived herself as taking on an additional metaphorical identity, i.e., an innocent victim of a sudden disaster.

Examples (12) and (13) show that highly traumatized participants exhibited an increased tendency to focus on the self. Previous trauma narrative research showed that frequencies of self-related expressions are often positively and significantly correlated with post-traumatic symptoms and disorders (e.g., Frewen et al. 2011; Gušić et al. 2018; Kaplow et al. 2018; Kleim et al. 2018; Todorov et al. 2018). As the traumatic event is totally unexpected and often contradictory to trauma victims' established knowledge of the self and the world (Janolff-Bulman 1989), the experience can lead to significant alterations in trauma victims' perceptions and understanding of the self such as altered physical sensations, distorted evaluations of the self, and disturbances in self-identity (Cox, Resnick & Kilpatrick 2014; Foa, Molnar & Cashman 1995; Janoff-Bulman 1989; Lanius, Terpou & McKinnon 2020; Schore 2003). The findings are also consistent with survey data reported by Berntsen et al. (2003): compared with individuals traumatized to a lesser extent, those with higher degrees of trauma tended to perceive tighter and very often negative connections between the self and the traumatic experience and view the trauma as a central part of their self-identity.

According to Moser (2007), knowledge about the inner self and experiences of self-changes can be highly abstract and complex. While numerous studies have highlighted self-related metaphors as an important linguistic and cognitive tool in processing post-traumatic experiences and attendant identity changes (e.g., Beck 2016, 2017; Foley 2015; Littlemore & Turner 2020), the present study further pinpoints the clinical importance of self-related metaphor variables in the evaluation of overall degrees of trauma.

The significant correlation between SELF AND SELF and overall degrees of trauma suggests that metaphorical meaning-making from the observer perspective might be a potential indicator of traumatization. No significant correlations were found for other target categories from the observer perspective, which means the relationship could be particularly strong in self-related metaphors. According to McIssac and Eich (2004), trauma memories accessed from the observer perspective are often experienced as less emotional and anxiety-provoking, which can be a reason why the perspective is more often adopted by people who experienced particularly severe post-traumatic stress as a strategy to mitigate their negative emotions (Berntsen, Willert & Rubin 2003; Kenny et al. 2009; McIsaac & Eich 2002, 2004; Nigro & Neisser 1983; Robinson & Swanson 1993). The relationship between metaphor use from this perspective and psychopathological experiences will be further elaborated in Section 4.4.3 in relation to symptom-related metaphor usage patterns.

4.4.2 Correlations between metaphor use and severities of ASD symptoms

Results of correlation analysis

Trauma victims' use of the selected metaphor variables was significantly correlated with the severities of three ASD symptoms, including re-experiencing, anxiety and hyperarousal, and impairment in functioning. The severity of re-experiencing was positively and significantly correlated with two emotion-related variables, i.e., the negative valence and emotional feelings and processes. These two symptoms also showed positive and significant correlations with SELF AND SELF and SELF AND SOCIAL SITUATION. Anxiety and hyperarousal scores had significant and positive correlations with two self-related variables, i.e., SELF AND SELF and self-references, while showing negative correlations with OTHERS. The severity of impairment in functioning was significantly related to metaphors in the negative valence. In contrast, dissociation and avoidance did not show significant correlations with any metaphor variables (all $ps>.05$). Significant correlations are summarized in Table 4.8 (non-significant results are marked as $n.s$; refer to Appendix 2 for the full correlation matrix).

Table 4.8: Significant correlations between metaphor use and severities of ASD symptoms.

Variables	Posttraumatic variables				
	Dissociation	Re-experiencing	Avoidance	Anxiety and hyperarousal	Impairment in functioning
Negative metaphors	n.s	r = .292, p = .049*	n.s	n.s	r = 0.462, p = .001**
OTHERS	n.s	n.s	n.s	r = −.319 p = .030*	n.s
SELF AND SELF	n.s	r = .385, p = .008**	n.s	r = .319 p = .031*	n.s
SELF AND SOCIAL SITUATION	n.s	r = .308, p = .037*	n.s	n.s	n.s
Emotional feelings and processes	n.s	r = .300, p = .043*	n.s	n.s	n.s
Self-references	n.s	n.s	n.s	r = .325, p = .028*	n.s

(Note: p-values less than .05 are indicated as * and those less than .01 as **)

Considering the strong correlations between the overall SASRQ scores and the symptom scores (refer to Table 4.6), it is unsurprising that significant indicators of high overall degrees of trauma, i.e., negative metaphors, SELF AND SELF, and self-references (refer to Section 4.4.1), also showed correlations with the three ASD symptoms. We can see each of the three symptoms was significantly correlated with at least one of the three self-related variables. Beyond the overlapping results, nuanced, symptom-specific patterns were found. Significant variables associated with each symptom also showed general tendencies that differ noticeably from those identified for overall degrees of trauma. Next, metaphor usage patterns that are specific to the three symptoms will be illustrated in turn.

Discussion

Re-experiencing

Re-experiencing is characterized by the recurrence of intrusive memories, emotions, and thoughts about the traumatic event. As the severity of re-experiencing increases, trauma victims become more inclined to metaphorize their emotional experiences during the traumatic event. Compared with those who were less disturbed by re-experiencing, individuals with more severe symptoms tend to use more negative metaphors. They were also more inclined to metaphorize the perceived incongruence within the self and the interactions between the self and the broader social situation (i.e., SELF AND SELF and SELF AND SOCIAL SITUATION).

The tendencies are illustrated by example (14). The example was generated by an interviewee whose re-experiencing score was 2.19 SD above the mean score of 5.98 (16 out of 30 points). It is a negative metaphor about EMOTIONAL FEELINGS AND PROCESSES, with a special emphasis on the incongruency between different aspects of the self (i.e., SELF AND SELF):

(14) 那个时候我的心情也是处于一种**撕扯**吧。一方面, 我要像老师说的那样理性地看待世界, 然后并且用我自己所学的知识来理解当下社会发生的一切。但是另一方面, 我**站在一个无辜卷入的被害、受害者的角度**, 我还是没有办法去理性地去认识他们(暴徒), 然后还是会很感情用事地觉得他们到底在干什么?

'At that time, my emotions were **tearing me apart**. On the one hand, I wanted to look at the world in a rational way just like what my supervisor said, and use the knowledge I learned to understand all that was happening in this society. But on the other hand, **standing in the position of an innocent victim, who was involuntarily drawn into this event**, I still can't understand them (the radical protesters) in a rational way. I am very emotional and keep asking myself what on earth are they doing?'

Two metaphor vehicle terms were used to describe the speaker's negative emotional feelings during the peak of the social unrest. In the first metaphor vehicle term, the confrontation between two different emotional and thought processes was conceptualized as the speaker being physically torn ("撕扯") into two different parts. One part stands for the speaker's rational thinking, which enables her to get rid of all personal feelings and make sense of the social unrest in a detached and objective way, and the other part represents the emotional aspect of the self, which is totally disconnected from the rational side of the self. The latter aspect is further elaborated by the second metaphor vehicle, which describes the self as an unlucky "victim" who was "involuntarily drawn into this event".

The tendency for individuals with severe re-experiencing symptoms to focus on emotions and express negative feelings is compatible with previous psychological research findings, which underscores negative emotional response as a key component of re-experiencing, alongside trauma-related sensory impressions and other substantive details of the traumatic event (e.g., Brewin, Christodoulides & Hutchinson 1996; Ehlers & Clark 2000; Ehlers, Hackmann & Michael 2004; Halligan et al. 2003; Hellawell & Brewin 2004; Jaeger et al. 2014; Kleim et al. 2013). According to the DMS-V, individuals exposed to trauma-related cues can experience intense or prolonged psychological distress as if the traumatic event is happening again. The positive and significant correlation between re-experiencing scores and emotion-related metaphors is also consistent with Fainsilber and Ortony's (1987) findings that descriptions of intense emotional experiences contain more emotion-related metaphors than accounts of milder emotions. As intense emotions are presumably more vivid and remarkable as compared to milder experiences, individuals may feel a more pressing need to provide detailed descriptions of their emotional states, which, in turn, leads to increased use of metaphorical expressions.

Compared with individuals who had less severe re-experiencing, those more disturbed by the symptom also generated more metaphors about SELF AND SELF and SELF AND SOCIAL SITUATION, which tap directly into the speakers' emotions and thoughts about the social unrest. The first metaphor vehicle term in example (14) ("撕扯") is a typical instance of SELF AND SELF metaphors. In contrast to SELF metaphors, which provide a self-immersed perspective on the speaker's thoughts and feelings, this target category opens a self-inspecting perspective on the speaker's emotions and thought processes. It captures the inconsistency between different emotions, thoughts, and the individual's pre- and post-trauma sense of self, which is a crucial cognitive challenge faced by all trauma victims when processing their experiences (Janoff-Bulman 1989). The increased use of SELF AND SELF metaphors reflects the imminent psychological need for trauma victims to reconcile the conflicts between their emotions and rational thinking and to make sense of the clash between their personal and social identities.

Topics about the current social situation are also frequently observed in trauma victims' conceptualization of their experiences. While SOCIAL SITUATION depicts trauma victims' perception and understanding of the societal status from a first-person perspective, SELF AND SOCIAL SITUATION places greater emphasis on how the speakers' everyday life and future development are connected to, and further influenced by the social unrest. It captures the participants' struggles in finding their roles in the rapidly changing social situation, which was, at the time of the social unrest, the most immediate and greatest psychological challenge faced by mainland Chinese immigrants.

The use of SELF AND SOCIAL SITUATION metaphors by high scorers on the re-experiencing subscale is illustrated by example (15). The speaker's re-experiencing score was 1.31 SD above the sample mean (12 out of 30 points).

(15) 对于未来你可能计划得很好, 然后你有一些你的打算, 但是**在这个时代的洪流面前, 你就直接被碾过去了**, 一点办法都没有。

'Maybe you have prepared very well your future, and you have some of your own plans, but **when faced with this flood torrent of history, you just get crushed over**, there's nothing you can do.'

The interviewee was a fresh graduate who planned to find a job and settle down in Hong Kong. However, the unfriendly atmosphere created by the social unrest, especially the protesters' destruction of the interviewee's laboratory in the university and the interpersonal conflicts arising from differing political views, made her realize that Hong Kong may not be a good place for mainland Chinese to stay. In this expression, the social unrest is interpreted as an event of great historical significance. A vivid metaphor scenario is constructed to express her idiosyncratic understanding of how ordinary people in Hong Kong were involuntarily affected by rapid social changes: the social unrest and its impact on Hong Kong society are interpreted as a gigantic and irresistible "flood torrent", which can lead to permanent and irreversible changes to the surrounding environment, and the impact of the social unrest on the speaker's study and future development is conceptualized as the speaker being physically "crushed over" by the "torrent" and straying away from the original position.

The positive and significant correlation between SELF AND SOCIAL SITUATION and re-experiencing is consistent with the observation that trauma victims under the influence of re-experiencing tend to concentrate on aspects of trauma that had the largest psychological impact on the individual (Christianson 1992; Ehlers et al. 2002). While previous research focused almost exclusively on concrete autobiographical details that are directly pertinent to the traumatic event (e.g., Ehlers et al. 2002; Ehlers, Hackmann & Michael 2004; Hellawell & Brewin 2004; Kleim et al. 2013), the present study shows that abstract thinking elicited by concrete traumatic experiences, reflected by metaphor use, can also be active among individuals with severe re-experiencing symptoms.

Anxiety and hyperarousal

The anxiety and hyperarousal subscale measures increased anxiety, sensitivity, and physiological arousal due to trauma exposure. Typical clinical manifestations include difficulty in sleeping and concentrating, hypervigilance, exaggerated startle response, irritable behaviors, and anger outbursts (American Psychiatric Association 2013). The severities of anxiety and hyperarousal were significantly correlated with increased use of self-related metaphors. Compared with individuals less disturbed by anxiety and hyperarousal, those experiencing more severe symptoms were more inclined to use SELF AND SELF metaphors to describe the conflicts between their thoughts and emotions. Moreover, this trauma population also generated more self-referential metaphors to account for the perceived changes in their self-identities. The use of self-related metaphors has been illustrated using examples (12) and (13) in Section 4.4.1 and example (14) presented earlier.

An interesting pattern that contrasts with the high scorers' inclination toward self-focus is the negative and significant correlation between anxiety and hyperarousal scores and the density of OTHERS metaphors. This suggests that individuals who experienced more severe anxiety and hyperarousal were less inclined to metaphorize other people's behaviors, feelings, and thoughts, in contrast to low scorers on this subscale. A close examination of OTHERS metaphors in the dataset reveals that the topics include people in the trauma victim's close interpersonal circle, such as family, friends, and colleagues, or people involved in the social unrest, such as the protesters, Hong Kong residents in general, and news media. Examples (16) and (17), which address the two topics, illustrate this pattern:

(16) 我身边同事有黄有蓝, 的确他们自己这么说自己, 我就引用一下。但是我心中没有蓝黄之说, 就是**没有颜色之分**。因为**每个人都是七色, 都是彩虹**。
'Some of my colleagues are yellow and some are blue, they did refer to themselves in this way, I'm just citing their words. But in my mind, there is no distinction between blue and yellow, I mean **there's no difference of color at all**. Because **everyone has seven different colors, everyone is a rainbow**.'

(17) 我们日常本来就局限在学校这个小圈子里。学校毕竟是个挺净土的一个地方, 之前愤怒也是因为你怎么**把手伸到**学校这块地方来了。
'Our daily life has always been restricted to the university, the small circle. The university is, after all, a place like a pure land. The university is, after all, like a pure land. The reason why I felt angry is how can you **lay your hands on this place**.

Example (16) was produced by an individual who got only 3 points on the anxiety and hyperarousal subscale; the score was 1.28 standard deviations below the sample mean of 10.37. As mentioned in Section 1.3.1, the two major political camps in Hong Kong are traditionally symbolized by different colors: the pro-establishment camp is often represented by "blue (藍)", and the pro-democracy camp by "yellow (黃)". Due to the social unrest, Hong Kong residents became increasingly attentive to their own and other individuals' political stances. Those who identified with the blue and the yellow camps frequently found themselves in opposition, and sometimes in direct confrontations. In this example, the speaker expresses her disagreement with the blue-versus-yellow division ("藍黃之說") by extending the POLITICAL STANCE IS COLOR metaphor. Instead of categorizing people using binary labels of blue and yellow, the speaker describes the complexity of human nature as a person having "seven different colors (七色)" and being a "rainbow (彩虹)" that cannot be described by a single color. Example (17) was produced by a participant who did not report evident anxiety and hyperarousal, as measured by the SASRQ. A metaphor describing radical protesters' acts was used right after a PERSONAL SITUATION metaphor, i.e., the university as a "pure land (淨土)" to express the speaker's disapproval of the protesters' vandalism of her university campus. The university, which was expected to stay clear from political activities, is compared to a sacred "pure land". The protesters' forceful imposition of their political views on the university staff and students is conceptualized as a physical act of "laying their hands" on a precious and revered object.

The others-focused tendency identified in low scorers was rarely found in individuals who experienced severe anxiety and hyperarousal. This can be a natural consequence of the self-focused tendency that accompanies anxiety and hyperarousal (Boehme, Miltner & Straube 2015; Todorov et al. 2018). While the symptom prompts the individual to allocate more cognitive resources to the processing of self-related thoughts and feelings, there would be correspondingly less attention available for matters considered "external" or less relevant to the self.

Impairment in functioning

Impairment in functioning measures the extent to which the individual's physical, cognitive, and social functioning is affected by the traumatic event. Individuals with higher scores on the impairment in functioning subscale showed a significantly stronger tendency to use metaphors with the negative valence. As the use of negative metaphors by severely traumatized people has been illustrated and thoroughly discussed in Section 4.4.1 (see example 11), no more examples will be provided here.

According to Jellestad et al. (2021), post-traumatic functional impairment manifests as perceived difficulties in accomplishing a wide range of real-world tasks, including but not limited to everyday self-care, managing domestic life, handling interpersonal interactions, and coping with general life tasks and demands. According to Ni et al. (2020), trauma victims of the social unrest perceived difficulties in maintaining their previous life routines, concentrating on work and studies, and preserving previous interpersonal interactions with friends and family. Individuals more severely affected by this symptom would experience heightened frustration and a greater sense of losing control when dealing with such functioning difficulties. This emotional response would then drive them to generate more negative metaphors in expressing their thoughts and feelings after trauma.

4.4.3 Summary of individual-level metaphor usage patterns

The individual-level correlation analyses established severities of traumatization as a previously neglected but important factor in shaping metaphor use and metaphor variations. The findings showed that trauma victims with differentiated experiences of ASD symptoms exhibited distinct preferences for different metaphor variables. As the severity of trauma and symptoms changed, the attention or preferences for the metaphor variables varied accordingly. While metaphorical thinking about abstract aspects of the traumatic event is not inherent to intrusive memories, the patterns still offer valuable insights into the speaker's immediate psychopathological experience.

An interesting observation is that there are both overlaps and contrasts between patterns associated with overall degrees of trauma and those identified for specific symptoms. Section 4.4.1 showed that as the overall degree of trauma went higher, the frequency of negative metaphors, SELF AND SELF metaphors, and self-referential metaphors increased correspondingly. These patterns reflect a general negative bias and self-focused tendency in severely traumatized people's metaphor use. Although these three variables were also correlated with the severities of more specific symptoms, the symptom-oriented analysis highlighted other groups of metaphor variables that are only significantly correlated with re-experiencing, anxiety and hyperarousal, and impairment in functioning (i.e., SELF AND SOCIAL SITUATION, EMOTIONAL FEELINGS AND PROCESSES, and OTHERS).

Clinical symptoms of a mental health disorder are usually strongly correlated with each other, but the symptoms are also sufficiently distinct from each other as they represent different dimensions of the disorder. This is clearly reflected by the patterns discussed in the two subsections. The overlaps and contrasts in the correlation results highlighted metaphor usage patterns as valid indicators of psychopathological experiences as well as their potential to capture nuanced physiological, emotional, and cognitive experiences.

Trauma victims with higher degrees of trauma, especially those with more severe re-experiencing and anxiety and hyperarousal, used more self-related target categories than the less traumatized. When the findings were examined in relation to the two psychological perspectives, more intriguing patterns emerge. Recall that SELF AND SELF and SELF AND SOCIAL SITUATION metaphors, both from the observer perspective, were significantly correlated with severities of re-experiencing, whereas their counterparts from the field perspective (i.e., SELF and SOCIAL SITUATION) were not. A similar pattern was found between SELF AND SELF metaphors and anxiety and hyperarousal scores. This suggests that individuals who were more affected by these symptoms exhibited a stronger preference for using metaphors from the observer perspective.

McIssac and Eich's (2004) study on perspective-taking in traumatic memories suggested that narrations in the field perspective contained richer details of the individual's affective reactions, somatic sensations, and psychological states during the traumatic event, whereas narrations in the observer perspective provided more factual details about the traumatic situation and less emotional content. Meanwhile, numerous studies on perspective-taking in trauma narratives showed that patients with PTSD tend to adopt an observer perspective when recalling trauma-related memories (McIssac & Eich 2005; Berntsen, Willert & Rubin 2003). At first glance, the two sets of findings might seem contradictory, as PTSD patients, who are typically overwhelmed by negative emotions, appear to prefer the less emotion-laden perspective. Clinical psychologists propose that the contradiction can be explained by trauma victims' tendency to maintain a psychological distance from extremely distressing memories (Ayduk & Kross 2010). While re-experiencing the traumatic event can be intrusive and overwhelming, adopting an external, self-observing perspective enables the individual to reprocess the traumatic experience from a safe psychological distance, preventing them from being overwhelmed again. This interpretation is supported by Robinson and Swanson's (1983) experimental studies on perspective changes. According to their findings, as the field perspective shifts to the observer perspective, the intensity of emotion experienced tends to decrease as the perspective shifts from the field to the observer perspective. In other words, the preference for the observer perspective over the field perspective in metaphor use might reflect the speakers' efforts to adopt a detached standing point when re-processing difficult traumatic memories.

We can see that the number of significant correlations differed across the five ASD symptoms. Re-experiencing and anxiety and hyperarousal showed the most robust correlations with metaphorical language, each significantly correlated with three metaphor variables; impairment in functioning scores was significantly correlated with one metaphor variable; dissociation and avoidance were not significantly related to any metaphor variables. The difference is likely related to the nature of the symptoms. Re-experiencing, anxiety and hyperarousal, and impairment in functioning entail heightened subjective experiences, including emotional feelings, thoughts, bodily sensations, responses to trauma-related cues, and reflections on details about the traumatic event and its impact on the self. As the symptom severity goes up, these subjective experiences become more intense and vivid, which would then compel trauma victims to provide more elaborate accounts of their feelings. In contrast, dissociation and avoidance are characterized by reduced awareness of the traumatic experience and trauma-related emotions and thoughts. Compared with re-experiencing, anxiety and hyperarousal, and impairment in functioning, the two symptoms are much less experientially prominent. Given that milder emotional experiences are less likely to trigger increased use of metaphors than intense feelings (Fainsilber & Ortony 1987), it is understandable that experiences of the latter two symptoms were less strongly correlated with quantitative metaphor usage patterns.

Another intriguing finding is that statistically significant correlations were mainly related to emotional valence, target categories, and discourse topics, rather than conventionality and vehicle terms. This does not necessarily mean that psychopathological experiences of symptoms are not relevant to trauma victims' metaphor use. As we have seen in Chapter 3, conventional and novel metaphors about different topics and perspectives were associated with different emotional valence. It is therefore possible that the relationship between conventionality and psychopathological experiences varies across other metaphor variables. Future research could explore this by breaking down conventional and novel metaphors into different emotional valence, topics, and perspectives, or by comparing the role of trauma-related variables that differ across different metaphor types.

Another explanation is that vehicle groupings in this project were identified in a top-down manner, based on the findings of previous trauma and metaphor research. While the coding method is helpful for exploring the relevance of clinically interesting metaphor variables to trauma evaluation, it may not fully capture the nuances of metaphor use in the current research context. It is also worth mentioning that previous trauma literature, from which the bodily experiences were selected, were all conducted in non-Asian contexts. While the speakers' socio-cultural backgrounds are widely acknowledged as a crucial factor influencing the choices of vehicle terms in emotion expression (Kövecses 2000, 2005, 2008; Meili, Heim & Maercker 2019; Rechsteiner, Tol & Maercker 2019; Rechsteiner et al. 2020; Wilson & Lindy 2013; Yu 1995, 2008), it is possible that trauma-related bodily experiences identified from non-Asian contexts differ from those that are prevalent in Asian linguistic communities. To explore the relationships between contextually motivated metaphor usage patterns and psychopathological experiences, follow-up studies can consider adopting systematic, bottom-up coding methods like the source domain verification procedure designed by Ahrens and Jiang (2020) and the two-tier coding proposed by Kimmel (2010).

4.5 Chapter conclusion

Metaphorical language serves as a vivid and compact means for trauma victims to transform their emotions and thought processes into more concrete and expressible forms, allowing them to share their unique perspectives and reflections on their traumatic experiences. Many mental health practitioners recognize the importance of attending to and exploring metaphors during psychotherapy (e.g., Kopp 1995; Siegelman 1990; Cox & Theilgaard 1987; Wilson & Lindy 2013). However, as diagnosis is often prior to and separated from therapeutic treatment, metaphors are usually not taken into account at the diagnostic stage.

This study illustrated the value of combining linguistic observations and psychometric data in exploring mental health metaphors. Compared with qualitative analysis based on introspective reports on psychological states, incorporating quantitative psychometric data into metaphor analysis enabled us to develop more precise and reliable accounts of clinically relevant metaphor usage patterns at the individual level. The findings showed that severities of traumatization are important sources of metaphor variations. Trauma victims' overall degrees of trauma were positively and significantly correlated with their use of negative metaphors and self-related metaphors. Different severities of specific clinical symptoms could be discerned from the speakers' metaphor use. Compared with the less traumatized, individuals who were more affected by re-experiencing generated more negative metaphors. They also used more metaphors in describing their emotions, inner conflicts, and their relationship with the social situation. Individuals who experienced more severe anxiety and hyperarousal showed a heightened self-related tendency and reduced attention to others. Those who experienced more severe impairment in functioning produced more metaphors in the negative valence.

The findings are consistent with the general theoretical view that metaphor use is intimately connected with the speaker's physical, emotional, and cognitive experiences (Kövecses 2000, 2010, 2015, 2020; Lakoff & Johnson 1980, 1999; Semino 2010; Semino et al. 2017; Tay 2013), and that speakers who have similar subjective experiences might have similar metaphor usage patterns (Charteris-Black 2012; Cameron & Maslen 2010). While previous studies mainly focused on the associations between metaphor use and broadly defined emotions, thoughts, and physical sensations, this study showed that systematic metaphor usage patterns can also reflect cross-individual differences in the speakers' psychopathological experiences. By breaking acute stress reactions down to specific clinical symptoms, this study illustrated how different emotional, cognitive, and physiological disturbances may prompt contrasting ways of metaphorical meaning-making.

The findings have obvious implications for understanding, assessing, and treating trauma. As mentioned in Section 2.4.2, clients' metaphors in conceptualizing the experiences are often regarded as irrelevant to clinical diagnosis and evaluations. This study, nevertheless, highlighted systematic metaphor usage patterns as expressive indicators of psychopathological experiences. Although findings generated from metaphor analyses alone may not be directly used to serve clinical purposes, they can still provide useful supporting information for diagnostic practices.

This study underlines the potential for metaphor analysis to provide informative guidance for understanding and managing mental health communication. The findings reveal the need for clinical practitioners to pay closer attention to trauma victims' metaphor use, especially general tendencies reflected by quantitative patterns. While this study is limited to a single traumatic context, it reveals the possibility for quantitative metaphor usage patterns to capture nuanced and clinically interesting subjective experiences. Patterns that are commonly identified across different contexts may also be incorporated as a convenient and informative reference in in-take interviews and subsequent therapy, or serve as references for developing new interview protocols and diagnostic tools.

Some limitations need to be noted. Firstly, as indicated in the preceding section, the use of top-down rather than bottom-up coding might leave some context-sensitive patterns undetected. It is also important to reiterate that correlational analyses only examine the degree to which two variables tend to vary together but do not reveal causal relationships; therefore, the interpretations provided in this chapter are only speculative. To obtain a more accurate understanding of the reported correlations, psycholinguistic and neurolinguistic experiments that focus specifically on metaphor use are needed. Lastly, data about trauma victims' baseline level metaphor use before the social unrest was not available. Owing to the unexpected nature of the social unrest, this study only focused on participants' spontaneous metaphor use right after the traumatic event. The longitudinal evolution of metaphors across different stages of trauma remains to be explored by future studies.

5 An image schematic analysis of metaphors in describing ASD symptoms

5.1 Chapter introduction

By contextualizing metaphor use into the clinical scenario of trauma evaluation, Chapter 4 examined the correlations between trauma victims' metaphor usage patterns and severities of psychopathological disturbances. While the significant results reflect different trauma populations' overall tendencies in metaphor use, they do not reflect how trauma victims in different clinical conditions perceive and conceptualize their psychopathological experiences. This chapter zooms in on a more specialized clinical context and probes into trauma victims' metaphorical conceptualizations of clinically present symptoms.[33] The focus is shifted from individual-level metaphor usage patterns to disorder/symptom-level metaphor use.

To extract patterns that are representative of the five ASD symptoms, psychometric data and therapeutic observations by mental health professionals were incorporated into qualitative metaphor analysis. As noted in Section 2.4, the clinical presence of a symptom is determined by the number of manifested clinical indicators, which means individuals above and below the diagnostic threshold may experience different ranges of psychopathological experiences. To ensure the comparability of the psychopathological experiences, in this chapter, the scope of participants was narrowed down to those above the diagnostic threshold of ASD. More details about participants in the reduced dataset are provided in Section 5.2.

Data coding in this chapter incorporated therapeutic insights about symptom relevance and discourse analytic findings about the semantic features of symptom-related expressions. Metaphors not directly related to the five ASD symptoms were filtered out, and then the remaining ones were categorized according to the symptoms they described. As I have shown in Section 2.2, embodied experiences are widely recognized as key components of trauma victims' metaphor use (e.g., Beck 2016; Gušić et al. 2018; Littlemore & Turner 2020; Tay 2014; Wilson & Lindy 2013). To extract potentially generalizable patterns of embodied experiences, symptom-specific metaphors were coded using Johnson's (1987) list of image schemas. The coding procedures are introduced in Section 5.3. Dominant image schematic patterns identified

---

33 Part of this chapter has been published as Qiu, Han, Bernadette Watson & Dennis Tay. 2022. Metaphors and Trauma: An Image Schematic Analysis of Symptom-specific Metaphors. *Lingua* 103244. The content has been substantially revised.

https://doi.org/10.1515/9783111346502-005

for each ASD symptom are illustrated and analyzed in Section 5.4. Implications, limitations, and future directions are discussed in Section 5.5.

5.2 Participants

This chapter examines metaphor use by trauma victims above the diagnostic threshold of ASD. As mentioned earlier, clinical diagnosis of ASD using the SASRQ relies more on the dichotomous coding of symptom presence. To identify participants who meet the diagnostic criteria of ASD, all participants' ratings on the 30 SASRQ items were converted from continuous scores to dichotomous outcomes (Cardeña et al. 2000): ratings between 0 and 2 were re-coded as 0 (non-presence), and those between 3 and 5 were recoded as 1 (presence). To receive a diagnosis of ASD, the individual must meet the diagnostic criteria for all five symptoms, including three for dissociation and at least one symptom for each of the remaining symptoms.

The 46 participants were sorted based on the number of clinically present symptoms (see Table 5.1). Among all, seven did not meet the diagnostic criteria for any symptoms. Thirty-four participants endorsed one to four symptoms: ten reported only one symptom, nine reported two, ten reported three, and five experienced four symptoms. These people were below the diagnostic threshold of ASD. A total of five participants were above the threshold, each reporting the clinical presence of all five symptoms. The ASD incidence rate in the current dataset was 10.87%, within the 7 to 28% range reported by Bryant et al. (2011). ASD and non-ASD participants' profiles, including their demographic information, overall SASRQ scores, and linguistic data are summarized in Table 5.2.

Table 5.1: Number of participants with one to five clinically present symptoms.

Number of clinically present symptoms	Number of participants
5	5
4	5
3	10
2	9
1	10
0	7
Total	46

Table 5.2: Descriptive statistics of the ASD and non-ASD datasets.

	ASD participants	Non-ASD participants
Number	5	41
Gender	4 females and 1 male	29 females and 5 males
Age	M=26.40, SD=2.51	M=26.63, SD=4.73
Overall SASRQ scores	M=82.80, SD=17.12	M=33.76, SD=18.36
Total lengths of interviews (Chinese Characters)	26,307	151,674
Average lengths of interviews (Chinese Characters)	M=5,261.40, SD=1,742.89	M=3,699.37, SD=1,695.92
Total number of metaphors	322	1,312
Average number of metaphors per interview	M=64.40, SD=30.03	M=32.00, SD=23.04
Average number of metaphors per thousand characters	M=12.02, SD=3.54	M=8.54, SD=3.45

The ASD group included four females and one male. Their average age was 26.40 years (SD=2.51), which was close to the non-ASD average of 26.63 years (SD=4.73). Their average SASRQ score was 82.80 out of 150 (SD=17.12), which was markedly higher than the non-ASD average of 33.76 (SD=18.36). The five ASD interviews comprised 26,307 Chinese characters. The average length of ASD interviews was 5,261.40 Chinese characters (SD=1,742.89), which was greater than the non-ASD average of 3,699.37 (SD=1,694.92). The five ASD interviews included a total of 332 metaphor vehicle terms, which took 19.7% of all metaphors in the dataset. The average number of metaphors per interview was 64.40 (SD=30.05), which was remarkably higher than the non-ASD average of 32.00 (SD=23.04). The density of metaphors per thousand Chinese characters was 12.02 (SD=3.54), also noticeably higher than the non-ASD average of 8.54 (SD=3.45).

Histograms of ASD and non-ASD participants' overall SASRQ scores, lengths of interviews, the average number of metaphors in interview, and density of metaphors per thousand characters are shown in Figure 5.1.

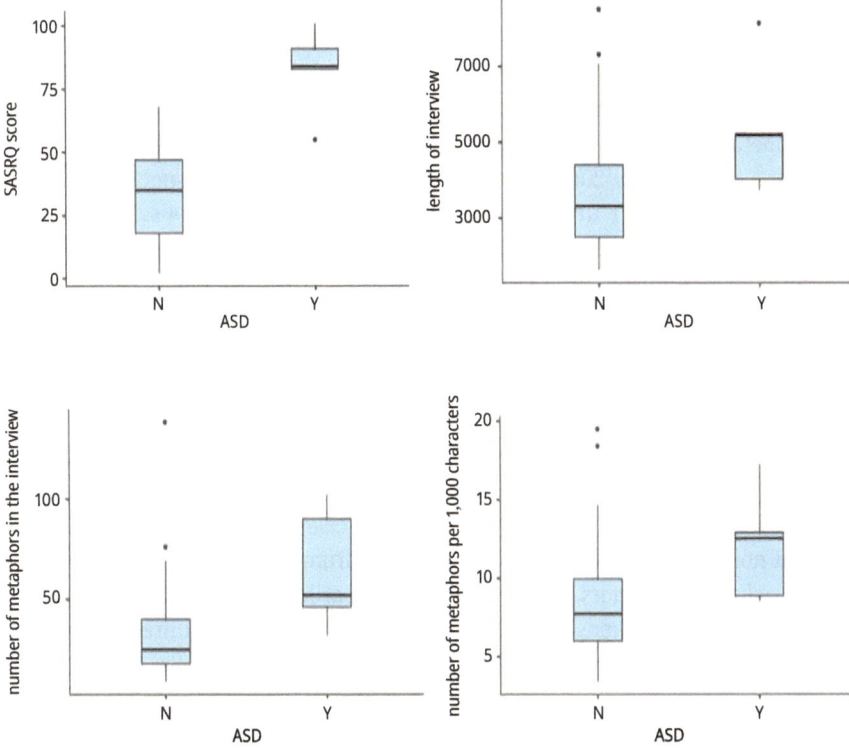

Figure 5.1: Psychometric and linguistic data generated by ASD and non-ASD participants.

5.3 Research questions and methods

The research questions are as follows:

(1a) How are image schematic metaphors used by trauma victims in describing their ASD symptoms, namely dissociation, re-experiencing, avoidance, anxiety and hyperarousal, and impairment in functioning?

(1b) How do the image schematic patterns differ across the five symptoms?

The coding was based on cross-disciplinary work that integrated clinical psychological insights with linguistic observations. Metaphors directly pertinent to the five major ASD symptoms were identified and further categorized in terms of image schemas. Data coding was jointly accomplished by two coders, including the author of this book, who received training in both cognitive linguistics and psychotherapy, and a psychologist and counseling supervisor who specializes in trauma therapy (refer to Section 1.3.2 for more information).

Pre-coding discussion was conducted to ensure that the coding was informed by both the clinical features of ASD symptoms and semantic meanings conveyed by the metaphors. As therapists and linguists may have different perspectives on metaphor (see Borbely 2008 for an exemplary therapeutic perspective), the two coders calibrated their understanding of metaphors and image schemas, using definitions, linguistic examples, and interpretations presented in previous linguistic works (e.g., Johnson 1987; Cameron & Maslen 2010). They also reviewed the clinical definitions and diagnostic criteria for all five ASD symptoms proposed by DSM-IV (American Psychiatric Association 1994).

The identification of symptom-specific metaphors was accomplished in three steps:

Step 1 All metaphor vehicle terms were examined for their relevance to trauma. Those that were not directly relevant to traumatic emotions, thoughts, and physiological experiences, such as descriptions of society, interpersonal relationships, and non-traumatic emotions, were excluded from the list. Below is an example of excluded metaphors, which was discussed earlier in Chapter 3. This metaphor describes the speaker's psychological state during the social unrest without addressing any specific aspect of her psychopathological experiences.

(1)　在我二十多年的人生里面, 应该是没有试过在短短的时间内情绪或者是心理状态会经历**那么大的起伏**。
'More than 20 years have passed in my life, I have never experienced **such great rises and falls** in emotions or psychological states within a short period of time'

Step 2 The remaining metaphor vehicle terms were examined for their relevance to the five ASD symptoms measured by the SASRQ. While some expressions were directly relevant to the speakers' traumatic experiences, the topics they described were not relevant to the five ASD symptoms. These expressions were excluded from the analysis. This step narrowed the scope of analysis down to 64 metaphor vehicle terms that were directly relevant to the five symptoms.

Step 3 The 64 symptom-related metaphors were examined for their underlying image schematic structures based on Johnson's (1987) inventory, which includes 27 image schemas (refer to Table 2.2 presented earlier). The inventory was chosen out of other existing inventories because it strikes a better balance between having a manageable number of categories and the ability to account for the current data (e.g., Lakoff 1987; Lakoff & Turner 1989; Clausner & Croft 1999; Hampe 2005).

Different from Chapters 3 and 4, inter-rater reliability of coding in this study was approached as "an ongoing process of refining skills, rather than a final process that can be adequately captured through a numerical measure" (Cameron et al. 2009: 73). To maximize the advantage of juxtaposing linguistic and therapeutic perspectives while avoiding potential "motivated looking" (Sarangi & Candlin 2001) from different disciplines, for each of the three steps, the coders first worked independently and then met to discuss problematic cases and inconsistencies in coding.

According to Kimmel (2005: 287), a metaphor may instantiate a "compound" of several simpler image schemas or be identified with different image schematic groundings. When this happens, the image schema that best captured the speaker's local expressive needs was selected, since the study of symptom-specific metaphors focuses not only on the linguistic features of the expressions but also on therapeutically relevant factors such as the speaker's immediate emotions, thoughts, personal experiences, and communicative intentions.

Upon completing the coding, correspondent analysis was conducted to identify the image schematic patterns associated with the five ASD symptoms. Observations derived from the psychotherapeutic perspective (Step 1 and Step 2) were juxtaposed with findings of linguistic discourse analysis (Step 3). The analysis reveals whether and how metaphors about the five ASD symptoms form recognizable patterns at the image schematic level, and how the patterns related to the symptoms' psychopathological features.

The findings yielded by the correspondent analysis will be presented in the next section. Major image schematic patterns identified for each ASD symptom will be illustrated using authentic linguistic examples and figures. The image schematic patterns will then be discussed from a qualitative discourse analytic perspective.

5.4 Results and discussion

5.4.1 Results of correspondent analysis

Twelve image schemas emerged from the 64 symptom-specific metaphors. The frequencies of metaphors and image schemas identified for the five symptoms are summarized in Table 5.3.

We can see that symptoms described by greater numbers of metaphors had more diversified image schematic groundings. Anxiety and hyperarousal were described by twenty-two metaphors that fell into four different image schemas, reexperiencing was represented by eighteen metaphors that instantiated six image schemas, and dissociation was described by seventeen metaphors from three image schemas. Avoidance and impairment in functioning had fewer metaphors:

Table 5.3: Total number of image schemas identified for the five ASD symptom.

Symptom	Image schemas (N)	Total number of metaphors	Total number of image schemas
Dissociation	DISABLEMENT (9) SPLITTING (5) SUPERIMPOSITION (3)	17	3
Re-experiencing	CONTAINER (8) COMPULSION (4) LINK (2) ATTRACTION (2) DISABLEMENT (1) SUPERIMPOSITION (1)	18	6
Avoidance	LACK OF CONTACT (4) MASS-COUNT (1)	5	2
Anxiety and hyperarousal	COMPULSION (15) CYCLE (5) SCALE (1) OBJECT (1)	22	4
Impairment in functioning	MASS-COUNT (2)	2	1
Total N of symptom-related metaphors		64	12

there were four metaphors for avoidance from two image schemas, and two for impairment in functioning, which instantiated the same image schema. The total numbers of metaphors identified for each symptom and symptom-specific metaphors produced by each participant are summarized in Table 5.4 and Figure 5.2.

Table 5.4: Total numbers of symptom-specific metaphors by participant.

	Dissociation	Re-experiencing	Avoidance	Anxiety and hyperarousal	Impairment in functioning	Total
1	2	9	2	13	0	26
2	5	5	0	2	0	12
3	1	0	3	2	0	6
4	6	0	0	5	2	13
5	3	4	0	0	0	7
Total	17	18	5	22	2	64

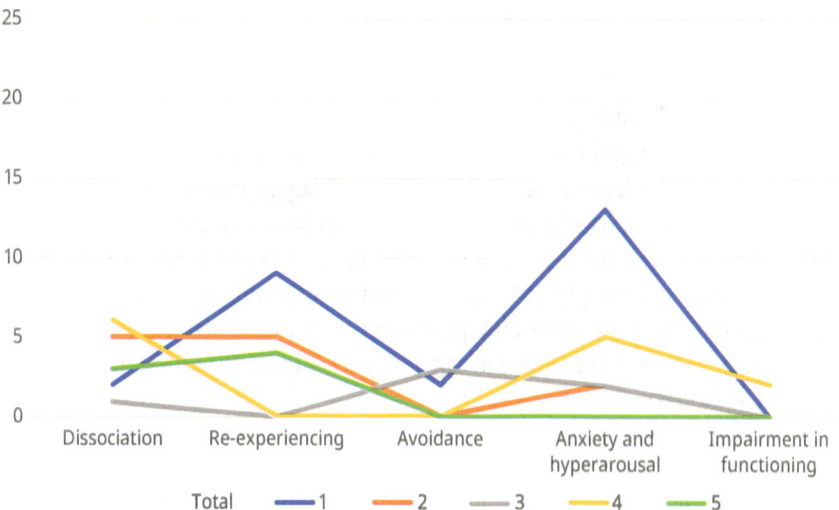

Figure 5.2: Distribution of symptom-specific metaphors across the five ASD participants.

Although all five participants involved in this study met the diagnostic criteria for all five symptoms, not all symptoms were addressed with metaphors. In other words, the clinical presence of symptoms was not always identifiable through metaphorical language. Each participant provided metaphorical accounts of two to four symptoms, with significant individual variation in symptom types and metaphor frequencies. For example, participant 1's metaphors covered all symptoms except for impairment in functioning, and most of the expressions were devoted to anxiety and hyperarousal (thirteen metaphors) and re-experiencing (nine metaphors). In contrast, participant 5 produced three metaphors about dissociation and four metaphors about re-experiencing but left the other three symptoms unaddressed. All five participants produced metaphors about dissociation, while only one (i.e., participant 4) used metaphors to describe impairment in functioning. The number of participants who provided metaphors about avoidance, re-experiencing, and anxiety and hyperarousal varied, ranging from two to four. As the interviewees were not guided to focus on any specific aspect of their psychopathological experiences, the patterns may reflect the natural distribution of symptom-specific metaphors in trauma narratives.

5.4.2 Symptom-level image schematic patterns

Dissociation

According to the DSM-V (American Psychiatric Association 2013: 291), dissociation is defined as a "disruption of and/or discontinuity in the normal integration of consciousness, memory, identity, emotion, perception, body representation, motor control, and behavior". Individuals suffering from dissociation often experience a disconnection between the mind and the body, detachment from the self and emotions, or a feeling that people and the surrounding environment become unreal. In the present dataset, seventeen metaphors were found for dissociation, and the image schemas formed three major categories, including DISABLEMENT, SPLITTING, and SUPERIMPOSITION.

As noted by Johnson (1987: 47), ENABLEMENT is characterized by "a felt sense of power to perform some action", while DISABLEMENT highlights the "lack of power" in manipulating or moving an object. In the five ASD participants' description of dissociation, this image schema is mainly used to describe the perceived deviation from, or loss of, the common sense of self. It was instantiated by nine metaphor vehicle terms, with "无力 (strengthless)" being the most frequent. The DISABLEMENT schema is illustrated by Figure 5.3 and example (18) below:

Figure 5.3: A diagram of the DISABLEMENT schema.

(18) 之前的压力是单纯的来自于学习上的压力, 但是我觉得那个东西是可以去努力的, 就是你**靠自己的行动去慢慢地缓解**的那种压力。但是现在这种情况就非常地**无力**, 就是我们控制不了的。

'The pressure I had before came from my schoolwork, but I think that is something that you can work on. It's the kind of pressure you can **resolve slowly through your own actions**. but the situation we are facing now makes me feel very **strengthless**, because we can't control it.'

The two metaphor vehicle terms in this example, structured by ENABLEMENT and DISABLEMENT, respectively, highlight the contrast between the adaptive and non-adaptive ways of coping with pressure. The first metaphor vehicle, which is about the speaker's life before the social unrest, depicts the healthy response to schoolwork pressure as a force-exerting process of "行动 (physical action)". This contrasts sharply with the traumatic condition described by the second metaphor: the lack of control over negative emotions is interpreted as the loss of physical strength and the inability to make any substantive changes. A similar expression is the "无力" (strengthless) metaphor presented earlier in Section 5.3.

SPLITTING and SUPERIMPOSITION, instantiated by five and three metaphor vehicles, respectively, are structurally alike as both involve the relocation of two entities. This is consistent with the sense of disconnection and discontinuity emphasized by the APA definition of dissociation. More nuanced differences between the two image schemas lie in the relationship between the two entities. The SPLITTING schema depicts the process of separating one single object into two different parts (see Figure 5.4). The schema is illustrated by example (12), which was discussed earlier in Chapter 4 as an instance of SELF AND SELF metaphors (reproduced below):

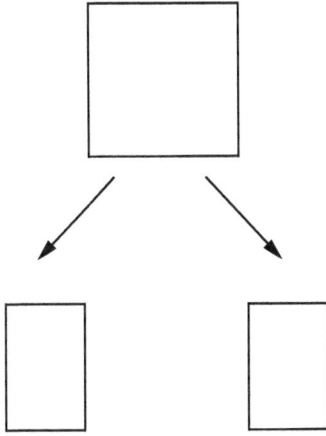

Figure 5.4: A diagram of the SPLITTING schema.

(12) **我仿佛身体里面有两个小人，然后一个小人喊着说**: "你要冷静地看一看这边啊, 你看一看这些民主社会"之类的,**另外一边就在说**: "你就是在这读一年书而已, 可是这一年已经被损失了这么多"。
      'It feels like there are two little persons in my body, and one is shouting: "You should be calm and see what happened here, you should see the democratic society" and the like. **The one on the other side says**: "You are just doing a master here for one year, but just in one year you have lost so much".'

This metaphor illustrates the confrontation between rational thinking and emotional feelings. According to Coons (1988), identity class and the loss of the normal sense of the self are typical manifestations of post-traumatic dissociation. The self, usually perceived as an integral whole under non-traumatic conditions, is depicted as "two little persons (两个小人)" who hold diametrically opposing views of the speaker's traumatic experiences. One person represents the speaker's rational thinking, which is accessed from an emotionally detached perspective, and the other stands for the speaker as an emotional and social being, expressing concerns over her study and life in Hong Kong.

The SPLITTING schema highlights the contrast and even confrontations between two entities while recognizing the entities as sub-components of a larger system. In example (18), both views held by the two little persons represent the speaker's genuine, although conflicting, thoughts about her own experiences. In contrast, SUPERIMPOSITION accounts for two entities that are perceived as separate and distinct from one another. The image schema is illustrated by Figure 5.5 and example (19).

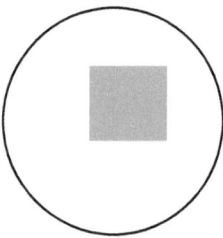

Figure 5.5: A diagram for the SUPERIMPOSITION schema.

(19)　我就算试图去理解他们, 也没有办法接受**发生在我身上**的这种 . . . . . . 就是
　　　我**成了**一个他们社会冲突的**无辜(受害)者**。这一点让我没有办法释怀。
　　　'Even if I try to understand them, I still can't accept what **happened onto my body** . . . it's like I **became an innocent victim** of their social conflicts. I can't get rid of this.'

In this example, two metaphor vehicle terms are used to interpret the speaker's perception of her new identity created by the social unrest. The first conceptualizes the abrupt and unexpected change in the speaker's self-identity as a tangible entity that happened "right onto" her body. The second metaphor further interprets the perceived change as the speaker taking up a new, metaphorical identity, i.e., "an innocent victim" (无辜者) of the social conflict. The two metaphors reflect the speaker's confusion over the sudden alteration in the sense of self as well as her inability to assimilate the traumatic experience into "existing meaning schemes" (Van Der Kolk & Ducey 1989: 270).

Re-experiencing

Re-experiencing is characterized by the re-occurrence of trauma-related memories and feelings. This symptom was described by eighteen metaphor vehicle terms with a diversified range of image schemas. Major categories include CONTAINER, LINK, and FORCE-related schemas like COMPULSION and ATTRACTION. In addition, two metaphor vehicle terms described re-experiencing as perceived DISABLEMENT of the human body and SUPERIMPOSITION of the political protests onto the speaker's personal life.

Eight metaphor vehicle terms were structured by the CONTAINER schema. A close reading of the data shows that both the self and trauma-related emotions can be conceptualized as the CONTAINER, or CONTENTS that are contained or blocked inside the CONTAINER. This is quite similar to the containment model of depression proposed by Charteris-Black (2012), in which the self can be either experienced as being CONTAINED within the state of depression, or perceived as a CONTAINER that holds negative feelings. A diagram of the CONTAINER schema is shown in Figure 5.6.

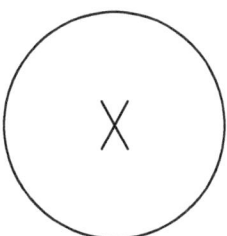

Figure 5.6: A diagram for the CONTAINER schema.

The conceptualizations of the self and traumatic feelings as the CONTAINER are illustrated by examples (20) and (11), respectively:

(20) 你可能看到很多人的那些不好的行为觉得特别不爽, 但是你又没有办法去讲, **心里就一直憋着气**。
'You might feel very uncomfortable when you see many people were doing those bad things, but you can't speak it out, so there is always **some air choked in your heart**.'

(11) 我自己甚至都可能会意识到我是不是就**像(进入)一个黑洞一样,被负面情绪吸进去了**。
'Even I myself realized, if I was, **just like (entered) a black hole**, if I was **absorbed by negative emotions**.'

Example (20) focuses specifically on the persistence of re-experiencing. Anger is described using a conventional metaphor of "气(air)", and the endurance of anger is conceptualized as gas being suppressed in the CONTAINER of the heart. This pattern contrasts with Example (11), which was discussed earlier in Chapter 4 as an instance of a negative metaphor. Different from example (20), example (11) highlights the overwhelmingness of the re-experiencing symptom. The negative emotions are conceptualized as the CONTAINER, and the self is interpreted as something being blocked in the CONTAINER: trauma-induced negative feelings are conceptualized as a black hole ("黑洞") that can absorb everything in the vicinity, and the self being overwhelmed by traumatic feelings is described as the self being involuntarily "absorbed" into the black hole.

The persistence of the re-experiencing symptom is represented by the LINK schema, which structures trauma as something that is enduringly linked to the self. The schema was instantiated by two metaphors. Figure 5.7 and example (21) are illustrative.

Figure 5.7: A diagram of the LINK schema.

(21) 你**没有办法完全去割掉这个东西**, 好像一旦出现了, 你就永远会记住。
'You **can never cut this thing off from you**, just like once it happened, you will remember it forever.'

This metaphor describes how the speaker felt when she saw radical protesters setting fire to public transportation and insulting people who held different political views. The recurrence of these memories is described as a tangible entity so tightly connected to the self that it has become an intrinsic, permanent part of the self. The difficulty of getting rid of the traumatic experience is described as the speaker's inability to "cut it off (割掉)".

FORCE-related schemas such as ATTRACTION and COMPULSION also contributed to ASD participants' conceptualization of re-experiencing. Unlike CONTAINER and LINK, FORCE-related schemas place a greater emphasis on the involuntary and uncontrollable nature of re-experiencing, which was noted by Brewin (2015) as a distinguishing feature of the symptom. The traumatic experiences are interpreted as an irresistible external force that causes the speaker to move in a certain direction or act in a specific way.

The two schemas were instantiated by two and four vehicle terms, respectively. The ATTRACTION schema is represented by Figure 5.8. The "吸进去 (attraction)"

Figure 5.8: A diagram of the ATTRACTION schema.

metaphor in example (11), which occurred right after the "black hole" metaphor, is a typical example of this schema. The self being troubled by negative emotions is interpreted as the self being physically "attracted" by an irresistible force.

Some participants described the enduring nature of the re-experiencing symptom with the COMPULSION schema, which involves a force vector, an entity affected by the force, and a potential trajectory along which the entity will move (Johnson 1987). The image schema is represented by Figure 5.9.

Figure 5.9: A diagram of the COMPULSION schema.

In the current dataset, trauma-related stimuli are often described as a constant external force acting upon the self. Example (22) is illustrative:

(22)　在你**被各种信息流不断冲刷**的这个过程中, 你肯定还是情绪会越来越激烈的。
'During the process of being **washed out by the information flows, again and again**, your emotions would definitely be more and more intense.'

In example (22), the speaker describes how media exposure to the social unrest leads to re-experiencing. Media reports, information disseminated via social media, and opinions expressed by the speaker's colleagues and friends are interpreted as rapid water flows ("信息流"). The recurrence of negative and intense emotions, which comes along with exposure to trauma-related cues, is conceptualized as the speaker being washed out ("冲刷") by these flows of information. It should be noted that the metaphor "washed out" has different interpretations in the Chinese and the English language. The basic meaning of "冲刷", according to the CCD 7, is shape changes in objects, soil, or rocks caused by water or flood. In example (22), this metaphor is used to highlight the repetitive and enduring impact of water, therefore, it was identified as an instance of re-experiencing metaphors. In contrast, the English meaning of "冲刷" emphasizes the consequent change more than the process leading to the change. According to the Longman Dictionary of Contemporary English, "washed out" has a basic meaning of "not brightly colored anymore" and a conventionalized metaphorical meaning of "(a person) feeling weak and looking unhealthy". If used by an English-speaking trauma victim, this metaphor may indicate a deviation from the normal sense of the self, and therefore, identified as an instance of dissociation metaphors. The contrasts between Chinese and English suggest that trauma victims' use of symptom-specific metaphors may differ across cultures.

Avoidance

Avoidance is a coping strategy used by trauma victims to protect themselves from overwhelming emotions and thoughts. The symptom was described by five metaphor vehicle terms, with four instantiating the LACK OF CONTACT schema (see Figure 5.10).

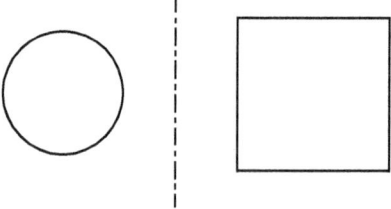

Figure 5.10: A diagram of the LACK OF CONTACT schema.

In Mandarin Chinese, knowing and learning about something is conventionally metaphorized as the individual having physical contact ("接触") with the surrounding environment. In the ASD participants' descriptions of avoidance, this metaphor is extended and elaborated in idiosyncratic ways: the trauma victim avoiding trauma-related people, events, places, and feelings is interpreted as the self being isolated from and having no physical contact with the external world. The following example is illustrative:

(23) 你会发现(暴乱)每天都在升级, 或者每个星期是也在升级的时候, 我就采取一个**龟缩**战术, 我就把我的社交软件除了微信以外都删掉了。
       'You would find that the scale (of the riot) gets larger every day, or it gets larger every week. The strategy I took was to **huddle up like a turtle**, I deleted all my social networking software except for WeChat.'

Here the speaker reflects on the strategies he used to cope with stress. Based on the conventional metaphor "KNOWING IS HAVING PHYSICAL CONTACT", the speaker describes his avoidance of social networking as the physical act of "huddling up like a turtle (龟缩)" and staying clear from the surrounding environment.

A less common but also therapeutically interesting schema found for avoidance-related metaphors is MASS-COUNT, which describes the transformation of dispersed individuals into a "single homogeneous mass" (Johnson 1987: 104). The schema is illustrated by Figure 5.11.

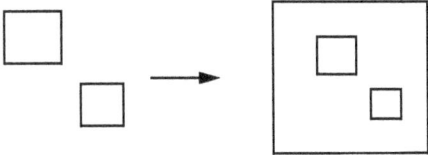

Figure 5.11: A diagram of the MASS-COUNT schema (in describing avoidance).

The image schema is only instantiated by one metaphor:

(24) 如果我出门去买东西, 还有说是去办事情, 就很会去考虑我在这个社会里边怎么样能更好的**融入进去**, 或者怎么样去**隐藏自己 (的大陆人特质)**。
'If I go out to buy something or do something, I would consider very carefully how to **merge myself** into the society, or to **hide myself (the mainland features)**.'

Hong Kong and the Chinese mainland differ markedly in terms of languages, social systems, and values; therefore, non-local students may perceive themselves as somewhat detached and even incompatible with the local community. In example (24), the self as a distinct, separate entity is compared against the conceptualization of Hong Kong society as "a single homogeneous mass" (Johnson 1987: 26). The speaker's strategic avoidance of trauma-related activities, places, and people, along with the concealment of her Chinese mainland identity, are conceptualized as acts of "merging (融入)" and "hiding (隐藏)" into the background of the local society.

Compared with the LACK OF CONTACT schema, which highlights the isolation of self from all possible trauma-related stimuli, the MASS-COUNT schema, as a precautionary measure to mitigate potential risks, appears to be a more active and adaptive approach to self-protection. Its relevance to trauma becomes evident only when the cultural divide between Hong Kong residents and Mainland Chinese immigrants is taken into account. The example clearly illustrates the speaker's conceptualization of herself as an outsider to Hong Kong society, someone who compromised her original socio-cultural identity to protect herself from risks targeted at her social group. This mindset is unlikely to be shared by local trauma victims.

Anxiety and hyperarousal

Trauma victims suffering from anxiety and hyperarousal may become overly sensitive and responsive to external stimuli, regardless of their relevance to the traumatic event. In the current dataset, this symptom was described by twenty-two metaphor vehicle terms with four image schemas. The majority of metaphors interpreted the symptom in terms of COMPULSION and CYCLIC CLIMAX. Two metaphors highlighted less commonly reported features of the symptom: one interpreted the intensification of anxiety as the expansion of space along the SCALE of size, and another represented the symptom as an OBJECT that has a perceivable weight.

The COMPULSION schema, instantiated by fifteen metaphor vehicle terms, was the most prevalent. It is illustrated by Figure 5.9. Similar to the COMPULSION schema that described the re-experiencing symptom (refer to example 22), the speaker's traumatic feelings are conceptualized as a potent force that can displace objects or cause them to fall to the ground, and the self under the influence of anxiety and hyperarousal is depicted as a passive recipient of this external force. Example (25) is illustrative.

(25) 我们都有一点害怕, 尤其是在路上看到戴口罩的人, 我当时心里面就会**"咯噔"一下**。
'All of us felt a little bit afraid, especially when seeing people with masks on the street. My heart would **quaver and make a noise of "gedeng"**.'

During the social unrest, rioters who committed vandalism and other criminal acts often wore face masks or Guy Fawkes masks to conceal their identities, so that they would not be recognized and tracked by the police after. Some also wore masks to express support for the radical protesters. In October 2019, the government implemented an anti-mask law, forbidding face-covering at unauthorized or illegal assemblies to prevent protesters from concealing their identities (Lau, Siu & Lum 2020). However, this did not stop radical protesters from masking or further vandalism. The sight of mask-wearing people was commonly regarded by local residents as a precursor to vandalism, violence, and injury. It was particularly anxiety-provoking to mainland Chinese immigrants, who faced higher risks of personal attacks due to their sociocultural identity (refer to Section 1.3.2).

In example (25), the emotional reaction to seeing mask-wearing people is interpreted as the movement of the heart. More specifically, the heart is conceptualized as an object that is abruptly pushed off from a high place, and the experience of anxiety and hyperarousal is described as the noise of "gedeng (咯噔)". The force relation is characterized by the abruptness of the force and the consequent movement of the object. It is markedly different from how it was instantiated in describing re-experiencing (refer to example 22). In example (22), the COMPULSION schema highlights the enduring nature of trauma-related emotions. While the speaker's psycho-pathological experience is likewise interpreted as an object under the influence of an external force, the self's movement is not a necessary consequence.

Apart from the force relation illustrated by example (25), there are also exceptional cases where the self is conceptualized as both the agent who exerts the force and the recipient who is influenced by the force. Take the following example:

(26) 然后就会觉得自己本来来香港就已经花了很多钱, 现在要花更多的钱, 却不能达到预期的学习效果, 然后在心理上也会**给自己增添很多负担, 就会给自己很多压力**。

'Then I would think that coming to study in Hong Kong has already cost me a lot of money, now I have to spend even more money, but can't learn what I expected to learn, then I will put **a lot of psychological burdens on myself, I will put a lot of pressure on myself**.'

At the most intense stage of social unrest, many students left Hong Kong for a safer environment. Example (26) describes the speaker's anxiety during this time. Worrying about extra expenditure caused by cross-border traveling and challenges in adapting to online learning, the speaker interprets her anxiety as self-imposed physical forces like burden "负担" and pressure "压力". In contrast to example (25), which focuses more on the hyperarousal side of the symptom, example (26) emphasizes the anxiety side, especially the persistent nature of anxiety.

Five metaphors described anxiety and hyperarousal as a repetitive phenomenon using a specific type of the CYCLE schema referred to as CYCLIC CLIMAX (represented by Figure 5.12).

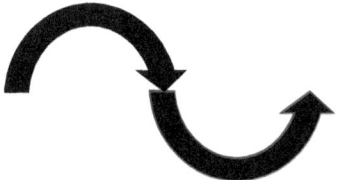

Figure 5.12: A diagram of the CYCLE schema.

In the current dataset, the participants presented two contrastive types of CYCLIC CLIMAX: the constant movement of an object between high and low spaces, and the alteration between two distinct physiological states. Both are captured by example (27), which occurred right after the "short-breathed (憋气)" metaphor in example (20):

(27)　因为(心情)总是**起起伏伏**的, 就是**一会憋气一会不憋气**这个样子。
'Because it (my mood) is always **going up and down**, it's just like **sometimes you feel there is some air choked in your heart, and then the next the air is out.**'

In contrast to example (20), which elaborates on the enduring nature of re-experiencing, the two metaphors in example (27) highlight the repetitive nature of anxiety and hyperarousal symptoms. The first metaphor ("起起伏伏") interprets the speaker's mood as an entity engaged in cyclic up-and-down movement. This experience is further elaborated through an extension of the "short-breathed" metaphor, comparing the alternation between hyperarousal and relaxation to the recurring pattern of being "short-breathed" and "not short-breathed".

Impairment in functioning
The term "impairment in functioning" is inherently metaphorical: the reduction in emotional, cognitive, and social functioning is compared to the mutilation of the human body or damage of a tangible entity. Despite the metaphoricity implied by the name of the symptom, only two metaphor vehicles, produced by the same interviewee, were directly relevant to impairment in functioning. Both metaphors instantiated the MASS-COUNT schema, which portrays the process of a massive complex breaking down into several different clusters. The embodied experience involved in this image schema is consistent with the metaphorical meaning conveyed by the symptom name. The image schema is illustrated by Figure 5.13 and example (28).

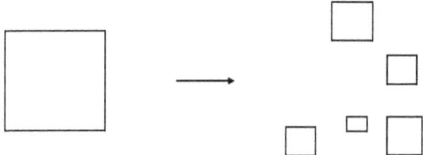

Figure 5.13: A diagram of the MASS-COUNT schema (in describing impairment in functioning).

(28)　而且原来来这里读书的那种心情已经完全**被破坏掉了**, 就是不知道自己到底学这些有什么意义。
'The mood I used to have about studying here **has been completely destroyed**, I have no idea why I'm still learning all these things.'

This metaphor describes how the speaker's motivation to sustain her study plan was destroyed (破坏). Based on the conceptualization of self-motivation as a tangible object, the speaker's traumatic experience is interpreted as a gigantic external power that causes the object to lose its original structure. Interestingly, the structure is precisely the reverse of the MASS-COUNT schema identified in the description of avoidance, which describes the speaker's avoidance as the aggregation of parts into a whole (refer to Figure 5.11).

5.4.3 Disorder-level image schematic patterns

In sum, this study investigated how trauma victims above the diagnostic threshold of ASD describe the five major symptoms with metaphors. Through the combination of linguistic data, psychometric data, and therapeutic observations, symptom-specific image schematic patterns were identified and discussed based on genuine linguistic examples.

The image schemas provided valuable insights into ASD participants' psychopathological experiences. COMPULSION (19 instances), DISABLEMENT (10 instances), and CONTAINER (8 instances) composed more than half of the ASD participants' symptom-specific metaphors. In other words, psychopathological experiences of ASD were most often conceptualized as external forces working on the self, reduced or loss of mobility, and the self being CONTAINED in trauma or the self CONTAINING various negative emotions. Image schemas such as SPLITTING, LACK OF CONTACT, and MASS-COUNT occurred less frequently. However, it is important to note that relatively low occurrence rates do not necessarily denote less clinical significance, especially when the observations were made based on a limited sample size.

Most of these embodied experiences have been recognized by previous research as key building blocks in the conceptualization of trauma-related emotions such as anger, sadness, depression, and anxiety (Charteris-Black 2012; Kövecses 2000; Yu & Tay 2020) and in describing different types of traumatic experiences (Foley 2015; Littlemore & Turner 2020; Rechsteiner, Tol & Maercker 2019; Rechsteiner et al. 2020; Wilson & Lindy 2013). Findings derived from this study further confirmed their clinical significance in trauma assessment and their relevance to more specific acute stress symptoms. An interesting observation is that although image schematic analysis captures universal rather than cultural-specific aspects of bodily experiences, results of the correspondent analysis showed that trauma victims' choices of image schemas in describing psychopathological symptoms (e.g., the use of MASS-COUNT in describing avoidance) were also informed by their sociocultural identities and shared mindset toward the traumatic event.

The patterns exhibited both convergence and divergence at the symptom level. The five symptoms were characterized by distinct sets of image schemas, and different image schemas identified for the same symptom often highlighted different clinical aspects of the symptom. In cases where overlaps were found, different clinical and experiential features were foregrounded. For example, both examples (22) and (25) instantiated the COMPULSION schema, conceptualizing trauma victims' emotional feelings as an entity under the influence of an external force. While example (22) described re-experiencing as an iterative movement, with a special focus on the process of the movement (i.e., the object being "washed out"), example (25) depicted anxiety and hyperarousal as a one-go movement, highlighting the consequence of the forced movement (i.e., the object falling and making a noise). Both examples (24) and (28) instantiated the MASS-COUNT schema. While example (24) described the experience of avoidance as the individual being integrated into a larger background, example (28) interpreted impairment in functioning as a reverse process, in which a massive complex was broken down into smaller segments. Compared with image schematic patterns previously identified for different emotions and mental health issues (e.g., Kövecses 2000; Yu & Tay 2020), the variations of metaphors across different symptoms of a given mental health disorder appeared to be more pronounced. As the study was based on a small sample size, this observation should be considered with caution. To draw more definite conclusions, studies on larger datasets and more diversified contexts are needed.

Notably, the frequency of metaphors and the number of image schemas were equally distributed across the five acute symptoms (refer to Table 5.3 and Figure 5.2). Dissociation, re-experiencing, and anxiety and hyperarousal attracted greater numbers of metaphors and image schemas. By contrast, avoidance and impairment in functioning were less likely to be represented by metaphors, and the numbers of image schemas were relatively lower. The frequency and category distribution of symptom-specific metaphors were also not balanced across the five participants (refer to Table 5.4). Some participants appeared to be more active than others in metaphor use. These differences may be related to the experiential features of the symptoms and their differentiated potential to be verbalized using metaphorical language. It is also possible that specific characteristics of the traumatic event, the participants' subjective experience of the symptoms, or their demographic features caused some symptoms to be more perceptually salient than others and therefore get greater chances of being represented in metaphorical language. These possibilities, while beyond the scope of the current study, offer promising avenues for future research.

5.5 Chapter conclusion

In contrast to Chapter 4, which investigated individual-level correlations between metaphor use and severities of traumatization, this chapter explored the qualitative features of trauma victims' metaphors about the five ASD symptoms (i.e., disorder/symptom-level metaphor usage patterns). Using correspondent analysis, the study illustrated how the incorporation of psychometric data and psychological observations can yield new insights for cognitive semantic analyses of mental health metaphors. It also demonstrated how an established inventory of image schemas could be used as a convenient and useful framework for therapeutic practitioners to probe into clients' conceptualizations of clinically interesting phenomena.

This study identified clear image schematic patterns for the five symptoms, highlighting varieties of psychopathological experiences as a crucial factor in explaining trauma metaphor variations. These findings, together with the patterns revealed by Chapter 4, contributed to a more comprehensive understanding of trauma victims' use of metaphors. The two clinically situated analyses revealed the need for future research to consider the interactions between metaphor use and more specific clinical features of mental disorders. A synthesized discussion of findings yielded by the two analyses will be provided in Section 6.2.1.

The findings hold practical implications for the clinical assessment and treatment of trauma. While trauma evaluation and diagnosis based on clinical guidelines such as DSM-V focus almost exclusively on objective and factual details, this study highlighted the possibility for psychopathological experiences of ASD symptoms to be captured in metaphorical language and further distinguished at the image schematic level. Although the patterns did not necessarily capture the core psychopathological features of the symptoms, they could still offer complementary information insights into trauma victims' psychopathological experiences. The patterns could enhance clinical practitioners' understanding of trauma victims' idiosyncratic, subjective experiences, which is helpful for fostering a "patient-centered" perspective on psychopathological experiences of trauma (Mead & Bower 2000; McWhinney 1993).

The findings highlighted the potential for symptom-related image schematic patterns to be integrated into clinical practices as referential points for identifying and exploring trauma victims' psychopathological experiences. Typical symptom-specific image schemas and linguistic expressions, especially those observed across different clinical contexts, may also be used as teaching or supporting materials in therapist training and education (e.g., Grove & Panzer 1989; Kopp 1995; Kopp & Craw 1998; Sims 2003; Sims & Whynot 1997). Furthermore, the patterns could serve as useful references for designing and translating psychometric tools, so that the linguistic descriptions can align more closely with the client's psychopathological experiences rather than the theory-informed professional perspective.

Several limitations must be acknowledged. First, given the small sample size, this study only investigated symptom-specific metaphors produced by speakers who are above the diagnostic criteria of ASD, the analysis was limited to qualitative features, therefore, the findings need to be interpreted with caution. To obtain a more comprehensive view of trauma victims' symptom-specific metaphors, future research can compare metaphor use by individuals with different numbers of symptoms and those who report different experiences of the same symptom. Quantitative analyses of larger sample sizes will also help identify more representative patterns. For example, categorical data analysis, regression analyses, and correlation analyses can be used to explore the quantitative relationships between trauma victims' experience of differential symptoms and their preference for symptom-specific metaphors. Second, while referring to an established inventory of image schema helps extract potentially generalizable patterns, the top-down coding did not consider idiosyncratic traumatic experiences. As idiosyncrasies of personal experiences can be more easily identified at the level of vehicle terms, future studies could consider using the two-tier coding (Kimmel 2010) that identifies both image schemas and vehicle terms (refer to Tay 2015 for an example of empirical research in the Chinese context).

In this study, the potential role of sociocultural knowledge in metaphor use was not addressed. Previous studies have shown that the perception of and recovery from trauma is often structured by cultural-specific constructs (Meili, Heim & Maercker 2019; Rechsteiner, Tol & Maercker 2019; Rechsteiner et al. 2020; Wilson & Lindy 2013). Findings of this study also showed that trauma victims' choices of image schemas can be informed by their sociocultural identities. However, as image schematic analysis focuses on universal aspects of embodied experiences and downplays potential sociocultural differences (Correa-Beningfield et al. 2005; Kimmel 2005), it may not be the best approach for exploring the role of these factors. Future research could compare the use of symptom-related metaphors in different cultural contexts and explore how such cultural sensitivity is reflected in the choice of more specific conceptual resources.

6 Conclusion

6.1 Chapter introduction

Chapters 3 to 5, together, presented a mixed-method, multi-level analysis of trauma metaphors elicited by the 2019–2020 Hong Kong social unrest: various therapeutically interesting patterns were extracted and examined at the text level, individual level, and disorder/symptom level. This chapter concludes the book with a retrospective summary of the findings from the three studies, their contribution to existing knowledge of trauma and mental health metaphors, and how the studies could be complemented by upcoming research. Section 6.2 will first summarize the major findings under the two major linguistic and clinical aims (outlined earlier in Section 1.4) and elaborate on the methodological implications of the multi-level analysis. Based on a holistic view of the three studies and a critical reflection on the whole research design, Section 6.3 offers an overarching account of the limitations, and Section 6.4 discusses future directions that emerged throughout the research process.

6.2 Summary of findings and implications

6.2.1 The linguistic and clinical aims

This book's primary, linguistic aim was to investigate previously neglected contextual characteristics of trauma metaphors. Two therapeutically interesting research avenues were pursued: 1) the multifaceted nature of metaphor use was investigated by examining systematic, quantitative interactions among multiple presentational and semantic features; 2) the role of subjective experiences in metaphor variation was explored by examining metaphor usage patterns by people with different severities of traumatization and different varieties of symptoms. A secondary, clinical aim was to explore the potential relevance of metaphorical language to psychopathological experiences of trauma. The aim was accomplished by juxtaposing linguistic data, psychometric data, and therapeutic observations.

The two research aims were addressed through three separate studies that focused on different aspects of metaphor use. A synthesized summary of major findings under the two research aims is shown in Figure 6.1.

As mentioned in Section 2.3, existing research on trauma and mental health metaphors mainly focused on semantic features like vehicle terms and topics. Only limited attention has been paid to presentational features that capture speakers' pre-

https://doi.org/10.1515/9783111346502-006

The linguistic aim	
The multifaceted nature of metaphor use can be captured through the interrelationships among semantic and presentational features: – Semantic features of metaphors can interact systematically with different presentational features (e.g., conventionality and emotional valence) – Multiple presentational features can also engage in systematic interactions with one another. – The relationship between two presentational features may vary at different levels of semantic specificity.	*Metaphor use may vary systematically with the speaker's subjective experiences:* Psychopathological experiences arising from spontaneous, emotionally charged events are important factors in shaping metaphor variation: – Different overall degrees of trauma and severities of symptoms are correlated with contrasting inclinations in the use of specific types of metaphors. – Experiences of different symptoms are often conceptualized using distinct sets of image schemas.

Relevance to therapeutic practices and therapist training:	Systematic metaphor usage patterns encode implicit yet clinically relevant information about the speaker's psychopathological experiences, for example:
Clinically situated metaphor analysis could: – reveal a mental health population's general, implicit tendency in packaging and presenting metaphorical ideas; – help validate prevailing assumptions and impressions about metaphor use; – serve as prompts or references in the practice of metaphor-based therapeutic protocols and techniques; – be included as supporting materials for therapist training and education;	*Systematic metaphor usage patterns encode implicit yet clinically relevant information about the speaker's psychopathological experiences, for example*: – The occurrence rates of specific types of metaphors can serve as indicators of the speakers' overall degrees of trauma and severities of more specific symptoms. – Preference for image schemas can be traced back to the client's experiences of ASD symptoms.

– assist in the development and refinement of psychometric and interview tools.

The clinical aim

Figure 6.1: A synthesized summary of major findings under the two research aims.

ferred ways of packaging and presenting metaphorical ideas, such as conventionality and emotional valences. If we consider different semantic and presentational features as discrete points in a three-dimensional space, then the relationships among multiple features can be conceived as facets formed by connecting the points. Chapter 3 of this book investigated the contextual characteristics of trauma metaphors by examining different facets formed by multiple presentational and semantic variables.

The findings showed that apart from semantic features, different information processing modes may also elicit varied ways of metaphorical meaning-making. Metaphors about the eight target categories and those generated from the two psychological perspectives exhibited contrasting associations with CONVENTIONALITY and EMOTIONAL VALENCE. The findings underline the potential for both semantic and presentational features to capture systematic patterns of metaphor use. More interestingly, the relationship between CONVENTIONALITY and EMOTIONAL VALENCE varied across different levels of semantic specificity (refer to Section 3.4.3). This reveals the potential for semantic and presentational features to capture different contextual characteristics, highlighting the theoretical and practical value of studying the multifacetedness of metaphor use.

This study also holds implications for therapeutic practices and therapist training. Firstly, the findings revealed general tendencies of metaphor use that are characteristic of the given trauma population, pointing toward metaphor usage patterns that are (un)likely to occur in real-world trauma talk. Secondly, the study offered empirical evidence that supported or supplemented existing knowledge about mental health metaphors, such as the emotional focuses identified for different target categories and the contrast between the two perspectives in conventionality. Some findings presented challenges to prevailing therapeutic assumptions, such as the relationship between conventionality and emotion expression. Thirdly, dominant patterns identified by this study, although not generalizable to all mental health contexts, could be incorporated as illustrative examples into teaching and training materials. Patterns that are verified in other mental health contexts can also serve as useful reference points for unpacking and extending client-generated metaphors in metaphor-based therapeutic protocols (e.g., Grove & Panzer 1989; Kopp 1995; Kopp & Craw 1998; Sims 2003; Sims & Whynot 1997).

Another focus of this book was the interaction between psychopathological experience and metaphor use. Chapter 4 investigated how trauma victims with different overall degrees of trauma and different severities of symptoms exhibited varying attention toward specific types of metaphors. Chapter 5 examined how different varieties of ASD symptoms, characterized by distinct emotional, cognitive, and physiological disturbances, were described using image schematic metaphors. Significant correlations with metaphor variables and dominant image schemas identified for the five ASD symptoms are summarized in Table 6.1.

Table 6.1: A summary of significant correlations and dominant image schematic patterns.

Symptom	Statistically Significant Correlations	Image schemas
Dissociation	–	DISABLEMENT SPLITTING SUPERIMPOSITION
Re-experiencing	Negative metaphors* (+) SELF AND SELF** (+) SELF AND SOCIAL SITUATION* (+) Emotional feelings and processes* (+)	CONTAINER COMPULSION LINK ATTRACTION DISABLEMENT SUPERIMPOSITION
Avoidance	–	LACK OF CONTACT MASS-COUNT
Anxiety and hyperarousal	OTHERS* (-) SELF AND SELF* (+) Self-references* (+)	COMPULSION CYCLE SCALE OBJECT
Impairment in functioning	Negative metaphors** (+)	MASS-COUNT
Overall degrees of trauma	Negative metaphors* (+) SELF AND SELF* (+) Self-references* (+)	DISABLEMENT COMPULSION CONTAINER

(Note: p-values less than .05 are indicated as * and those less than .01 as **, and positive and negative correlations are marked as + and -, respectively. The image schemas are listed in the order of occurrence rate).

Chapter 4 showed that individuals with different overall degrees of trauma and different severities of symptoms exhibited differential attention to/preference for specific types of metaphors. Among all, negative metaphors, SELF AND SELF, and self-referential metaphors were particularly expressive markers of traumatization; as the degrees of traumatization increased, trauma victims became more inclined to use these metaphors. Chapter 5 showed that trauma victims above the diagnostic criteria of ASD employed distinct sets of image schemas when describing different symptoms. DISABLEMENT, COMPULSION, and CONTAINER were the most frequently observed image schemas in describing ASD symptoms.

While a large body of metaphor research established long-term, recurrent human experiences as the primary source of conceptual elements for metaphorical meaning-making, the two clinically situated studies revealed that subjective experiences arising from spontaneous, emotionally charged events may influence how these conceptual resources are accessed and presented with metaphors. Consistent with earlier works on metaphor variations (e.g., Kövecses 2010, 2015, 2020), the studies demonstrated that quantitative differences in subjective experiences may manifest as heightened or lowered inclinations toward certain types of metaphors, and qualitative differences in subjective experiences may prompt the speakers to draw on distinct sets of conceptual resources in metaphorical meaning-making.

We have seen that trauma victims' metaphor use encodes rich information about their psychopathological experiences, and that different clinical conditions are characterized by distinct (although sometimes overlapping) metaphor usage patterns. Although patterns revealed by metaphor-based analysis alone are not sufficient to serve formal diagnostic purposes, they can nonetheless offer valuable supplementary information about clients' subjective experiences. These insights can assist clinical practitioners in developing a client-centered perspective regarding the mental health conditions under examination and the client's implicit treatment needs. Moreover, patterns confirmed by other studies can also be used as quick references when therapists want to get a rough estimate of clients' psychopathological conditions and recovery progress during therapy. In therapeutic treatment, the patterns could be usefully adapted as references in exploring disorder- and symptom-related imageries and thinking patterns and eliciting alternative conceptualizations (Cirillo & Crider 1995; Kopp 1995; Witztum, Van Der Hart & Friedman 1988). The patterns may also serve as convenient references in clinical scenarios where psychometric information is not yet available, such as the initial stages of in-take interviews and crisis intervention. Like the patterns revealed by Chapter 3, the disorder- and symptom-level patterns and typical linguistic examples could be included in therapist education and training schemes (e.g., Mathieson et al. 2016) to enhance therapists' sensitivity to metaphors as potential linguistic markers of psychopathology.

Another promising avenue for applying metaphor-based research findings is the development and refinement of psychometric tools. A quick look at commonly used questionnaires and interview tools for trauma diagnosis showed that the use of metaphorical expressions is by no means uncommon. For example, five questionnaire items in the original version of SASRQ (Cardeña et al. 2000) used obviously metaphorical expressions (italicized): "I felt hypervigilant or *'on edge'*" (item 12) "I experienced myself *as though I were a stranger*" (item 13), "I felt *distant from* my own memories" (Item 20), "my mind *went blank*" (item 24), and "I felt estranged or *detached from* other people" (item 28). In the Chinese-translated version of the SASRQ (Hou 2008), most of the metaphorical meanings were retained. Metaphorical expressions were also found in diagnostic instruments on other mental health disorders or psychological phenomena, for example, Depression Anxiety Stress Scales (DASS; Lovibond & Lovibond 1995), Anxiety Sensitivity Profile (ASP; Taylor & Cox 1998), and Meta-Cognitions Questionnaire (MCQ; Cartwright-Hatton & Wells 1997). Metaphor-based analysis, like the patterns reported in Chapters 4 and 5, could provide clinical psychologists with evidence-based conclusions about which type of metaphors is commonly shared by people of higher degrees of trauma, how metaphors are used by those who are particularly disturbed by a symptom, and how metaphors can be phrased to describe the symptom from the client's perspective. Common patterns identified across different mental health contexts and those characteristic of specific socio-cultural contexts could also assist decision-making during the development process, such as which metaphors to include (or avoid).

6.2.2 The multi-level analysis

The three main body chapters, together, presented a multi-level analysis that dissects metaphor use in mental health contexts through text-level, individual-level, and disorder/symptom-level analyses (refer to Figure 1.2, reproduced as Figure 6.2 below). The approach not only provides a comprehensive view of contextual characteristics of metaphor use by the target population but also highlights the link between these characteristics and the speakers' psychopathological experiences.

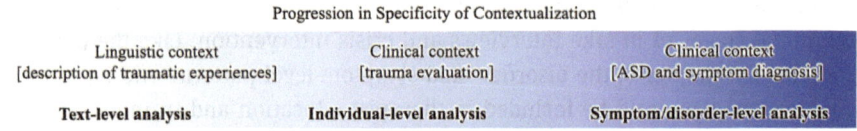

Figure 6.2: Structure of the multi-level analysis.

The text-level analysis, exemplified by Chapter 3 of this book, examines the speakers' choices and packaging of specific metaphor variables without considering any clinical input. The aim was to offer a broad overview of a target mental health population's general yet implicit tendencies in metaphor use. In the current research context, this was achieved by probing into the multifaceted nature of metaphor use reflected by the interrelationships among multiple variables and their subcategories.

The individual-level analysis and the disorder/symptom-level analysis identify metaphor usage patterns that are potentially related to the mental health issue under examination. Both require the incorporation of psychometric data (and clinical observations wherever relevant) into metaphor analysis. The individual-level analysis focuses specifically on metaphor variations across individuals with different severities of psychopathological experiences. This analysis highlights the heterogeneity within the target mental health population. The disorder/symptom-level analysis focuses on metaphor usage patterns that are pertinent to disorder- and symptom-specific emotional, cognitive, and physiological disturbances. In contrast to the individual-level analysis, the disorder/symptom-level analysis places more emphasis on the unique aspects of different psychopathological experiences. In the current research context, the individual-level analysis probed into the correlations between severities of traumatization and frequencies of therapeutically interesting metaphor variables, and the disorder/symptom-level analysis worked on dominant image schematic patterns in ASD participants' descriptions of clinically present symptoms. The findings can be used to develop more effective communication and intervention strategies, as well as foster a client-centered perspective on focal psychopathological experiences.

Bridging the gap between linguistic patterns and psychopathological experiences, the multi-level analysis presents a feasible and practical framework for cross-disciplinary research on metaphor use in specific mental health contexts. The approach is inherently flexible and can be adapted to extract both quantitative and qualitative patterns, depending on the research objectives and the nature of the data. Apart from following the research avenues and methods demonstrated by this book, future research using this approach could explore other aspects of metaphor use using more flexible combinations of quantitative and qualitative methods (summarized in Sections 3.4, 4.5, and 5.5). Some potential research directions and methods beyond the current research context are listed in Section 6.4. This approach can also be applied to the study of other linguistic phenomena of clinical interest.

6.3 Limitations

Sections 3.5, 4.5, and 5.5 provided focused reflections on the limitations identified for the three studies, with special attention to the selection of variables and choices of research methods. In addition, some key limitations in research design and analytic strategies also need to be considered.

First of all, this study is limited in the use of convenience sampling and snowball sampling. Since the sampling was non-randomized, the participants had homogeneous demographic characteristics, such as age, nationality, and educational background. The proportion of females and males was also not balanced (N=33 and 13, respectively). The limitation in sampling hinders comparative analyses across different demographic features. To capture the psychological impact of large-scale traumatic events, especially in culturally diverse contexts such as Hong Kong, stratified random sampling would be preferable, although this method is not always feasible in situations requiring urgent response. If possible, preparing a sampling plan that captures the region's true demographic landscape would be beneficial for future studies. This approach would ensure a more representative and diverse participant pool, allowing for a more accurate understanding of the impact of large-scale emergency events.

Another drawback of using convenience sampling and snowball sampling is that the findings might have been influenced by potential confirmation bias. For instance, as the social unrest is politically sensitive, trauma victims who had concerns about targeted harassment or other negative repercussions for commenting on the protests were unlikely to sign up for the study. Similarly, individuals who were particularly affected by avoidance might feel reluctant to talk and think about their traumatic experiences, and those who developed severe impairment in functioning might not participate in the study, as they might experience greater challenges in engaging in interpersonal interactions.

Secondly, psychometric data examined in this book were collected using the SASRQ, which took clinical symptoms outlined in the DSM-IV as the entry point for evaluating ASD (American Psychiatric Association 1994). The diagnostic criteria were updated in DSM-V, which was released in 2013 (American Psychiatric Association 2013; refer to Bryant et al. 2015 for a comparison of the two diagnostic criteria and their predictive validity of PTSD). However, at the time of this project, psychometric tools that incorporated the DSM-V criteria (e.g., the SASRQ-II, Lötvall, Palmborg & Cardeña 2022) were not available. Nonetheless, it is essential for mental health communication researchers to check for the most up-to-date instruments that reflect the latest clinical understanding.

Thirdly, while the DSM-IV symptoms served as convenient starting points for exploring the role of psychopathological experiences in metaphor use, the psychometric data may not reflect more subtle individual differences in symptom experiences. As noted by Galatzer-Levy and Bryant (2013), people who meet the DSM-IV diagnostic criteria of trauma-related disorder may experience various combinations and subsets of symptoms. According to the diagnostic criteria of PTSD specified in DSM-IV, there could be 31 possible combinations of dissociation-related symptoms, 99 possible combinations of avoidance symptoms, and 26 possible combinations of hyperarousal symptoms (Galatzer-Levy and Bryant 2013: 656). The complexity in PTSD symptomatology applies to ASD as well and could be a potential factor influencing variations in metaphor use. Furthermore, Bryant et al. (2011) noted that acute stress reactions may encompass a broader range of clinical manifestations than what is described in the DSM diagnostic criteria; reactions like prolonged grief (Ozer et al. 2003), shock, disgust, and somatic reactions (Isserlin, Zerach & Solomon 2008) such as fatigue, nausea, and muscle pain might also have diagnostic significance. In addition, individuals exposed to trauma may develop co-morbid depression, anxiety, and other mental health disorders alongside acute stress reactions (Gradus et al. 2015). To gain a more nuanced account of the interplay between metaphor use and these psychopathological aspects, analyses based on finer as well as broader psychometric categories are needed.

Another key limitation, as mentioned earlier in Chapters 3 and 4, lies in the use of top-down coding schemes (Kopp 1995; Nigro & Neisser 1983; O'Kearney & Perrott 2006) rather than the bottom-up approach. As the top-down approach searches for trauma-related metaphor usage patterns from clinical aspects highlighted by previous clinical research, it minimizes the risk of detecting spurious relationships in quantitative analyses and adds to the replicability across studies and clinical contexts. However, the top-down approach may not fully capture the particularistic qualities of metaphor use that are specific to a traumatic context. To complement this limitation, future research could adopt bottom-up approaches (e.g., Ahrens & Jiang 2020; Kimmel 2010; Cameron & Maslen 2010) to identify contextually motivated vehicle terms and target topics.

It is crucial to acknowledge that manual metaphor identification, including drawing the boundaries, identifying vehicle terms and topics, and assigning coding categories, inherently relies on subjective decisions. Even the use of top-down coding schemes does not entirely eliminate the subjectivity in coding. This inherent subjectivity is a methodological challenge faced by metaphor analysis in general (Armstrong Davis, & Paulson 2011). A standardized, reliable, and preferably automatic approach, if available, would greatly enhance the reliability of metaphor identification and the comparability of findings across different research contexts. However, manual coding of metaphors does have the advantage of capturing contextually motivated patterns, providing clinical practitioners with the flexibility to tailor their analysis to emergent themes and therapeutic objectives. With this approach, clinical practitioners can convert their observations into quantifiable data points, assess the validity of their impressions based on the derived patterns, and adjust their ways of managing these metaphors in future sessions. It is important for future researchers to recognize that both manual and potential automated approaches have an edge in extracting clinically interesting patterns, and the choice of method should be based on a careful consideration of research needs and objectives.

6.4 Future directions

This section discusses some future directions for studying trauma and mental health metaphors. In Section 6.4.1, I outline some clinical factors that are beyond the scope of the book but hold significance for future studies, including metaphoric behaviors and somatic reactions, indirect exposure to traumatic events, emotional disorders triggered by trauma, and Type II trauma. In Section 6.4.2, I will discuss the potential influence of some non-clinical factors, including socio-cultural background, political stances, demographic features, and the types of traumatic events. The three studies presented in this book represented some exploratory attempts to address the linguistic and clinical aims outlined in Section 1.3. In Section 6.4.3, I will introduce some alternative pathways for addressing the linguistic and clinical aims. Special focus will be placed on the prediction of psychopathological experiences based on metaphor usage patterns and the study of natural groupings within metaphor use.

6.4.1 Metaphor use and other important clinical factors

Metaphoric behaviors and somatic reactions elicited by trauma
An emerging research avenue in both trauma and metaphor studies is trauma victims' metaphoric behaviors and somatic reactions. As noted by Wilson and Lindy (2013), traumatic experiences can be expressed not only through linguistic resources but also through trauma victims' body language like gestures and repetitive compulsive behaviors, somatic experiences like chest pain, hypersensitivity, and heart racing, and symbolic behaviors such as substance abuse and avoidance behaviors. These non-verbal expressions arise directly from past traumatic experiences and intrude spontaneously into the present and foreseeable future when triggered by trauma-related stimuli. They can impede trauma victims' adaptive functioning in the present, confining their personalities to the emergency defense field of trauma (Wilson & Lindy 2013). Through an in-depth analysis of a multimodal text by an eight-year-old refugee, Busch (2020) showed that the intense but "bottled" feelings of fear and helplessness can be vividly represented through both verbal and non-verbal artistic methods. In a study of metaphor use by bereaved parents, Littlemore and Turner (2020) identified more deliberate and adaptive metaphoric behaviors as explicit signs of traumatic experiences. For example, a father wanted to metaphorically "share a beer" with his stillborn son. This symbolic behavior, which usually takes place when a boy of the family reaches adulthood, is believed to "bring a salient moment from a hoped for, but non-existent future into the present". In the context of bereavement, this behavior served as a possible way to reconcile between the two incompatible realities (Littlemore & Turner 2020: 58).

Participants of the present study also reported interesting metaphoric behaviors. As mentioned earlier, a large number of mainland Chinese immigrants chose to leave Hong Kong temporarily due to safety concerns. However, a participant deliberately chose to stay despite the potential risks, inconvenience in daily life, and immense emotional distress. In the interview, he interpreted the reasons as he was "taking up a challenge (接受挑战)" posed by the reality and holding on in a battle that he did not want to lose ("好像一个战争一样,不想这么就输了"). Some participants also reported somatic experiences, such as shortness of breath and palpitation, and built their metaphors upon these experiences (see example 27 discussed in Section 5.4.2). These metaphoric behaviors and somatic experiences are apparently related to the participants' idiosyncratic ways of perceiving and interpreting the traumatic event. Their interactions with metaphor use and psychopathological experiences remain an intriguing area to be explored.

Metaphors in describing indirect trauma exposure

Another clinical aspect interesting to metaphor research is psychological disturbances caused by indirect exposure to a traumatic event, known as secondary traumatic stress (STS; Figley 1983). STS refers to psychological distress induced by empathetic engagement with trauma victims and is sometimes interchangeably referred to as "vicarious trauma" (McCann & Pearlman 1990). Examples of indirect trauma exposure include media exposure to traumatic events such as flooding, air crashes, and war, witnessing healthcare emergencies caused by the COVID-19 pandemic, and personal communication with trauma victims. Although traumatic feelings associated with such experiences do not meet the current diagnostic criteria for ASD and PTSD, they may also trigger mental health issues like depression and anxiety (Pfefferbaum & North 2020).

Given the wide reach of social media, even individuals who were not personally involved in the traumatic event may experience overwhelming negative feelings. This differs from individuals with direct trauma exposure, who experienced both negative emotions and bodily, sensory, and physiological experiences of the life-threatening situation. This disparity presents a fascinating avenue for metaphor research. Does the amount of trauma exposure influence the overall rates of metaphor use? Do individuals with and without direct trauma exposure use describe their subjective experiences with different sets of vehicle terms and image schemas? How do metaphors produced by these two groups of individuals differ in presentational features? Exploring these questions could not only enrich our knowledge about the contextual features of trauma metaphors but also open a new perspective on the role of embodied experiences in metaphorical meaning-making.

Metaphors about other trauma-related emotions

This study explored trauma-metaphor interactions based on psychometric measures of ASD and its subordinate symptoms. However, there is a broader spectrum of trauma-related emotions and psychopathological experiences that may influence metaphor use. Apart from the clinical manifestations described in DSM-IV, emotions such as depression, fear, and grief, as indicated by research from Ozer et al. (2003) and Isserlin, Zerach, & Solomon (2008), also play a significant role in the aftermath of trauma. Exploring trauma victims' metaphors in relation to these emotions would be an intriguing direction for future research. For example, how do specific emotional disorders like depression, fear, and grief shape the use of metaphors? Can the comorbidity of trauma and different emotional disorders be distinguished from the individuals' language and metaphor use? Which vehicles and topics are more prevalent or distinct in expressing emotional disorders associated with trauma? The findings could complement the findings presented in this book and contribute to our knowledge about the interplay between metaphor use and emotional afflictions in general.

Type II trauma and cross-domain mappings

This book focused on trauma induced by a discrete, unanticipated, and extremely overwhelming event. The psychological consequences of such events are termed by Terr (1991) as *Type I trauma*. In juxtaposition, Terr (1991) identifies a contrasting phenomenon of *Type II trauma*, which refers to the experience of long-standing or repeated ordeals over the entire life span, such as domestic violence and childhood abuse. Victims of Type II trauma may experience depression, chronic anxiety, dissociation, and difficulties with self-regulation (Terr 1991). Compared with victims of one-time traumatic events, those who have Type II trauma may experience more complex and enduring psychological disturbances. They may also have higher risks of developing PTSD on later exposure to Type I trauma (Ford & Courtois 2009).

Type II trauma is particularly interesting to metaphor research as it may damage a person's ability to establish metaphoric connections between past experiences and the present (refer to Borbely 2008 for an example). This impairment may manifest as an unconscious tendency to transfer emotions, behaviors, and thought patterns from significant past experiences to current life situations. Type II trauma can be worked through in psychotherapy by establishing cross-domain mappings between the client's past and present experiences. An example of non-metaphorical cross-domain mapping, presented in Tay (2016), is reproduced below. The extract was selected from a series of therapeutic sessions aiming to elucidate how the client's current interpersonal relationships were influenced by her past relationship with her father:

T: 我感觉你是在用对待你父亲的方法来对待我。
'I feel that **you are treating me like how you treated your father**.'
[. . . . . .]
T: 哦。你看看,你说这些哦,有时候我都分不清哪个是爸爸,哪个是你。 你们真的很像诶!

'Oh. See, when you say these things, **sometimes I cannot tell which is father, and which is you. You are really alike!**'

The two examples draw explicit connections between the patient in the present and her father in the past. Despite the apparent mappings between the two temporal domains, such expressions do not involve the contrast and transfer between two different meanings (Cameron & Maslen 2010); therefore, they are not metaphorical in the linguistic sense.

Alternatively, Type II trauma can also be worked through by establishing metaphorical cross-domain mappings. An example is cited from Qiu and Tay (under review). The extract was selected from a therapeutic session with a Dependent Personality Disorder client, who exhibits a strong inclination to interpret her current interpersonal relationships and work situations based on her past interactions with her parents.

C: 这些(痛苦)都没意义,那我不想活了。'All these (miseries) make no sense at all. I don't want to live anymore.'
[......]
T: 你就像一个小孩子撒泼一样,躺在地上说"我不玩了,我不过了,你非得给我买这个玩具"是一样的道理。'**You are just like a child in a tantrum, lying on the ground and saying, "I'm not going, I won't do anything unless you buy me this toy"**. What you are doing is just like that.'

In this conversation, the client showing an uncooperative and playful attitude in therapy was identified by the therapist as a sign of the client transferring her interactional mode with her parents onto the ongoing therapy. To facilitate the client's reflection on her unconscious psychological activity, the therapist metaphorized the client as a child throwing a tantrum and asking for toys. Compared with non-metaphorical cross-domain comparisons, the construction of metaphorical cross-domain mappings promotes the client's self-reflection in a less intrusive way.

Therapeutic conversations on Type II trauma offer a unique opportunity for comparing these two forms of cross-domain mappings. Findings about the contextual features of their linguistic expressions and the response they elicit from the other speaker can provide a new perspective on the role of metaphoricity in articulating complex, emotion-laden ideas. An exploratory study of the two types of cross-domain mappings can be found in Qiu and Tay (under review). While the study presents a frequency-based exploratory analysis of a small number of sessions (N=7), future research could conduct quantitative analyses on larger sample sizes to extract systematic patterns of metaphor use and variation. A comparative study of metaphor usage patterns associated with Type I and Type II trauma recovery would also be an interesting direction.

6.4.2 Metaphor use and non-clinical factors

Socio-cultural background

Numerous studies have shown that people with different sociocultural backgrounds may use metaphors in different ways. For example, Musolff (2017) identified intriguing cultural differences in NATION metaphors produced by 31 individuals from 10 countries. While NATION AS GEOBODY and NATION AS FUNCTIONAL WHOLE were used by participants across all cultural backgrounds, these two metaphors were used at contrasting rates among Chinese and Western participants. Many Chinese participants interpreted the geographical shape of the nation as the shape of a human body, for example, Beijing as the heart and brain, and Hong Kong and Taiwan as the feet. In contrast, participants from Western countries were more inclined to conceptualize the nation as functions and features of the body, for example, Britain as "a vast, churning body [. . .] sucking in resources, processing them, and spewing out fumes and ideas" (Musolff 2017: 10).

Studies that adopted a sociocultural perspective on trauma metaphors (e.g., Rechsteiner et al. 2019, 2020; Meili et al. 2020; Wilson & Lindy 2013) showed that individuals with different sociocultural knowledge and religious beliefs may interpret their traumatic and psychopathological experiences in contrasting ways. However, the analyses were mostly qualitative in nature and the sample sizes were relatively small. Systematic, quantitative patterns within large-scale data, especially in ethnically diverse contexts such as Hong Kong and Singapore, remain unexplored. This direction was not pursued by this book owing to logistical constraints. Did mainland Chinese immigrants, local residents, and immigrants from other parts of the world experience the social unrest in different ways? Did individuals with and without overseas experiences perceive the social unrest differently? Which dimension of sociocultural experiences is the most influential in shaping the individuals' interpretations and their psychopathological experiences? These questions remain open for future researchers.

Political stances

The relationship between trauma victims' political stances and metaphor use is also an interesting question in the current research context. A large body of research has shown that individuals with different ideologies and political positions may interpret social and political issues in different ways, and that these divergences can be clearly observed from their metaphor use. For example, Boers (1997) found that in the United Kingdom during the 1980s, the shift to the right in the political atmosphere triggered more active use of "safety net" metaphors in describing the welfare state, which, contrary to the "shelter" alternative, de-emphasizes the vulnerability of citizens. In a study of metaphor use in right-wing and left-wing British magazines, Caers (2006) found that right-wing authors made more active use of health, conflict, and mobility metaphors, whereas left-wing authors used more metaphors about crime and living organisms.

As mentioned earlier, the Hong Kong social unrest was characterized by high political tension with the involvement of several different political powers (Shek 2020). According to the survey conducted by Ni et al. (2020) on Hong Kong residents' psychological well-being during the social unrest, political stances may be linked to the risks of mental health disorders: non-involvement in initial protests and neutrality towards the extradition bill halved the risk of suspected PTSD, although neither support nor opposition to the bill extradition, nor participation in protests, was significantly associated with probable psychopathological distress. The survey results pointed to interesting interactions between political stances and psychopathological experiences. In the present study, the participants' political stances and views were not solicited due to their concerns about personal safety. How the interactions may manifest in trauma victims' metaphor use remains an intriguing question for future researchers, especially political psychology researchers and linguists who apply Critical Discourse Analysis. The findings would also generate practical guidance for providing therapeutic treatment and social support after traumatic events of a similar nature, such as war and armed conflicts.

Demographic characteristics and type of traumatic event

Findings summarized in Section 2.2 show that different demographic characteristics (e.g., age, gender, educational background) and types of traumatic events (e.g., natural disaster, large-scale public event, traffic accident) may also influence trauma victims' interpretation of their experiences. While this book is based on a relatively homogenous sample collected in a single traumatic context, future research could replicate the methods on larger sample sizes with more heterogeneous demographic profiles or a more diversified range of traumatic contexts. Is there any gender-specific pattern in trauma victims' metaphor use? How does educational background influence the semantic and presentational features of metaphors? Do different types of traumatic events, which involve distinct types of bodily experiences, trigger different metaphor usage patterns? Investigations along these lines could enhance our understanding of how the same traumatic event may be perceived and interpreted in idiosyncratic ways. The insights may also pave the way for more personalized and effective therapeutic approaches.

6.4.3 Quantitative analyses of mental health metaphors

Natural groupings of metaphors

In this book, statistical analyses and interpretation followed the p-value paradigm,[34] assessing the likelihood of observing the data under the null hypothesis (i.e., no statistical relationship exists between the observed and the measured phenomena). A fixed p-value of .05 was used as the threshold for rejecting the null hypothesis. Relationships with p-values above the threshold were regarded as statistically significant and of greater research interest; patterns of theoretical concern but below the threshold were not considered in the analysis.

This approach is not without limitations. According to Dick and Tevaearai (2015: 815), fixed p-value provides only "a crude orientation regarding the probable realness of specific group differences", offering a simplistic explanation of the big picture. Nevertheless, this strategy can be helpful for exploratory research that aims to highlight potentially clinically relevant patterns and derive clear-cut conclusions, which is the reason why it was adopted in this book. Following the American Statistical Association statement and guidelines, descriptive statistics such as Cramer's V, adjusted residuals, and correlation coefficients were used in the studies to provide supplementary information for understanding and comparing the relationships.[35]

Apart from following the p-value paradigm as this book did, future researchers could also adopt a more descriptive or modeling approach, interpreting p-values as a continuous measure and supplementing the results with more descriptive statistics (e.g., confidence intervals, maximum and minimum values, and data distribution). An interesting direction following this approach is the study of the natural groupings of mental health metaphors, which highlights how individuals with certain psychopathological conditions tend to use various types of metaphors in similar or different ways. Two feasible ways of extracting natural groupings are cluster analysis and association rule mining. Cluster analysis groups data points into clus-

---

34 The p-value paradigm is also called the frequentist statistical inferencing, as it assesses the likelihood of a phenomenon happening in a large number of repeated experiments as its frequency of occurring.

35 An alternative paradigm for assessing statistical evidence is Bayesian inference, which calculates the probability of a hypothesis being true given the data (see Tay 2020b for exemplary applications in metaphor research).

ters based on the inherent similarities of the data points; members within each identified group share a maximal similarity, and the groups themselves are maximally different from each other (refer McMullen 1985; Tay 2020a; Tay & Qiu 2022 for examples in the study of mental health metaphors). Association rule mining identifies variables or categories that are likely to co-occur in different contexts (see Tay & Qiu 2024 for examples), revealing patterns of association and relationships among metaphorical expressions within the same group. Both methods can reveal distinguishing features of the clinical groups under examination.

The study of natural groupings of metaphors is expected to lead to a deeper and more precise understanding of metaphor variations. The statistical patterns, especially when interpreted in relation to psychometric data, demographic information, and therapeutic outcomes, could provide a comprehensive account of interesting but not necessarily statistically significant patterns (Wasserstein, Schirm & Lazar 2019; refer to Tay 2022 for an example); this may help to uncover factors that were not readily apparent in research following the *p*-value paradigm. The findings could also offer valuable insights for psychology researchers' understanding of relevant psychological phenomena and generate useful information for clinical practitioners' reflection and refinement of their own practices.

Putting metaphor analysis into the predictive context

The three studies presented in this book were descriptive in nature. The focus was the multifaceted nature of trauma metaphors and potentially trauma-related variables. As the primary goal of mental health communication is to provide reliable diagnoses and in-time evaluations of the client's clinical conditions, another promising direction in the study of mental health metaphors would be to put metaphor analysis into the predictive context, that is, to examine how metaphor usage patterns can be used to predict a larger trauma populations' psychopathological experience.

In this scenario, a particularly useful statistical technique is regression, which investigates the relationship between one outcome variable and multiple predictor variables. Two methods that could be usefully applied to the study of mental health metaphors are multiple regression and logistic regression. Multiple regression can be used to predict the values of continuous outcome variables such as psychometric scores. The method can examine the amount of change in the outcome variable explained by a unit change in the predictor variables. For example, if we have strong evidence that one or more metaphor variables are associated with high levels of stress, multiple regression could quantify the strength of this association and predict the speaker's stress level based on the prevalence of the variable(s) in her/his language use. In studies of mental health communication, participant clustering, for example, caused by including different types of traumatic events, age groups, and ethnic groups, may introduce significant variability in language use. In multiple mixed effects regression, these factors can be included as random factors so that their effects on the study outcomes are appropriately accounted for. In contrast to multiple regression, logistic regression predicts binary outcomes like the clinical presence of symptoms and disorders and positive versus negative therapeutic outcomes. It could be used to determine the likelihood that certain metaphor variables are correlated with the presence or absence of a given clinical condition (refer to Plug, Sharrack & Reuber 2009 for an example).

This book, together with previous research on trauma narratives and metaphors, has highlighted several variables relevant to psychopathological experiences of trauma (summarized in Sections 2.2 and 2.3). Future research could therefore adopt regression methods to transform the descriptive insights provided by existing studies into quantitative indicators of psychopathology. The methods could also be applied to other mental health contexts where metaphors have been shown to play an essential role in reflecting psychological afflictions and changes. For example, in personal narratives about depression, multiple types of metaphors have been identified as potential markers of psychopathology, therapeutic change, and recovery (e.g., Charteris-Black 2012; Levitt, Korman & Angus 2000; Littlemore 2019; McMullen & Conway 2002; Pritzker 2007; Yu 2008; Yu & Tay 2020). Using regression, future research could work out the predictive value of these metaphor types and potentially establish a systematic link between specific metaphor usage and various stages or severity of depression. The findings are expected to offer a more nuanced and precise way of monitoring and understanding an individual's psychological progress throughout therapy.

The application of these quantitative methods can be seen as an attempt to further the linguistic and clinical aims pursued by this book. However, it is important to reiterate that in the study of mental health communication, quantitative methods should better be supplemented or informed by qualitative insights to ensure that statistically significant patterns are interpreted from a context-situated perspective. This is particularly important when the analysis aims to address the roles of sociocultural backgrounds, political stances, demographic features, and other nuanced clinical aspects of trauma.

6.5 Chapter conclusion

This chapter summarized the major findings, implications, and limitations of the book. Based on an overview of the three main body chapters, the findings and implications were discussed in a synthesized way under the proposed linguistic and clinical aims. Besides the limitations identified for each of the studies, I have also summarized the limitations at the more general level of research design and analytic strategies, highlighting areas where further research and refinement are needed.

It is hoped that the findings and reflections could provide a comprehensive view of the systematicity underlying trauma metaphors and the dynamic interactions between metaphor use and the speakers' psychopathological experiences. As exploratory research on a large-scale traumatic event, these studies are also expected to provide an immediate sense of how metaphor analyses, especially those grounded in real-life socio-cultural settings, could open new perspectives for understanding mental health communication, and potentially, inform clinical practice of and research on mental health assessment, diagnosis, and treatment.

This chapter has also outlined some future directions that emerged through the course of this study. It is hoped that these directions could inspire more empirical works on mental health metaphors and explorative applications of metaphor research findings in clinical contexts. These attempts would help us complete the jigsaw puzzle of contextualized metaphors and mental health issues, piece by piece, and work out collaborative and better ways for coping with human emotions and thoughts.

Appendix 1: Reflexivity statement

Researcher's professional background

The researcher (and author of this book) received systematic training in designing and conducting semi-structured interviews in the mental health context. Before the data collection started, she received professional training in trauma theories and psychometric testing and underwent 20 hours of supervision in interview and therapy with trauma victims. She had extensive experience in conducting semi-structured interviews with victims of different traumatic events. In terms of professional background in linguistics, the researcher was primarily trained in cognitive linguistics, especially metaphor analysis following the discourse dynamics approach. She is particularly experienced in identifying and analyzing metaphorical language in mental health communication.

The therapist who was involved in this study held a master's degree in psychotherapy. He is also a therapist supervisor certified by the Chinese Psychological Association (APA). At the time of the study, he had 25 years of experience in psychoanalytic therapy and 13 years of experience in trauma treatment and therapist training.

Biases and impact on data collection

Like the participants of this study, the researcher experienced stress during the social unrest due to exposure to life-threatening situations, violence, and abuse. To mitigate the potential influence of her own traumatic experience on the interview, she consulted the therapist supervisor before commencing the study. Under the supervisor's guidance, the researcher practiced psychological and interview strategies for dealing with intense emotions. The supervisor reviewed the recruitment message, consent form, information sheet, interview questions, and verbal instructions for administering the SASRQ. Special attention was given to potential interviewer biases and non-neutral expressions.

The researcher shares the same socio-cultural identity with participants of the project. In this research context, this similarity could have facilitated access to a wider range of participants. As mainland Chinese were a major target group of protest-related violence and abuse, this shared identity also enabled the participants to express their irrational fear, anger, and other negative opinions more freely, without the psychological defense often present when facing an interviewer from another socio-cultural background. Nevertheless, the researcher's

https://doi.org/10.1515/9783111346502-007

positionality could have introduced potential biases. The commonalities in ethnic and sociocultural background might have led some participants to unconsciously rely more on collective beliefs shared by mainland Chinese when interpreting their traumatic experiences rather than dig deep into their personal thoughts and feelings.

Hong Kong local residents and other socio-cultural groups were not included in the recruitment plan. This was partly because these sociocultural groups do not share the same mother tongue, which may affect the comparability of the data. In addition, the recruitment was expected to be challenging, as people were generally reluctant and even fearful to openly express their opinions due to the distrust and tension brought about by the social unrest.

Researcher's role

All interviews and psychometric assessments were conducted by the researcher. In the interview, she served as an active listener and empathetic interlocutor. Although not therapeutic in nature, the interview, by allowing the participant to narrate personal traumatic experiences in a safe and comfortable environment, was expected to provide the participants with an opportunity to reorganize their thoughts and feelings and establish a new perspective to reflect on her/his own trauma. When the participant's responses were ambiguous or ambivalent, the interviewer acted as a facilitator, guiding her/him to reflect on the experience and further explore the associated feelings and thoughts.

In the subsequent psychometric assessment, the researcher served as an instructor and assistant. Her main responsibilities were to introduce the questionnaire and address participants' questions about questionnaire items and test results.

Ethical considerations

The researcher was aware that simply talking about a traumatic event may re-trigger the participant's distress. At the end of each interview, the researcher checked whether the interviewee was not feeling distressed or experienced discomfort due to participation in the study. When transcribing the interview, the researcher re-evaluated the participant's psychological states, using the test results as supplementary information. Free access to professional therapists would be provided if the participant reported negative interview experiences or requested counselling support, though no such cases arouse during the study. Recognizing that individuals' views on their participation may shift over time, the researcher rechecked each interviewee's willingness to be involved in the study at the end of each interview. Despite the sensitive subject matter, none expressed the desire to withdraw from the study.

Appendix 2: Correlations between trauma victims' metaphor use and severities of trauma

		Overall degrees of trauma	Dissociation	Re-experiencing	Avoidance	Anxiety and hyperarousal	Impairment in functioning
Density of metaphors	Pearson Correlation	.105	.082	.189	.106	.006	.099
	Sig. (2-tailed)	.488	.588	.209	.485	.969	.513
Negative metaphors	Pearson Correlation	.318*	.250	.292*	.253	.260	.462**
	Sig. (2-tailed)	.031	.094	.049	.090	.081	.001
Neutral metaphors	Pearson Correlation	-.084	-.080	.047	-.023	-.182	-.175
	Sig. (2-tailed)	.580	.599	.758	.877	.226	.245
Positive metaphors	Pearson Correlation	-.091	-.022	-.015	-.103	-.106	-.234
	Sig. (2-tailed)	.549	.887	.921	.496	.481	.117
Novel metaphors	Pearson Correlation	.140	.157	.199	.106	.038	.132
	Sig. (2-tailed)	.353	.298	.186	.482	.804	.381
Conventional metaphors	Pearson Correlation	.035	-.014	.109	.065	-.024	.033
	Sig. (2-tailed)	.819	.928	.472	.666	.875	.829
Sensory information	Pearson Correlation	.004	-.025	.106	.035	-.100	.048
	Sig. (2-tailed)	.978	.870	.484	.819	.510	.752

(continued on the next page)

https://doi.org/10.1515/9783111346502-008

(continued from the previous page)

		Overall degrees of trauma	Dissociation	Re-experiencing	Avoidance	Anxiety and hyperarousal	Impairment in functioning
War and threat	Pearson Correlation	.079	.204	.160	.004	-.085	.063
	Sig. (2-tailed)	.604	.174	.287	.978	.575	.677
Physical activity	Pearson Correlation	.040	-.019	.137	.077	-.024	.010
	Sig. (2-tailed)	.794	.899	.363	.613	.875	.950
Space and spatial relations	Pearson Correlation	.129	.106	.080	.050	.196	.186
	Sig. (2-tailed)	.393	.481	.598	.740	.192	.215
Emotional feelings and processes	Pearson Correlation	.259	.183	.300*	.197	.249	.247
	Sig. (2-tailed)	.083	.224	.043	.190	.095	.098
Self-references	Pearson Correlation	.311*	.271	.249	.247	.325*	.264
	Sig. (2-tailed)	.036	.069	.095	.098	.028	.076
Thinking and understanding	Pearson Correlation	-.031	-.088	.089	.029	-.095	-.079
	Sig. (2-tailed)	.837	.560	.557	.848	.530	.604
SELF	Pearson Correlation	.114	.061	.117	.057	.145	.205
	Sig. (2-tailed)	.450	.686	.438	.707	.336	.173
OTHERS	Pearson Correlation	-.271	-.185	-.198	-.259	-.319*	-.197
	Sig. (2-tailed)	.068	.218	.187	.082	.030	.190

PERSONAL SITUATION	Pearson Correlation	-.143	-.234	-.146	-.012	-.120	-.126
	Sig. (2-tailed)	.342	.117	.333	.939	.428	.404
SOCIAL SITUATION	Pearson Correlation	.061	.126	.084	.101	-.108	.019
	Sig. (2-tailed)	.688	.406	.577	.503	.477	.898
SELF AND SELF	Pearson Correlation	.339*	.267	.385**	.280	.319*	.212
	Sig. (2-tailed)	.021	.073	.008	.059	.031	.158
SELF AND OTHERS	Pearson Correlation	.147	.082	.056	.222	.118	.139
	Sig. (2-tailed)	.330	.589	.709	.137	.437	.356
SELF AND PERSONAL SITUATION	Pearson Correlation	-.058	-.191	.021	.027	.009	-.160
	Sig. (2-tailed)	.700	.203	.890	.858	.955	.288
SELF AND SOCIAL SITUATION	Pearson Correlation	.213	.278	.308*	.103	.081	.198
	Sig. (2-tailed)	.154	.062	.037	.498	.591	.187

**Correlation is significant at the 0.01 level (2-tailed).
*Correlation is significant at the 0.05 level (2-tailed).

References

Agresti, Alan. 2002. *Categorical Data Analysis*. New York: John Wiley & Sons. https://doi.org/10.1002/0471249688.

Ahrens, Kathleen & Menghan Jiang. 2020. Source Domain Verification Using Corpus-based Tools. *Metaphor and Symbol* 35(1). 43–55. https://doi.org/10.1080/10926488.2020.1712783.

Alvarez-Conrad, Jennifer, Lori A. Zoellner & Edna B. Foa. 2001. Linguistic predictors of trauma pathology and physical health. *Applied Cognitive Psychology* 15(7). S159–S170. https://doi.org/10.1002/acp.839.

American Psychiatric Association. 1994. *Diagnostic and statistical manual of mental disorders (4th ed.)*. Washington DC: American Psychiatric Association.

American Psychiatric Association. 2013. *Diagnostic and Statistical Manual of Mental Disorders (5th ed.)*. Washington DC: American Psychiatric Association.

Amir, Marianne, Zeev Kaplan & Moshe Kotler. 1996. Type of Trauma, Severity of Posttraumatic Stress Disorder Core Symptoms, and Associated Features. *The Journal of General Psychology* 123(4). 341–351. https://doi.org/10.1080/00221309.1996.9921286.

Badour, Christal L., Heidi S. Resnick & Dean G. Kilpatrick. 2017. Associations Between Specific Negative Emotions and *DSM-5* PTSD Among a National Sample of Interpersonal Trauma Survivors. *Journal of Interpersonal Violence* 32(11). 1620–1641. https://doi.org/10.1177/0886260515589930.

Barlow, Jack M., Howard R. Pollio & Harold J. Fine. 1977. Insight and figurative language in psychotherapy. *Psychotherapy: Theory, Research & Practice* 14(3). 212–222. https://doi.org/10.1037/h0086530.

Batten, Sonja V., Victoria M. Follette, Mandra L. Rasmussen Hall & Kathleen M. Palm. 2002. Physical and psychological effects of written disclosure among sexual abuse survivors. *Behavior Therapy* 33(1). 107–122. https://doi.org/10.1016/S0005-7894(02)80008-9.

Beck, Cheryl Tatano. 2016. Posttraumatic Stress Disorder After Birth: A Metaphor Analysis. *MCN: The American Journal of Maternal/Child Nursing* 41(2). 76–83. https://doi.org/10.1097/NMC.0000000000000211.

Beck, Cheryl Tatano. 2017. The Anniversary of Birth Trauma: A Metaphor Analysis. *The Journal of Perinatal Education* 26(4). 219–228. https://doi.org/10.1891/1058-1243.26.4.219.

Berntsen, Dorthe, Morten Willert & David C. Rubin. 2003. Splintered memories or vivid landmarks? Qualities and organization of traumatic memories with and without PTSD. *Applied Cognitive Psychology* 17(6). 675–693. https://doi.org/10.1002/acp.894.

Boehme, Stephanie, Wolfgang H.R. Miltner & Thomas Straube. 2015. Neural correlates of self-focused attention in social anxiety. *Social Cognitive and Affective Neuroscience* 10(6). 856–862. https://doi.org/10.1093/scan/nsu128.

Boers, Frank. 1997. No pain, no gain in a free-market rhetoric: A test for cognitive semantics? *Metaphor and Symbol* 12(4). 231–241.

Boers, Frank. 1999. When a bodily source domain becomes prominent: The joy of counting metaphors in the socio-economic domain. In Raymond W. Gibbs & Gerard J. Steen (eds.), *Metaphor in Cognitive Linguistics*, 47–56. Amsterdam, Philadelphia: John Benjamins Publishing Company.

Bolognesi, Marianna, Roosmaryn Pilgram & Romy Van Den Heerik. 2017. Reliability in content analysis: The case of semantic feature norms classification. *Behavior Research Methods* 49(6). 1984–2001. https://doi.org/10.3758/s13428-016-0838-6.

https://doi.org/10.1515/9783111346502-009

Borbely, Antal F. 1998. A psychoanalytic concept of metaphor. *The International Journal of Psychoanalysis* 79(5). 923–936.

Borbely, Antal F. 2008. Metaphor and psychoanalysis. In Raymond W. Gibbs, Jr. (ed.), *The Cambridge Handbook of Metaphor and Thought*, 412–424. Cambridge: Cambridge University Press.

Bowdle, Brian F. & Dedre Gentner. 2005. The Career of Metaphor. *Psychological Review* 112(1). 193–216. https://doi.org/10.1037/0033-295X.112.1.193.

Bradley, Margaret M. & Peter J. Lang. 1994. Measuring emotion: The self-assessment manikin and the semantic differential. *Journal of Behavior Therapy and Experimental Psychiatry* 25(1). 49–59. https://doi.org/10.1016/0005-7916(94)90063-9.

Brewin, Chris R. 2015. Re-experiencing traumatic events in PTSD: new avenues in research on intrusive memories and flashbacks. *European Journal of Psychotraumatology* 6(1). 27180. https://doi.org/10.3402/ejpt.v6.27180.

Brewin, Chris R., Bernice Andrews & John D. Valentine. 2000. Meta-analysis of risk factors for posttraumatic stress disorder in trauma-exposed adults. *Journal of Consulting and Clinical Psychology* 68(5). 748–766. https://doi.org/10.1037/0022-006X.68.5.748.

Brewin, Chris R., James Christodoulides & Gary Hutchinson. 1996. BRIEF REPORT: Intrusive Thoughts and Intrusive Memories in a Nonclinical Sample. *Cognition & Emotion* 10(1). 107–112. https://doi.org/10.1080/026999396380411.

Briere, John. 1995. *Trauma Symptom Inventory Professional Manual*. Odessa, FL: Psychological Assessment Resources.

Bryant, Richard A., Matthew J. Friedman, David Spiegel, Robert Ursano & James Strain. 2011. A review of acute stress disorder in DSM-5. *Depression and Anxiety* 28(9). 802–817. https://doi.org/10.1002/da.20737.

Bryant, Richard A. & Rachel M. Guthrie. 2007. Maladaptive self-appraisals before trauma exposure predict posttraumatic stress disorder. *Journal of Consulting and Clinical Psychology* 75(5). 812–815. https://doi.org/10.1037/0022-006X.75.5.812.

Bryant, Richard A., Allison G. Harvey, Suzanne T. Dang & Tanya Sackville. 1998. Assessing acute stress disorder: Psychometric properties of a structured clinical interview. *Psychological Assessment* 10 (3). 215–220. https://doi.org/10.1037/1040-3590.10.3.215.

Bryant, Richard A., Michelle L. Moulds & Rachel M. Guthrie. 2000. Acute stress disorder scale: A self-report measure of acute stress disorder. *Psychological Assessment* 12(1). 61–68. https://doi.org/10.1037/1040-3590.12.1.61.

Busch, Brigitta. 2020. Message in a Bottle: Scenic Presentation of the Unsayable. *Applied Linguistics* 41 (3). 408–427. https://doi.org/10.1093/applin/amaa001.

Caers, E. 2006. When ministers were digging in for a fight. Metaphors of liberal common sense during the Winter of Discontent, 1978–1979. *Belgian journal of English language and literatures* N.R.4. 5–20.

Cahill, Shawn P. & Kristin Pontoski. 2005. Post-traumatic stress disorder and acute stress disorder I: their nature and assessment considerations. *Psychiatry (Edgmont)* 2(4). 14–25.

Cameron, Lynne. 1999. Identifying and describing metaphor in spoken discourse data. In Lynne Cameron & Graham Low (eds.), *Researching and Applying Metaphor*, 105–132. Cambridge: Cambridge University Press.

Cameron, Lynne & Robert Maslen (eds.). 2010. *Metaphor analysis: research practice in applied linguistics, social sciences and the humanities*. Oakville, Conn: Equinox Pub.

Cameron, Lynne, Robert Maslen, Zazie Todd, John Maule, Peter Stratton & Neil Stanley. 2009. The Discourse Dynamics Approach to Metaphor and Metaphor-Led Discourse Analysis. *Metaphor and Symbol* 24(2). 63–89. https://doi.org/10.1080/10926480902830821.

Cardeña, Etzel & Eve Carlson. 2011. Acute Stress Disorder Revisited. *Annual Review of Clinical Psychology* 7(1). 245–267. https://doi.org/10.1146/annurev-clinpsy-032210-104502.

Cardeña, Etzel, Cheryl Koopman, Catherine Classen, Lynn C. Waelde & David Spiegel. 2000. Psychometric properties of the Stanford Acute Stress Reaction Questionnaire (SASRQ): A valid and reliable measure of acute stress. *Journal of Traumatic Stress* 13(4). 719–734. https://doi.org/10.1023/A:1007822603186.

Carlson, Eve B. 1997. *Trauma assessments: a clinician's guide*. New York: Guilford Press.

Cartwright-Hatton, Sam & Adrian Wells. 1997. Beliefs about worry and intrusions: the Meta-Cognitions Questionnaire and its correlates. *Journal of Anxiety Disorders* 11(3). 279–296. https://doi.org/10.1016/S0887-6185(97)00011-X.

Charteris-Black, Jonathan. 2004. *Corpus Approaches to Critical Metaphor Analysis*. London: Palgrave Macmillan. https://doi.org/10.1057/9780230000612.

Charteris-Black, Jonathan. 2012. Shattering the bell jar: metaphor, gender, and depression. *Metaphor and Symbol* 27(3). 199–216. https://doi.org/10.1080/10926488.2012.665796.

Chen, Zheng. 2016. *Measuring Police Subcultural Perceptions*. Singapore: Springer. https://doi.org/10.1007/978-981-10-0096-6.

Cheung, Elizabeth. 2019. December 02. Polytechnic University facing immeasurable loss to research projects after radicals trashed campus in battle with police, chairman says. *South China Morning Post*. https://www.scmp.com/news/hong-kong/health-environment/article/3040165/polytechnic-university-facing-immeasurable-loss. (last accessed 23 September, 2023).

China Daily. 2019a. August 09. Hong Kong airport on alert ahead of fresh wave of protests. *China Daily*. https://www.chinadailyhk.com/articles/228/68/165/1565320445142.html. (last accessed 23 September, 2023).

China Daily. 2019b. September 05. Lam withdraws HK extradition bill. *China Daily*. https://www.chinadaily.com.cn/a/201909/05/WS5d6f8e47a310cf3e35569bc1.html. (last accessed 23 September, 2023).

Christianson, Sven-Åke. 1992. Emotional stress and eyewitness memory: A critical review. *Psychological Bulletin* 112(2). 284–309. https://doi.org/10.1037/0033-2909.112.2.284.

Cirillo, Leonard & Cathleen Crider. 1995. Distinctive therapeutic uses of metaphor. *Psychotherapy: Theory, Research, Practice, Training* 32(4). 511–519. https://doi.org/10.1037/0033-3204.32.4.511.

Clausner, Timothy C. & William Croft (eds.). 1999. Domains and image schemas. *Cognitive Linguistics* 10(1). 1–31. https://doi.org/10.1515/cogl.1999.001.

Cohn, Michael A., Matthias R. Mehl & James W. Pennebaker. 2004. Linguistic markers of psychological change surrounding September 11, 2001. *Psychological Science* 15(10). 687–693. https://doi.org/10.1111/j.0956-7976.2004.00741.x.

Coons, Philip M. 1988. Psychophysiologic aspects of multiple personality disorder: A review. *Dissociation: Progress in the Dissociative Disorders* 1(1). 47–53.

Costa, Adriana & Gerard Steen. 2014. Metaphor as a window on talk about trauma and post traumatic growth. *Scripta* 18(34). 283–299. https://doi.org/10.5752/P.2358-3428.2014v18n34p283.

Cox, Keith S., Heidi S. Resnick & Dean G. Kilpatrick. 2014. Prevalence and correlates of posttrauma distorted beliefs: evaluating DSM-5 PTSD expanded cognitive symptoms in a national sample. *Journal of Traumatic Stress* 27(3). 299–306. https://doi.org/10.1002/jts.21925.

Cox, Murray & Alice Theilgaard. 1987. *Mutative metaphors in psychotherapy: The Aeolian Mode*. New York: Tavistock/Routledge.

Creswell, John W. 2014. *Research design: qualitative, quantitative, and mixed methods approaches*. 4th ed. Thousand Oaks, CA: SAGE Publications.

Cronbach, Lee J. 1951. Coefficient alpha and the internal structure of tests. *Psychometrika* 16(3). 297–334. https://doi.org/10.1007/BF02310555.

Demjén, Zsófia, Agnes Marszalek, Elena Semino & Filippo Varese. 2019. Metaphor framing and distress in lived-experience accounts of voice-hearing. *Psychosis* 11(1). 16–27. https://doi.org/10. 1080/17522439.2018.1563626.

Dick, Florian & Hendrik Tevaearai. 2015. Significance and Limitations of the p Value. *European Journal of Vascular and Endovascular Surgery* 50(6). 815. https://doi.org/10.1016/j.ejvs.2015.07.026.

Dunmore, Emma, David M. Clark & Anke Ehlers. 1999. Cognitive factors involved in the onset and maintenance of posttraumatic stress disorder (PTSD) after physical or sexual assault. *Behaviour Research and Therapy* 37(9). 809–829. https://doi.org/10.1016/S0005-7967(98)00181-8.

Eckstein, Sarah, Jennifer Straub, Nicole Russo & Daniel Eckstein. 2012. Into The Woods: Introducing the Couples Metaphoric Interview Matrices. *The Family Journal* 20(1). 70–78. https://doi.org/10. 1177/1066480711429545.

Ehlers, Anke & David M. Clark. 2000. A cognitive model of posttraumatic stress disorder. *Behaviour Research and Therapy* 38(4). 319–345. https://doi.org/10.1016/S0005-7967(99)00123-0.

Ehlers, Anke, David M. Clark, Emma Dunmore, Lisa Jaycox, Elizabeth Meadows & Edna B. Foa. 1998. Predicting response to exposure treatment in PTSD: The role of mental defeat and alienation. *Journal of Traumatic Stress* 11(3). 457–471. https://doi.org/10.1023/A:1024448511504.

Ehlers, Anke, Thomas Ehring & Birgit Kleim. 2012. Information Processing in Posttraumatic Stress Disorder. In J. Gayle Beck & Denise M. Sloan (eds.), *The Oxford Handbook of Traumatic Stress Disorders*, 191–218. Oxford: Oxford University Press. https://doi.org/10.1093/oxfordhb/ 9780195399066.013.0014.

Ehlers, Anke, Ann Hackmann & Tanja Michael. 2004. Intrusive re-experiencing in post-traumatic stress disorder: Phenomenology, theory, and therapy. *Memory* 12(4). 403–415. https://doi.org/10. 1080/09658210444000025.

Ehlers, Anke, Ann Hackmann, Regina Steil, Sue Clohessy, Kerstin Wenninger & Heike Winter. 2002. The nature of intrusive memories after trauma: the warning signal hypothesis. *Behaviour Research and Therapy* 40(9). 995–1002. https://doi.org/10.1016/S0005-7967(01)00077-8.

Elliott, Gregory C. 1988. Interpreting higher order interactions in log-linear analysis. *Psychological Bulletin* 103(1). 121–130. https://doi.org/10.1037/0033-2909.103.1.121.

Espuny, Javier, Laura Jiménez-Ortega, Pilar Casado, Sabela Fondevila, Francisco Muñoz, David Hernández-Gutiérrez & Manuel Martín-Loeches. 2018. Event-related brain potential correlates of words' emotional valence irrespective of arousal and type of task. *Neuroscience Letters* 670. 83–88. https://doi.org/10.1016/j.neulet.2018.01.050.

Fainsilber, Lynn & Andrew Ortony. 1987. Metaphorical Uses of Language in the Expression of Emotions. *Metaphor and Symbolic Activity* 2(4). 239–250. https://doi.org/10.1207/ s15327868ms0204_2.

Feldman Barrett, Lisa, James Gross, Tamlin Conner Christensen & Michael Benvenuto. 2001. Knowing what you're feeling and knowing what to do about it: Mapping the relation between emotion differentiation and emotion regulation. *Cognition & Emotion* 15(6). 713–724. https://doi.org/10. 1080/02699930143000239.

Ferrara, Kathleen Warden. 1994. *Therapeutic ways with words*. New York, Oxford: Oxford University Press.

Figley, Charles R. 1983. Catastrohes: An overview of family reactions. In Charles R. Figley & Hamilton I. McCubbin (eds.), *Stress and the Family: Coping With Normative Transitions*, 3–20. New York: Brunner/Mazel.

Foa, Edna B., Chris Molnar & Laurie Cashman. 1995. Change in rape narratives during exposure therapy for posttraumatic stress disorder. *Journal of Traumatic Stress* 8(4). 675–690. https://doi. org/10.1002/jts.2490080409.

Foley, Patrick S. 2015. The metaphors they carry: Exploring how veterans use metaphor to describe experiences of PTSD. *Journal of Poetry Therapy* 28(2). 129–146. https://doi.org/10.1080/08893675.2015.1011375.

Ford, Julian D. & Christine A. Courtois. 2009. Defining and understanding complex trauma and complex traumatic stress disorders. In Christine A. Courtois & Julian D. Ford (eds.), *Treating complex traumatic stress disorders: An evidence-based guide*, 13–30. New York: The Guilford Press.

Frank, Roslyn M. 2008. Introduction: Sociocultural Situatedness. In Roslyn M. Frank, René Dirven, Tom Ziemke & Enrique Bernárdez (eds.), *Body, Language and Mind: Volume 2: Sociocultural Situatedness*, 1–18. Berlin, New York: De Gruyter Mouton.

Frewen, Paul A., David J. A. Dozois, Richard W. J. Neufeld, Maria Densmore, Todd K. Stevens & Ruth A. Lanius. 2011. Self-referential processing in women with PTSD: Affective and neural response. *Psychological Trauma: Theory, Research, Practice, and Policy* 3(4). 318–328. https://doi.org/10.1037/a0021264.

Fullagar, Simone & Wendy O'Brien. 2012. Immobility, Battles, and the Journey of Feeling Alive: Women's Metaphors of Self-Transformation Through Depression and Recovery. *Qualitative Health Research* 22(8). 1063–1072. https://doi.org/10.1177/1049732312443738.

Fuoli, Matteo, Jeannette Littlemore & Sarah Turner. 2022. Sunken ships and screaming banshees: metaphor and evaluation in film reviews. *English Language and Linguistics* 26(1). 75–103. https://doi.org/10.1017/S1360674321000046.

Galatzer-Levy, Isaac R. & Richard A. Bryant. 2013. 636,120 Ways to Have Posttraumatic Stress Disorder. *Perspectives on Psychological Science* 8(6). 651–662. https://doi.org/10.1177/1745691613504115.

Geeraerts, Dirk, Gitte Kristiansen & Yves Peirsman. 2010. *Advances in cognitive sociolinguistics*. Berlin: De Gruyter Mouton.

Gelo, Omar Carlo Gioacchino & Erhard Mergenthaler. 2012. Unconventional metaphors and emotional-cognitive regulation in a metacognitive interpersonal therapy. *Psychotherapy Research* 22(2). 159–175. https://doi.org/10.1080/10503307.2011.629636.

Gentner, Dedre, Brian Bowdle, Phillip Wolff & Consuelo Boronat. 2001. Metaphor is like analogy. In Dedre Gentner, Keith J Holyoak & Boicho N Kokinov (eds.), *The analogical mind: Perspectives from cognitive science*, 199–253. Cambridge: MIT Press.

Gentner, Dedre, Brian Falkenhainer & Janice Skorstad. 1988. Viewing Metaphor as Analogy. In David H. Helman (ed.), *Analogical Reasoning*, 171–177. Dordrecht: Springer. https://doi.org/10.1007/978-94-015-7811-0_8.

Gibbs, Raymond W. & Heather Franks. 2002. Embodied Metaphor In Women's Narratives About Their Experiences With Cancer. *Health Communication* 14(2). 139–165. https://doi.org/10.1207/S15327027HC1402_1.

Gilbert, G. Nigel. 1993. *Analyzing tabular data: loglinear and logistic models for social researchers*. London: UCL Press.

Giora, Rachel. (2002). Literal vs. figurative language: Different or equal? Journal of Pragmatics 34(4). 487–506. https://doi.org/10.1016/S0378-2166(01)00045-5.

Gök, Ayşe & Ahmet Kara. 2022. Individuals' conceptions of COVID-19 pandemic through metaphor analysis. *Current Psychology* 41(1). 449–458. https://doi.org/10.1007/s12144-021-01506-z.

Gradus, Jaimie L., Sussie Antonsen, Elisabeth Svensson, Timothy L. Lash, Patricia A. Resick & Jens Georg Hansen. 2015. Trauma, Comorbidity, and Mortality Following Diagnoses of Severe Stress and Adjustment Disorders: A Nationwide Cohort Study. *American Journal of Epidemiology* 182(5). 451–458. https://doi.org/10.1093/aje/kwv066.

Grant, Jan & Jim Crawley. 2002. *Transference And Projection: Mirrors to the Self*. Buchkingham: Open University Press.

Greenacre, Michael & Jorg Blasius (eds.). 2006. *Multiple Correspondence Analysis and Related Methods*. New York: Chapman and Hall/CRC. https://doi.org/10.1201/9781420011319.

Grove, David J. & Basil I. Panzer. 1989. *Resolving traumatic memories: metaphors and symbols in psychotherapy*. New York: Irvington.

Guité-Verret, Alexandra, Melanie Vachon, Deborah Ummel, Emilie Lessard & Camille Francoeur-Carron. 2021. Expressing grief through metaphors: family caregivers' experience of care and grief during the Covid-19 pandemic. *International Journal of Qualitative Studies on Health and Well-being* 16(1). 1996872. https://doi.org/10.1080/17482631.2021.1996872.

Gušić, Sabina, Andrea Malešević, Etzel Cardeña, Hans Bengtsson & Hans Peter Søndergaard. 2018. "I feel like I do not exist": A study of dissociative experiences among war-traumatized refugee youth. *Psychological Trauma: Theory, Research, Practice, and Policy* 10(5). 542–550. https://doi.org/10.1037/tra0000348.

Haen, Craig. 2020. The Roles of Metaphor and Imagination in Child Trauma Treatment. *Journal of Infant, Child, and Adolescent Psychotherapy* 19(1). 42–55. https://doi.org/10.1080/15289168.2020.1717171.

Halligan, Sarah L., Tanja Michael, David M. Clark & Anke Ehlers. 2003. Posttraumatic stress disorder following assault: The role of cognitive processing, trauma memory, and appraisals. *Journal of Consulting and Clinical Psychology* 71(3). 419–431. https://doi.org/10.1037/0022-006X.71.3.419.

Hampe, Beate. 2005. Image schemas in Cognitive Linguistics: Introduction. In Beate Hampe & Joseph E. Grady (eds.), *From Perception to Meaning*, 1–14. Berlin, Boston: De Gruyter Mouton. https://doi.org/10.1515/9783110197532.0.1.

Harvey, Allison G. & Richard A. Bryant. 1999. A qualitative investigation of the organization of traumatic memories. *British Journal of Clinical Psychology* 38(4). 401–405. https://doi.org/10.1348/014466599162999.

He, Shusi & Kathy Zhang. 2020. May 16. Violence drags HK into era of terror: report. *China Daily*. https://global.chinadaily.com.cn/a/202005/16/WS5ebf3c87a310a8b241156202.html. (last accessed 23 September, 2023).

Hellawell, Steph J & Chris R Brewin. 2004. A comparison of flashbacks and ordinary autobiographical memories of trauma: content and language. *Behaviour Research and Therapy* 42(1). 1–12. https://doi.org/10.1016/S0005-7967(03)00088-3.

Holman, E. Alison, Dana Rose Garfin & Roxane Cohen Silver. 2014. Media's role in broadcasting acute stress following the Boston Marathon bombings. *Proceedings of the National Academy of Sciences* 111(1). 93–98. https://doi.org/10.1073/pnas.1316265110.

Hou, Cailan. 2008. 成人自评 [Self-assessment for adults]. In Fujun Jia & Cailan Hou (eds.), 心理应激与创伤评估手册 [*The Handbook of Psychological Stress and Trauma Measurement*], 29–33. Beijing: People's Medical Publishing House.

Isserlin, Leanna, Gadi Zerach & Zahava Solomon. 2008. Acute stress responses: A review and synthesis of ASD, ASR, and CSR. *American Journal of Orthopsychiatry* 78(4). 423–429. https://doi.org/10.1037/a0014304.

Jaeger, Jeff, Katie M. Lindblom, Kelly Parker-Guilbert & Lori A. Zoellner. 2014. Trauma narratives: It's what you say, not how you say it. *Psychological Trauma: Theory, Research, Practice, and Policy* 6(5). 473–481. https://doi.org/10.1037/a0035239.

Janoff-Bulman, Ronnie. 1989. Assumptive Worlds and the Stress of Traumatic Events: Applications of the Schema Construct. *Social Cognition* 7(2). 113–136. https://doi.org/10.1521/soco.1989.7.2.113.

Jellestad, Lena, Nicolà A. Vital, Jolanda Malamud, Jan Taeymans & Christoph Mueller-Pfeiffer. 2021. Functional impairment in Posttraumatic Stress Disorder: A systematic review and meta-analysis. *Journal of Psychiatric Research* 136. 14–22. https://doi.org/10.1016/j.jpsychires.2021.01.039.

Jiao, Allan Y. 2001. Police and Culture: A Comparison between China and the United States. *Police Quarterly* 4(2). 156–185. https://doi.org/10.1177/109861101129197789.

Johnson, Mark Leonard. 1987. *The body in the mind: the bodily basis of meaning, imagination, and reason*. Chicago: University of Chicago Press.

Joseph, Stephen & P. Alex Linley. 2006. Growth following adversity: Theoretical perspectives and implications for clinical practice. *Clinical Psychology Review* 26(8). 1041–1053. https://doi.org/10.1016/j.cpr.2005.12.006.

Jubinville, Jodi, Christine Newburn-Cook, Kathleen Hegadoren & Thierry Lacaze-Masmonteil. 2012. Symptoms of Acute Stress Disorder in Mothers of Premature Infants. *Advances in Neonatal Care* 12(4). 246–253. https://doi.org/10.1097/ANC.0b013e31826090ac.

Kaplow, Julie B., Britney M. Wardecker, Christopher M. Layne, Ethan Kross, Amanda Burnside, Robin S. Edelstein & Alan R. Prossin. 2018. Out of the Mouths of Babes: Links Between Linguistic Structure of Loss Narratives and Psychosocial Functioning in Parentally Bereaved Children. *Journal of Traumatic Stress* 31(3). 342–351. https://doi.org/10.1002/jts.22293.

Kauschke, Christina, Daniela Bahn, Michael Vesker & Gudrun Schwarzer. 2019. The Role of Emotional Valence for the Processing of Facial and Verbal Stimuli – Positivity or Negativity Bias? *Frontiers in Psychology* 10. 1654. https://doi.org/10.3389/fpsyg.2019.01654.

Keating, Elizabeth & RJ Reinhart. 2020. February 10. Hong Kongers' Confidence in Institutions Damaged in Unrest. *Gallup*. https://news.gallup.com/poll/284189/hong-kongers-confidence-institutions-damaged-unrest.aspx. (last accessed 23 September, 2023).

Kenny, Lucy M. & Richard A. Bryant. 2007. Keeping memories at an arm's length: Vantage point of trauma memories. *Behaviour Research and Therapy* 45(8). 1915–1920. https://doi.org/10.1016/j.brat.2006.09.004.

Kenny, Lucy M., Richard A. Bryant, Derrick Silove, Mark Creamer, Meaghan O'Donnell & Alexander C. McFarlane. 2009. Distant Memories: A Prospective Study of Vantage Point of Trauma Memories. *Psychological Science* 20(9). 1049–1052. https://doi.org/10.1111/j.1467-9280.2009.02393.x.

Kimmel, Michael. 2005. Culture regained: Situated and compound image schemas. In Beate Hampe & Joseph E. Grady (eds.), *From Perception to Meaning*, 285–312. Berlin/Boston: De Gruyter Mouton. https://doi.org/10.1515/9783110197532.4.285.

Kimmel, Michael. 2010. Why we mix metaphors (and mix them well): Discourse coherence, conceptual metaphor, and beyond. *Journal of Pragmatics* 42(1). 97–115. https://doi.org/10.1016/j.pragma.2009.05.017.

Kleim, Birgit, Belinda Graham, Richard A. Bryant & Anke Ehlers. 2013. Capturing intrusive re-experiencing in trauma survivors' daily lives using ecological momentary assessment. *Journal of Abnormal Psychology* 122(4). 998–1009. https://doi.org/10.1037/a0034957.

Kleim, Birgit, Andrea B. Horn, Rainer Kraehenmann, Matthias R. Mehl & Anke Ehlers. 2018. Early Linguistic Markers of Trauma-Specific Processing Predict Post-trauma Adjustment. *Frontiers in Psychiatry* 9. 645. https://doi.org/10.3389/fpsyt.2018.00645.

Knapton, Olivia. 2016. Experiences of Obsessive-Compulsive Disorder: Activity, State, and Object Episodes. *Qualitative Health Research* 26(14). 2009–2023. https://doi.org/10.1177/1049732315601666.

Knapton, Olivia & Gabriella Rundblad. 2018. Metaphor, discourse dynamics and register: applications to written descriptions of mental health problems. *Text & Talk* 38(3). 389–410. https://doi.org/10.1515/text-2018-0005.

Kopp, Richard R. 1995. *Metaphor therapy: using client-generated metaphors in psychotherapy*. New York: Brunner/Mazel.

Kopp, Richard R. & Michael Jay Craw. 1998. Metaphoric language, metaphoric cognition, and cognitive therapy. *Psychotherapy: Theory, Research, Practice, Training* 35(3). 306–311. https://doi.org/10.1037/h0087795.

Kopp, Richard R. & Daniel Eckstein. 2004. Using early memory metaphors and client-generated metaphors in Adlerian therapy. *Journal of Individual Psychology* 60(2). 163–174.

Kövecses, Zoltán. 2000. *Metaphor and emotion: language, culture, and body in human feeling*. Cambridge, New York, Paris: Cambridge University Press.

Kövecses, Zoltán. 2005. *Metaphor in Culture: Universality and Variation*. Cambridge: Cambridge University Press. https://doi.org/10.1017/CBO9780511614408.

Kövecses, Zoltán. 2010[2002]. *Metaphor: a practical introduction*, 2nd edn. New York: Oxford University Press.

Kövecses, Zoltán. 2015. *Where metaphors come from: reconsidering context in metaphor*. New York: Oxford University Press.

Kövecses, Zoltán. 2020. *Extended Conceptual Metaphor Theory*. Cambridge: Cambridge University Press. https://doi.org/10.1017/9781108859127.

Krippendorff, Klaus. 1970. Estimating the Reliability, Systematic Error and Random Error of Interval Data. *Educational and Psychological Measurement* 30(1). 61–70. https://doi.org/10.1177/001316447003000105.

Krippendorff, Klaus. 2004[1980]. *Content analysis: an introduction to its methodology*, 2nd edn. Thousand Oaks, CA: SAGE Publications.

Kross, Ethan, Ozlem Ayduk & Walter Mischel. 2005. When asking "why" does not hurt. Distinguishing rumination from reflective processing of negative emotions. *Psychological Science* 16(9). 709–715. https://doi.org/10.1111/j.1467-9280.2005.01600.x.

Kuo, Lily & Guardian reporter. 2019. September 04. Hong Kong's leader withdraws extradition bill that ignited mass protests. *The Guardian*. Beijing and Hong Kong. https://www.theguardian.com/world/2019/sep/04/hong-kong-lam-to-withdraw-extradition-bill-say-reports. (last accessed 23 September, 2023).

Kweon, Yong-Sil, Na Young Jung, Sheng-Min Wang, Sheila A.M. Rauch, Jeong Ho Chae, Hae-Kook Lee, Chung Tai Lee & Kyoung-Uk Lee. 2013. Psychometric Properties of the Korean Version of Stanford Acute Stress Reaction Questionnaire. *Journal of Korean Medical Science* 28(11). 1672–1676. https://doi.org/10.3346/jkms.2013.28.11.1672.

Lakoff, George. 1987. *Women, fire, and dangerous things: What categories reveal about the mind*. Chicago, IL, US: University of Chicago Press.

Lakoff, George. 1990. The Invariance Hypothesis: is abstract reason based on image-schemas? *Cognitive Linguistics* 1(1). 39–74. https://doi.org/10.1515/cogl.1990.1.1.39.

Lakoff, George. 1992. Multiple Selves: The Metaphorical Models of the Self Inherent In Our Conceptual System. *UC Berkeley: Department of Linguistics*. https://escholarship.org/uc/item/53g1n5b2 (last accessed 23 September, 2023).

Lakoff, George & Mark Leonard Johnson. 1980. *Metaphors we live by*. Chicago, London: University of Chicago press.

Lakoff, George & Mark Leonard Johnson. 1999. *Philosophy in the flesh: the embodied mind and its challenge to western thought*. New York: Basic books.

Lakoff, George & Zoltán Kövecses. 1987. The cognitive model of anger inherent in American English. In Dorothy Hollan & Naomi Quinn (eds.), *Cultural models in language and thought*, 195–221. Cambridge: Cambridge University Press. https://doi.org/10.1017/CBO9780511607660.009.

Lakoff, George & Mark Turner. 1989. *More than cool reason: a field guide to poetic metaphor*. Chicago: University of Chicago Press.

Lanius, Ruth A., Braeden A. Terpou & Margaret C. McKinnon. 2020. The sense of self in the aftermath of trauma: lessons from the default mode network in posttraumatic stress disorder. *European Journal of Psychotraumatology* 11(1). 1807703. https://doi.org/10.1080/20008198.2020.1807703.

Lau, Chris, Jasmine Siu & Alvin Lum. 2020. April 09. Hong Kong mask ban legal when aimed at unauthorised protests, Court of Appeal rules in partially overturning lower court verdict. *South China Morning Post*. https://www.scmp.com/news/hong-kong/law-and-crime/article/3079197/hong-kong-mask-ban-legal-when-aimed-unauthorised. (last accessed 23 September, 2023).

Leung, Hillary. 2022. January 17. Hong Kong court jails 7 for up to 40 months for rioting during 2019 PolyU siege. *Hong Kong Free Press*. https://hongkongfp.com/2022/01/17/hong-kong-court-jails-7-for-up-to-40-months-for-rioting-during-2019-polyu-siege/. (last accessed 23 September, 2023).

Levitt, Heidi, Yifaht Korman & Lynne Angus. 2000. A metaphor analysis in treatments of depression: Metaphor as a marker of change. *Counselling Psychology Quarterly* 13(1). 23–35. https://doi.org/10.1080/09515070050011042.

Levy, Kenneth N. & J. Wesley Scala. 2012. Transference, transference interpretations, and transference-focused psychotherapies. *Psychotherapy* 49(3). 391–403. https://doi.org/10.1037/a0029371.

Liao, Changju, Linghong Guo, Cuicui Zhang, Meiqi Zhang, Wenjing Jiang, Ying Zhong, Qingfang Lin & Yin Liu. 2021. Emergency stress management among nurses: A lesson from the COVID-19 outbreak in China–a cross-sectional study. *Journal of Clinical Nursing* 30(3–4). 433–442. https://doi.org/10.1111/jocn.15553.

Littlemore, Jeannette. 2019. *Metaphors in the Mind: Sources of Variation in Embodied Metaphor*. Cambridge: Cambridge University Press. https://doi.org/10.1017/9781108241441.

Littlemore, Jeannette & Sarah Turner. 2019. What Can Metaphor Tell Us About Experiences of Pregnancy Loss and How Are These Experiences Reflected in Midwife Practice? *Frontiers in Communication* 4. 42. https://doi.org/10.3389/fcomm.2019.00042.

Littlemore, Jeannette & Sarah Turner. 2020. Metaphors in communication about pregnancy loss. *Metaphor and the Social World* 10(1). 45–75. https://doi.org/10.1075/msw.18030.lit.

Long, Philippa Shadrach & Georgia Lepper. 2008. Metaphor in psychoanalytic psychotherapy: a comparative study of four cases by a practitioner researcher. *British Journal of Psychotherapy* 24(3). 343–364. https://doi.org/10.1111/j.1752-0118.2008.00090.x.

Lötvall, Rebecka, Åsa Palmborg & Etzel Cardeña. 2022. A 20-years+ review of the Stanford Acute Stress Reaction Questionnaire (SASRQ): Psychometric properties and findings. *European Journal of Trauma & Dissociation* 6(3). 100269. https://doi.org/10.1016/j.ejtd.2022.100269.

Lovibond, Peter. & Sydney Harold Lovibond. 1995. The structure of negative emotional states: comparison of the Depression Anxiety Stress Scales (DASS) with the Beck Depression and Anxiety Inventories. *Behaviour Research and Therapy* 33(3). 335–343. https://doi.org/10.1016/0005-7967(94)00075-u.

Low, Graham, Zazie Todd, Alice Deignan & Lynne Cameron (eds.). 2010. *Researching and applying metaphor in the real world*. Amsterdam, Philadelphia: John Benjamins Publishing Company.

Luno, Jeremy A., Max Louwerse & J. Gayle Beck. 2013. Tell Us Your Story: Investigating the Linguistic Features of Trauma Narrative. *Proceedings of the Annual Meeting of the Cognitive Science Society* 35(35). https://escholarship.org/uc/item/95n9p15n. (22 September, 2023).

Luo, Yu, Xiangcai He, Shaofeng Wang, Jinjin Li & Yu Zhang. 2021. Media exposure predicts acute stress and probable acute stress disorder during the early COVID-19 outbreak in China. *PeerJ* 9. e11407. https://doi.org/10.7717/peerj.11407.

Palmborg, Åsa, Rebecka Lötvall & Etzel Cardeña. 2022. Acute Stress among Nurses in Sweden during the COVID-19 Pandemic. *European Journal of Trauma & Dissociation* 6(3). 100283. https://doi.org/10.1016/j.ejtd.2022.100283.

Manne, Sharon. (2002). Language Use and Post-Traumatic Stress Symptomatology in Parents of Pediatric Cancer Survivors. *Journal of Applied Social Psychology* 32(3). 608–629. https://doi.org/10.1111/j.1559-1816.2002.tb00233.x

Mathieson, Fiona, Jennifer Jordan, James Bennett-Levy & Maria Stubbe. 2018. Keeping metaphor in mind: training therapists in metaphor-enhanced cognitive behaviour therapy. *The Cognitive Behaviour Therapist* 11. e8. https://doi.org/10.1017/S1754470X18000077.

Mathieson, Fiona, Jennifer Jordan, Janet D. Carter & Maria Stubbe. 2015. The metaphoric dance: co-construction of metaphor in cognitive behaviour therapy. *The Cognitive Behaviour Therapist* 8. e24. https://doi.org/10.1017/S1754470X15000628.

Mathieson, Fiona, Jennifer Jordan, Janet D. Carter & Maria Stubbe. 2016. Nailing Down Metaphors in CBT: Definition, Identification and Frequency. *Behavioural and Cognitive Psychotherapy* 44(2). 236–248. https://doi.org/10.1017/S1352465815000156.

Mathieson, Fiona, Jennifer Jordan & Maria Stubbe. 2020. Recent applications of metaphor research in cognitive behaviour therapy. *Metaphor and the Social World* 10(2). 199–213. https://doi.org/10.1075/msw.00003.mat.

McCann, I. Lisa & Laurie Anne Pearlman. 1990. Vicarious traumatization: A framework for understanding the psychological effects of working with victims. *Journal of Traumatic Stress* 3(1). 131–149. https://doi.org/10.1007/BF00975140.

McIsaac, Heather K. & Eric Eich. 2002. Vantage point in episodic memory. *Psychonomic Bulletin & Review* 9(1). 146–150. https://doi.org/10.3758/BF03196271.

McIsaac, Heather K. & Eric Eich. 2004. Vantage Point in Traumatic Memory. *Psychological Science* 15 (4). 248–253. https://doi.org/10.1111/j.0956-7976.2004.00660.x.

McMullen, Linda M. 1985. Methods for studying the use of novel figurative language in psychotherapy. *Psychotherapy: Theory, Research, Practice, Training* 22(3). 610–619. https://doi.org/10.1037/h0085547.

McMullen, Linda M. 1989. Use of Figurative Language in Successful and Unsuccessful Cases of Psychotherapy: three Comparisons. *Metaphor and Symbolic Activity* 4(4). 203–225. https://doi.org/10.1207/s15327868ms0404_1.

McMullen, Linda M. 1996. Studying the Use of Figurative Language in Psychotherapy: The Search for Researchable Questions. *Metaphor and Symbolic Activity* 11(4). 241–255. https://doi.org/10.1207/s15327868ms1104_1.

McMullen, Linda M. 2008. Putting It in Context: Metaphor and Psychotherapy. In Raymond W. Gibbs, Jr. (ed.), *The Cambridge Handbook of Metaphor and Thought*, 397–411. Cambridge: Cambridge University Press. https://doi.org/10.1017/CBO9780511816802.024.

McMullen, Linda M. & John B. Conway. 2002. Conventional metaphors for depression. In Susan R. Fussell (ed.), *The Verbal Communication of Emotions: Interdisciplinary Perspectives*, 167–181. London: Taylor & Francis Inc.

McWhinney, Ian. R. 1993. Why we need a new clinical method. *Scandinavian Journal of Primary Health Care* 11(1). 3–7. https://doi.org/10.3109/02813439308994894.

Mead, Nicola. & Peter Bower. 2000. Patient-centredness: a conceptual framework and review of the empirical literature. *Social Science & Medicine* 51(7). 1087–1110. https://doi.org/10.1016/s0277-9536(00)00098-8.

Meili, Iara, Eva Heim & Andreas Maercker. 2019. Culturally shared metaphors expand contemporary concepts of resilience and post-traumatic growth: contrasting an indigenous Brazilian community and a Swiss rural community. *Medical Humanities* 45(4). 335–345. https://doi.org/10.1136/medhum-2018-011450.

Metcalfe, Janet & Walter Mischel. 1999. A hot/cool-system analysis of delay of gratification: Dynamics of willpower. *Psychological Review* 106(1). 3–19. https://doi.org/10.1037/0033-295X.106.1.3.

Michael, Tanja, Sarah L. Halligan, David M. Clark & Anke Ehlers. 2007. Rumination in posttraumatic stress disorder. *Depression and Anxiety* 24(5). 307–317. https://doi.org/10.1002/da.20228.

Mogul, Rhea. 2019. December 15. PTSD and protests: How the violence on Hong Kong's streets impacts mental health. *Hong Kong Free Press*. https://hongkongfp.com/2019/12/15/ptsd-protests-violence-hong-kongs-streets-impacts-mental-health/. (last accessed 23 September, 2023).

Mok, Danny. 2019. December 02. Hong Kong protests: more petrol bombs and offensive weapons found at Polytechnic University on Sunday. *South China Morning Post*. https://www.scmp.com/news/hong-kong/politics/article/3040136/hong-kong-protests-more-petrol-bombs-and-offensive-weapons. (last accessed 23 September, 2023).

Moser, K. S. 2004. The role of metaphors in acquiring and transmitting knowledge. In Martin Fischer, Nicholas Borehan & Barry Nyhan (eds.), *European perspectives on learning at work: The acquisition of work process knowledge*, 148–163. Luxembourg: Cedefop Reference Series 56. https://www.cedefop.europa.eu/files/3033_en.pdf. (last accessed 25 September, 2023).

Moser, Karin. 2007. Metaphors as symbolic environment of the self: How self-knowledge is expressed verbally. *Current Research in Social Psychology* 12(12). 151–178.

Moser, Karin. 2000. Metaphor Analysis in Psychology – Method, Theory, and Fields of Application. *Forum: Qualitative Social Research* 1(2). 21. https://doi.org/10.17169/FQS-1.2.1090.

Musolff, Andreas. 2004. *Metaphor and Political Discourse*. London: Palgrave Macmillan. https://doi.org/10.1057/9780230504516.

Musolff, Andreas. 2017. Metaphor and Cultural Cognition. In Farzad Sharifian (ed.), *Advances in Cultural Linguistics*, 325–344. Singapore: Springer.

Ng, Roger M. K. 2020. January 15. Mental Health Crisis in Hong Kong. *Psychiatric Times*. https://www.psychiatrictimes.com/view/mental-health-crisis-hong-kong. (last accessed 23 September, 2023).

Ni, Michael Y, Xiaoxin I Yao, Kathy S M Leung, Cynthia Yau, Candi M C Leung, Phyllis Lun, Francis P Flores, Wing Chung Chang, Benjamin J Cowling & Gabriel M Leung. 2020. Depression and post-traumatic stress during major social unrest in Hong Kong: a 10-year prospective cohort study. *The Lancet* 395(10220). 273–284. https://doi.org/10.1016/S0140-6736(19)33160-5.

Nigro, Georgia & Ulric Neisser. 1983. Point of view in personal memories. *Cognitive Psychology* 15(4). 467–482. https://doi.org/10.1016/0010-0285(83)90016-6.

Nijenhuis, Ellert, Onno Van Der Hart & Kathy Steele. 2010. Trauma-related Structural Dissociation of the Personality. *Activitas Nervosa Superior* 52(1). 1–23. https://doi.org/10.1007/BF03379560.

O'Kearney, Richard & Kelly Perrott. 2006. Trauma narratives in posttraumatic stress disorder: A review. *Journal of Traumatic Stress* 19(1). 81–93. https://doi.org/10.1002/jts.20099.

Orsillo, Susan M. 2001. Measures for Acute Stress Disorder and Posttraumatic Stress Disorder. In Martin M. Antony, Susan M. Orsillo & Lizabeth Roemer (eds.), *Practitioner's guide to empirically based measures of anxiety*, 255–307. Amsterdam: Kluwer Academic Publishers.

Ozer, Emily J., Suzanne R. Best, Tami L. Lipsey & Daniel S. Weiss. 2003. Predictors of posttraumatic stress disorder and symptoms in adults: A meta-analysis. *Psychological Bulletin* 129(1). 52–73. https://doi.org/10.1037/0033-2909.129.1.52.

Palmborg, Åsa, Rebecka Lötvall & Etzel Cardeña. 2022. Acute Stress among Nurses in Sweden during the COVID-19 Pandemic. *European Journal of Trauma & Dissociation* 6(3). 100283. https://doi.org/10.1016/j.ejtd.2022.100283.

Pedersen, Anette Fischer & Robert Zachariae. 2010. Cancer, acute stress disorder, and repressive coping. *Scandinavian Journal of Psychology* 51(1). 84–91. https://doi.org/10.1111/j.1467-9450.2009.00727.x.

Pennebaker, James W. 1993. Putting stress into words: Health, linguistic, and therapeutic implications. *Behaviour Research and Therapy* 31(6). 539–548. https://doi.org/10.1016/0005-7967(93)90105-4.

Pennebaker, James W. & Martha E. Francis. 1996. Cognitive, Emotional, and Language Processes in Disclosure. *Cognition and Emotion* 10(6). 601–626. https://doi.org/10.1080/026999396380079.

Pennebaker, James W, Ryan L. Boyd, Kayla Jordan, Kate Blackburn. 2015. *The development and psychometric properties of LIWC2015*. Austin, TX: University of Texas at Austin.

Pennebaker, James W., Tracy J. Mayne & Martha E. Francis. 1997. Linguistic predictors of adaptive bereavement. *Journal of Personality and Social Psychology* 72(4). 863–871. https://doi.org/10.1037/0022-3514.72.4.863.

Perry, Viviana. 2021. October 20. Acute Stress Disorder (ASD) vs. Post Traumatic Stress Disorder (PTSD). *Remedy Psychiatry*. https://remedypsychiatry.com/acute-stress-disorder-asd-vs-post-traumatic-stress-disorder-ptsd/. (last accessed 23 September, 2023)

Pfefferbaum, Betty & Carol S. North. 2020. Mental Health and the Covid-19 Pandemic. *New England Journal of Medicine* 383(6). 510–512. https://doi.org/10.1056/NEJMp2008017.

Plug, Leendert, Basil Sharrack & Markus Reuber. 2009. Seizure metaphors differ in patients' accounts of epileptic and psychogenic nonepileptic seizures. *Epilepsia* 50(5). 994–1000. https://doi.org/10.1111/j.1528-1167.2008.01798.x.

Pollio, Howard R. & Jack M. Barlow. 1975. A Behavioural Analysis of Figurative Language in Psychotherapy: One Session in a Single Case-Study. *Language and Speech* 18(3). 236–254. https://doi.org/10.1177/002383097501800306.

Pollio, Howard R., Jack M. Barlow, Harold J. Fine & Marilyn R. Pollio. 1977. *Psychology and the Poetics of Growth: Figurative Language in Psychology, Psychotherapy, and Education*. London: Routledge. https://doi.org/10.4324/9781003454656.

Pragglejaz Group. 2007. MIP: A Method for Identifying Metaphorically Used Words in Discourse. *Metaphor and Symbol*. 22(1). 1–39. https://doi.org/10.1080/10926480709336752.

Pritzker, Sonya. 2007. Thinking Hearts, Feeling Brains: Metaphor, Culture, and the Self in Chinese Narratives of Depression. *Metaphor and Symbol* 22(3). 251–274. https://doi.org/10.1080/10926480701357679.

Qiu, Han. & Dennis Tay. (under review). Cross-domain mappings in therapeutic interpretations of transference: the use of and response to metaphors and non-metaphors.

Radvansky, Gabriel A. & Connie Svob. 2019. Observer memories may not be for everyone. *Memory* 27 (5). 647–659. https://doi.org/10.1080/09658211.2018.1550093.

Rasmussen, A. S. & D. Berntsen. 2009. Emotional valence and the functions of autobiographical memories: Positive and negative memories serve different functions. *Memory & Cognition* 37(4). 477–492. https://doi.org/10.3758/MC.37.4.477.

Rechsteiner, Karin, Andreas Maercker, Eva Heim & Iara Meili. 2020. Metaphors For Trauma: A Cross-Cultural Qualitative Comparison in Brazil, India, Poland, and Switzerland. *Journal of Traumatic Stress* 33(5). 643–653. https://doi.org/10.1002/jts.22533.

Rechsteiner, Karin, Varsha Tol & Andreas Maercker. 2019. "It should not have happened": metaphorical expressions, idioms, and narrative descriptions related to trauma in an indigenous community in India. *International Journal of Qualitative Studies on Health and Well-being* 14(1). 1667134. https://doi.org/10.1080/17482631.2019.1667134.

Reijnierse, Gudrun, Christian Burgers, Tina Krennmayr, Gerard J. Steen. 2018. DMIP: A Method for Identifying Potentially Deliberate Metaphor in Language Use. Corpus Pragmatics 2.129–147. https://doi.org/10.1007/s41701-017-0026-7.

Rhodes, John E., & Simon Jakes. 2004. The Contribution of Metaphor and Metonymy to Delusions. Psychology and Psychotherapy: Theory, Research and Practice 77(1). 1–17. https://doi.org/10.1348/147608304322874227.

Robinson, John A. & Karen L. Swanson. 1993. Field and observer modes of remembering. *Memory* 1 (3). 169–184. https://doi.org/10.1080/09658219308258230.

Rowat, Ronda, Jack De Stefano & Martin Drapeau. 2008. The role of patient-generated metaphors on in-session therapeutic processes. *Archives of Psychiatry and Psychotherapy* 10(1). 21–27.

Sarangi, Srikant & Christopher N. Candlin. 2001. 'Motivational relevancies': Some methodological reflections on social theoretical and sociolinguistic practice. In Coupland Nikolas, Sarangi Shrikant & Christopher N. Candlin (eds.), *Sociolinguistics and Social Theory*, 350–388. London: Routledge.

Schore, Allan N. 2003. *Affect regulation and the repair of the self*. New York: W. W Norton & Company.

Semino, Elena. 2008. *Metaphor in discourse*. Cambridge, New York: Cambridge University Press.

Semino, Elena. 2010. Descriptions of Pain, Metaphor, and Embodied Simulation. *Metaphor and Symbol* 25(4). 205–226. https://doi.org/10.1080/10926488.2010.510926.

Semino, Elena. 2011. Metaphor, Creativity and the Experience of Pain across Genres. In Joan Swann, Rob Pope & Ronald Carter (eds.), *Creativity, Language, Literature: The State of the Art*, 83–102. Basingstoke: Palgrave Macmillan. https://doi.org/10.1007/978-1-349-92482-0_6.

Semino, Elena, Zsófia Demjén, Andrew Hardie, Sheila Payne & Paul Rayson. 2017. *Metaphor, Cancer and the End of Life: A Corpus-Based Study*. London: Routledge. https://doi.org/10.4324/9781315629834.

Shalev, Arieh. Y., Tuvia Peri, Laura Canetti & Shaul Schreiber. 1996. Predictors of PTSD in injured trauma survivors: a prospective study. *The American Journal of Psychiatry* 153(2). 219–225. https://doi.org/10.1176/ajp.153.2.219.

Shek, Daniel T. L. 2020. Protests in Hong Kong (2019–2020): a Perspective Based on Quality of Life and Well-Being. *Applied Research in Quality of Life* 15(3). 619–635. https://doi.org/10.1007/s11482-020-09825-2.

Siegelman, Ellen Y. 1990. *Metaphor and meaning in psychotherapy*. New York: Guilford Press.

Sims, Peter A. 2003. Working with Metaphor. *American Journal of Psychotherapy* 57(4). 528–536. https://doi.org/10.1176/appi.psychotherapy.2003.57.4.528.

Sims, Peter A. & Christopher A. Whynot. 1997. Hearing Metaphor: An Approach to Working with Family-Generated Metaphor. *Family Process* 36(4). 341–355. https://doi.org/10.1111/j.1545-5300.1997.00341.x.

South China Morning Post. 2019. January 22. Hong Kong protests: call for peace from son of Luo Changqing, killed by brick hurled during Sheung Shui clash. *South China Morning Post*. https://today.line.me/hk/v2/article/0XDE23. (last accessed 23 September 2023).

Spong, Sheila. 2010. Discourse analysis: Rich pickings for counsellors and therapists. *Counselling and Psychotherapy Research* 10(1). 67–74. https://doi.org/10.1080/14733140903177052.

Stanley, B. Liahnna, Alaina C. Zanin, Brianna L. Avalos, Sarah J. Tracy & Sophia Town. 2021. Collective Emotion During Collective Trauma: A Metaphor Analysis of the COVID-19 Pandemic. *Qualitative Health Research* 31(10). 1890–1903. https://doi.org/10.1177/10497323211011589.

Steen, Gerard. 2008. The Paradox of Metaphor: Why We Need a Three-Dimensional Model of Metaphor. *Metaphor and Symbol* 23(4). 213–241. https://doi.org/10.1080/10926480802426753.

Steen, Gerard. 2011. The contemporary theory of metaphor – now new and improved! *Review of Cognitive Linguistics* 9(1). 26–64. https://doi.org/10.1075/rcl.9.1.03ste.

Steen, Gerard J., Aletta G. Dorst, J. Berenike Herrmann, Anna Kaal, Tina Krennmayr & Trijntje Pasma. 2010. *A Method for Linguistic Metaphor Identification: From MIP to MIPVU*. Amsterdam: John Benjamins Publishing Company. https://doi.org/10.1075/celcr.14.

Stott, Richaard, Warren Mansell, Paul Salkovskis, Anna Lavender, & Sam Cartwright-Hatton. 2010. Oxford Guide to Metaphors in CBT: Building Cognitive Bridges. Oxford: Oxford University Press.

Stroinska, Magda. 2014. Metaphors we li(v)e by: Disease as a conceptual metaphor for sextual assault. In Magda Stroinska, Vikki Cecchetto & Kate Szymanski (eds.), *The Unspeakable: Narratives of Trauma*, 183–198. Frankfurt, Berlin: Peter Lang.

Substance Abuse and Mental Health Services Administration. 2014. Trauma-Informed Care in Behavioral Health Services. Substance Abuse and Mental Health Services Administration (US). https://www.ncbi.nlm.nih.gov/books/NBK207201/. (last accessed 23 September 2023).

Swanepoel, Marlize. 2011. Meeting with the Metaphor: The Impact of the Dramatic Metaphor on the Therapeutic Relationship. *Dramatherapy*. 33(2). 101–113. https://doi.org/10.1080/02630672.2011.582778.

Szabo, Yvette Z., Ashlee J. Warnecke, Tamara L. Newton & Jeffrey C. Valentine. 2017. Rumination and posttraumatic stress symptoms in trauma-exposed adults: a systematic review and meta-analysis. *Anxiety, Stress, & Coping* 30(4). 396–414. https://doi.org/10.1080/10615806.2017.1313835.

Tabachnick, Barbara G. & Linda S. Fidell. 2007. *Using multivariate statistics*. 5th ed. Boston: Pearson Education Limited.

Talmy, Leonard. 2003. *Toward a cognitive semantics. 1: Concept structuring systems*. Cambridge: MIT Press.

Tao, Jiong, Shenglin Wen, Xianglan Wang, Zhaoyu Gan, Leijun Li, Liangrong Zheng, Hong Shan, Jinbei Zhang & Lingjiang Li. 2008. 汶川地震安置点灾民急性应激障碍及影响因素分析 [Experience and influencing factors of Acute Stress Disorder induced by the Wenchuan earthquake]. *Chinese Journal of Nervous and Mental Diseases* 34(10). 618–620. https://doi.org/10.3969/j.issn.1002-0152.2008.10.013.

Tay, Dennis. 2013. *Metaphor in psychotherapy: a descriptive and prescriptive analysis*. Amsterdam, Philadelphia: John Benjamins Publishing Company.

Tay, Dennis. 2014. Bodily experience as both source and target of meaning making: Implications from metaphors in psychotherapy for Posttraumatic Stress Disorder. *Cognitive Linguistic Studies* 1(1). 84–100. https://doi.org/10.1075/cogls.1.1.04tay.

Tay, Dennis. 2015. Metaphor in case study articles on Chinese university counseling service websites. *Chinese Language and Discourse* 6(1). 28–56. https://doi.org/10.1075/cld.6.1.02tay.

Tay, Dennis. 2016. Metaphor and Psychological Transference. *Metaphor and Symbol* 31(1). 11–30. https://doi.org/10.1080/10926488.2016.1116903.

Tay, Dennis. 2017. Quantitative metaphor usage patterns in Chinese psychotherapy talk. *Communication and Medicine* 14(1). 51–68. https://doi.org/10.1558/cam.27688.

Tay, Dennis. 2018. Metaphors of movement in psychotherapy talk. *Journal of Pragmatics* 125. 1–12. https://doi.org/10.1016/j.pragma.2017.12.009.

Tay, Dennis. 2019. *Time series analysis of discourse: method and case studies*. New York, London: Routledge.

Tay, Dennis. 2020a. A Computerized Text and Cluster Analysis Approach to Psychotherapy Talk. *Language and Psychoanalysis* 9(1). 4–25. https://doi.org/10.7565/landp.v9i1.1701.

Tay, Dennis. 2020b. Affective Engagement in Metaphorical versus Literal Communication Styles in Counseling. *Discourse Processes* 57(4). 360–375. https://doi.org/10.1080/0163853X.2019.1689086.

Tay, Dennis. 2021. Is the Social Unrest like COVID-19 or Is COVID-19 like the Social Unrest? A Case Study of Source-target Reversibility. *Metaphor and Symbol* 36(2). 99–115. https://doi.org/10.1080/10926488.2021.1887708.

Tay, Dennis. 2022. *Navigating the Realities of Metaphor and Psychotherapy Research*. Cambridge: Cambridge University Press. https://doi.org/10.1017/9781108975049.

Tay, Dennis & Xie Pan (eds.). 2022. *Data analytics in cognitive linguistics: methods and insights*. Berlin, Boston: De Gruyter Mouton.

Tay, Dennis & Han Qiu. 2022. Modeling Linguistic (A)Synchrony: A Case Study of Therapist–Client Interaction. *Frontiers in Psychology* 13. 903227. https://doi.org/10.3389/fpsyg.2022.903227.

Tay, Dennis & Han Qiu. 2024. Source domain association as conceptual assemblages in trauma talk – an association rule mining approach. *Metaphor and Symbol* 39(2). 96–109. https://doi.org/10.1080/10926488.2023.2300431.

Taylor, Steven. & Brian. J. Cox. 1998. Anxiety sensitivity: multiple dimensions and hierarchic structure. *Behaviour Research and Therapy* 36(1). 37–51. https://doi.org/10.1016/s0005-7967(97)00071-5.

Tedeschi, Richard & Lawrence Calhoun. 1995. *Trauma & Transformation: Growing in the Aftermath of Suffering*. California: SAGE Publications, https://doi.org/10.4135/9781483326931.

Terr, Lenore. C. 1991. Childhood traumas: an outline and overview. *The American Journal of Psychiatry* 148(1). 10–20. https://doi.org/10.1176/ajp.148.1.10.

The Government of the Hong Kong Special Administrative Region Press Releases. 2019. November 13. Special announcement by Education Bureau (2). https://www.info.gov.hk/gia/general/201911/13/P2019111300679.htm. (last accessed 23 September 2023).

The Government of the Hong Kong Special Administrative Region Press Releases. 2021. July 09. HKSAR Government condemns European Parliament's resolution. https://www.info.gov.hk/gia/general/202107/09/P2021070900704.htm. (last accessed 23 September, 2023).

Todorov, German I., Karthikeyan Mayilvahanan, Christopher K Cain & Catarina Cunha. 2018. *Screening word usage in people affected by PTSD: an unbiased, cost effective, and novel screening method?* Preprint. PsyArXiv. https://doi.org/10.31234/osf.io/y68fx.

Turner, Sarah, Jeannette Littlemore, Danielle Fuller, Karolina Kuberska & Sheelagh McGuinness. 2020. The production of time-related metaphors by people who have experienced pregnancy loss. In John Barnden & Andrew Gargett (eds.), *Figurative Thought and Language*, 389–418. Amsterdam: John Benjamins Publishing Company. https://doi.org/10.1075/ftl.10.14tur.

Van Der Kolk, Bessel A. & Charles P. Ducey. 1989. The psychological processing of traumatic experience: Rorschach patterns in PTSD. *Journal of Traumatic Stress* 2(3). 259–274. https://doi.org/10.1002/jts.2490020303.

Wagener Alwin. 2017. Metaphor in Professional Counseling. *Professional Counselor* 7(2). 144–54. https://doi.org/10.15241/aew.7.2.144.

Wallace-Hadrill, Sophie M. A. & Sunjeev K. Kamboj. 2016. The Impact of Perspective Change As a Cognitive Reappraisal Strategy on Affect: A Systematic Review. *Frontiers in Psychology* 7. 1715. https://doi.org/10.3389/fpsyg.2016.01715.

Wang, Xinting, Jihong Zhao & Hongwei Zhang. 2020. The Impact of Two Different Cultures on Juvenile Attitudes Toward the Police in China. *International Journal of Offender Therapy and Comparative Criminology* 64(1). 124–143. https://doi.org/10.1177/0306624X19872971.

Wardecker, Britney M., Robin S. Edelstein, Jodi A. Quas, Ingrid M. Cordón & Gail S. Goodman. 2017. Emotion Language in Trauma Narratives Is Associated With Better Psychological Adjustment Among Survivors of Childhood Sexual Abuse. *Journal of Language and Social Psychology* 36(6). 628–653. https://doi.org/10.1177/0261927X17706940.

Wasserstein, Ronald L., Allen L. Schirm & Nicole A. Lazar. 2019. Moving to a World Beyond "p< 0.05." *The American Statistician* 73(sup1). 1–19. https://doi.org/10.1080/00031305.2019.1583913.

Williams, Alishia D. & Michelle L. Moulds. 2007. Cognitive avoidance of intrusive memories: Recall vantage perspective and associations with depression. *Behaviour Research and Therapy* 45(6). 1141–1153. https://doi.org/10.1016/j.brat.2006.09.005.

Wilson, John P. & Jacob D. Lindy. 2013. *Trauma, Culture, and Metaphor*. New York: Routledge. https://doi.org/10.4324/9780203893579.

Witztum, Eliezer, Haim Dasberg & Abraham Bleich. 1986. Use of a Metaphor in the Treatment of Combat-induced Posttraumatic Stress Disorder. *American Journal of Psychotherapy* 40(3). 457–465. https://doi.org/10.1176/appi.psychotherapy.1986.40.3.457.

Witztum, Eliezer, Onno Van Der Hart & Barbara Friedman. 1988. The use of metaphors in psychotherapy. *Journal of Contemporary Psychotherapy* 18(4). 270–290. https://doi.org/10.1007/BF00946010.

World Health Organization. 2019. International Statistical Classification of Diseases and Related Health Problems 10th Revision. https://icd.who.int/browse10/2019/en (last accessed 23 September, 2023).

Wong, Brian. 2020. July 09. Hong Kong protests: man set on fire says he was standing up for justice when confronting black-clad mob. *South China Morning Post*. https://www.scmp.com/news/hong-kong/law-and-crime/article/3092549/hong-kong-protests-man-set-fire-says-he-was-standing. (last accessed 23 September 2023).

Yau, Cannix. 2020. January 08. HK$65 million bill for repairs on public facilities vandalised by anti-government protesters. *South China Morning Post*. https://www.scmp.com/print/news/hong-kong/transport/article/3045180/hk65-million-bill-repairs-public-facilities-vandalised. (last accessed 23 September, 2023).

Yiu, William. 2021. November 25. Hong Kong Polytechnic University leaders say unrest of 2019 is firmly in the past at anniversary celebration. *South China Morning Post*. https://www.scmp.com/news/hong-kong/education/article/3157394/hong-kong-polytechnic-university-leaders-say-unrest-2019. (last accessed 23 September, 2023).

Yu, Ning. 1995. Metaphorical Expressions of Anger and Happiness in English and Chinese. *Metaphor and Symbolic Activity* 10(2). 59–92. https://doi.org/10.1207/s15327868ms1002_1.

Yu, Ning. 2008. The Chinese heart as the central faculty of cognition. In Sharifian, Farzad, René Dirven, Ning Yu & Susanne Niemeier (eds), *Culture, Body, and Language: Conceptualizations of internal body organs across cultures and languages*, 131–168. Berlin, Boston: Mouton de Gruyter. http://www.scopus.com/inward/record.url?scp=84882259920&partnerID=8YFLogxK. (last accessed 25 September, 2023).

Yu, Yating & Dennis Tay. 2020. A mixed-method analysis of image-schematic metaphors in describing anger, anxiety, and depression. *Metaphor and the Social World* 10(2). 253–272. https://doi.org/10.1075/msw.00006.yu.

Zanotto, Mara Sophia, Lynne Cameron & Marilda do Couto Cavalcanti (eds.). 2008. *Confronting metaphor in use: an applied linguistic approach*. Amsterdam, Philadelphia: John Benjamins Publishing Company.

Zapf, Antonia, Stefanie Castell, Lars Morawietz & André Karch. 2016. Measuring inter-rater reliability for nominal data – which coefficients and confidence intervals are appropriate? *BMC Medical Research Methodology* 16. 93. https://doi.org/10.1186/s12874-016-0200-9.

Zhang, Yi, Yi Zhang & Kaiyi Dai. 2019. August 13. Signs of 'terrorism' seen in HK unrest. *China Daily*. https://www.chinadailyhk.com/articles/250/250/246/1565630378909.html. (last accessed 23 September, 2023).

Zhao, G. 2015. The Contemporary Chinese Dictionary. *International Journal of Lexicography* 28(1). 107–123. https://doi.org/10.1093/ijl/ecu030.

Zoellner, Lori A. & Joyce N. Bittenger. 2004. On the Uniqueness of Trauma Memories in PTSD. In Gerald M. Rosen (ed.), *Posttraumatic Stress Disorder*, 147–162. Chichester: John Wiley & Sons. https://doi.org/10.1002/9780470713570.ch8.

Index

https://doi.org/10.1515/9783111346502-010